# Religion, Beliefs,
# and
# International Human Rights

Religion and Human Rights Series

Series Editors
John Witte Jr.
Abdullahi Ahmed An-Na'im
Emory University

Other Books Published in the Series

*Proselytization and Self-Determination in Africa*
    Abdullahi Ahmed An-Na'im, Editor
*Religious Freedom and Evangelization in Latin America: The Challenge of Religious Pluralism*
    Paul E. Sigmund, Editor
*Proselytism and Orthodoxy in Russia: The New War for Souls*
    John Witte Jr. and Michael Bourdeaux, Editors
*Sharing the Book: Religious Perspectives on the Rights and Wrongs of Mission*
    John Witte Jr. and Richard C. Martin, Editors

RELIGION AND HUMAN RIGHTS SERIES

# Religion, Beliefs, and International Human Rights

## Natan Lerner

ORBIS BOOKS

**Maryknoll, New York 10545**

Copyright © 2000 by the Law and Religion Program at Emory University, Atlanta, Georgia.

Published by Orbis Books, Maryknoll, New York, U.S.A.

Manufactured in the United States of America.

Manuscript editing and typesetting by Joan Weber Laflamme.

**Library of Congress Cataloging-in-Publication Data**

Lerner, Natan.
   Religion, beliefs, and international human rights   /   Natan Lerner.
     p.   cm.   —   (Religion and human rights series)
   Includes bibliographical references and index.
   ISBN 1-57075-301-6 (pbk.)
    1. Human rights—Religious aspects. 2. Religion and international affairs. I. Title. II. Religion & human rights series

   BL65.H78.L47 2000
   323.44'2'09—dc21                                99-086309

*For*
*Bertha*
*Lidia, Rut, Ana, and Isar*
*and my grandchildren, Roni and Gil*

*With the hope that in the world in which my*
*grandchildren will grow, freedom of religion and*
*beliefs and human rights will be fully respected.*

# CONTENTS

# THE RELIGION AND HUMAN RIGHTS SERIES PREFACE

The relationship between religion and human rights is both problematic and unavoidable in all parts of the world. Religion, broadly defined to include various traditional, cultural, and customary institutions and practices, is unquestionably a formidable force for violence, repression, and chauvinism of untold dimensions. But religion is also a natural and necessary ally in the global struggle for human rights. For human rights norms are inherently abstract ideals—universal statements of the good life and the good society. They depend upon the visions and values of human communities to give them content, coherence, and concrete manifestation. Religion is an inherent condition of human lives and human communities. Religion invariably provides the sources and scales of dignity and responsibility, shame and respect, restitution and reconciliation that a human rights regime needs to survive and to flourish.

This book series explores the interaction of religious ideas and institutions with human rights principles and practices. It seeks to discover the religious sources of human rights—both their cultivation and their corruption in the discourse of sacred texts, the activism of religious organizations, and the practices of religious polities. It seeks to uncover the legal sources of human rights—both their protection and their abridgment in international human rights instruments and in domestic constitutions, statutes, and cases. It seeks to address some of the cutting edge issues of religion and human rights in theory and practice.

This series is made possible, in part, by the generous funding of The Pew Charitable Trusts, Inc. and the Ford Foundation. Pew's support came through its funding of a three-year project on "Soul Wars: The Problem and Promise of Proselytism in the New World Order." Ford's support came through its funding of a three-year project on "Cultural Transformation in Africa: Legal, Religious, and Human Rights Perspectives." Several of the early volumes in this series are parts and products of these two projects. They provide pilots and prototypes for the type of rigorous interdisciplinary and interreligious analysis that the subject of religion and human rights requires.

We wish to express our gratitude to our friends at the two foundations for their generous support of this effort. We also wish to thank the Maryknoll Fathers and Brothers and Bill Burrows and Bernadette Price of Orbis for their sage stewardship of this series.

— JOHN WITTE JR.
ABDULLAHI AHMED AN-NA'IM
EMORY UNIVERSITY, ATLANTA

# Preface and Acknowledgments

This book addresses human rights related to religion and beliefs. In part, it draws together and updates several articles and chapters previously published. Each of these earlier works dealt in part with discrimination, group and minority rights, and the protection of these rights by international law, essentially in the United Nations era. Each dealt with freedoms related to religion and beliefs, as well as with the position of religious groups or religious minorities within society. Each explored the relationship between these religious groups and their members, between the groups and the state, and between the state and individual members of the religious groups. I felt that updating and incorporating these writings into a single volume would provide a helpful contribution to an area of legal research that has been largely neglected until recently.

This volume builds on the assumption that freedom of religion and belief is a fundamental right of each person, and that it is also a right of groups, communities, and congregations. This right is interwoven with many other human rights, individual and collective, and illustrates how human rights are indivisible. Ideally, each society should provide a framework allowing a harmony between the rights and duties of the state, individuals, and groups within each state and internationally.

My perspective is that of a lawyer of international human rights, with particular interest in rights related to religion and beliefs. The recognition of these religious rights in positive legal terms is largely a phenomenon of the United Nations era that began in the aftermath of World War II—and, to some extent, was a consequence of the lessons of the war. Not only United Nations organizations, however, but also regional organizations have been active in the cultivation of religious rights, and I shall also take note of these. My emphasis will be on the texts of positive international law that have emerged in the half century since the adoption of the Universal Declaration of Human Rights (1948) and the Convention on the Prevention and Punishment of the Crime of Genocide (1948) immediately following the war. Sixteen appendices to this volume provide the reader with immediate access to the basic texts of international law on religious rights.

This book is designed to be accessible not only to fellow lawyers and law students but also to a more general audience, including theologians, ethicists, historians, human rights advocates, and those with interests in international politics and international organizations. I try so far as possible to avoid technical legal jargon. Although an in-depth analysis of the sociological and philosophical issues related to religion is beyond the scope of these pages, I make some references to the legal implications of these issues. Likewise, although a careful review of interreligious and international conflicts that affect the law of religious rights is beyond the scope of these pages, I make some reference to these conflicts to understand how they can affect the formulations and applications of international human rights instruments respecting religion.

I am deeply indebted and grateful to Professor John Witte Jr., director of the Law and Religion Program at Emory University and general co-editor of this new book series on religion and human rights. He encouraged me to prepare this volume and provided guidance, constructive criticisms, and advice throughout. I also wish to extend my thanks to Joel Nichols and Henry Kimmel for their dedicated and highly professional editorial assistance. Because English is not my mother tongue, I found comfort in having their able and creative cooperation.

Hili Mudrik and Miri Hart, my research assistants at the Interdisciplinary Center in Herzliya, helped me with the collection of the material for various chapters. Liz Nadel, the director of the center's library, and her staff also provided important help. Mrs. Einat Gabay, also part of the center's library staff, and Mr. Yehuda Mechaber, a staff member of the United Nations Library of the Israeli Ministry for Foreign Affairs, provided me with indispensable documents. The library at the Faculty of Law of Tel Aviv University was an outstanding resource and enormously facilitated my work.

The Pew Charitable Trusts, Inc. funded the Religious Human Rights Project (1992-95) and The Problem of Proselytism Project (1995-98), of which I was a part, and sponsored several research and lecture trips to Atlanta. The Niwano Foundation (Tokyo) extended support for the research done in connection with some of the chapters of this volume. I express my thanks to both institutions.

Finally, my thanks are due to the following publishers for permission to adopt and adapt for this volume materials originally published by them: Martinus Nijhoff Publishers; Sijthoff & Noordhoff and Kluwer Law International and its publishing director, Mr. Alan Stephens; *Israel Yearbook on Human Rights* and its editor, Professor Yoram Dinstein, then president of Tel Aviv University; and the *Emory International Law Review.*

— NATAN LERNER
KIRIAT ONO, ISRAEL

# INTRODUCTION

◆

This book deals with the approach of the international community, through its main institutions, to the issue of religious human rights since the establishment of the United Nations (U.N.). Since the end of World War II and the San Francisco Conference of 1945, during which the U.N. was established, a wide spectrum of global and regional instruments intended to protect human rights has been developed, although not necessarily with the same emphasis and structure. Religious human rights—or human rights related to religion and beliefs—are recognized as protected rights. No global treaty has yet been adopted. The 1981 U.N. Declaration on the Elimination of All Forms of Intolerance and Discrimination Based on Religion or Belief comes closest, but acceptance of this declaration is not mandatory.

Even in the absence of a specific treaty, however, mandatory provisions regarding religious human rights are contained in the International Covenant on Civil and Political Rights (1966) and in corresponding provisions in regional human rights instruments. Some of these instruments reflect customary international law and thus bind not only the states that have ratified such agreements but other states as well. Additional obligatory texts were introduced at several global and regional conventions, though these were more limited in scope and authority. I shall review all these provisions in this volume with the goal of reaching some coherent conclusions and making some recommendations on how to make further progress in the protection of religious human rights.

Adequate protection of religious human rights has become all the more pressing in recent years. Religious intolerance and persecution are at the forefront of many recent tragic conflicts around the world involving ethnicity, racism, group hatred, minority rights, self-determination, and segregation. Religious intolerance has fueled tragic campaigns of genocide and ethnic cleansing. Religion has thus become an increasingly central factor in international politics. For some observers, the Cold War between the major powers is being replaced by "a clash of civilizations," defined in religious and cultural terms.[1]

Moreover, persecution on religious grounds is a grave and present danger, as can be seen in current conflicts between believers and nonbelievers, or between different cults or churches in multi-religious states, or between states with an official or preferred religion and individuals and communities not

1

belonging to it. In some cases the conflict is between a church and its own members, and the law is expected to introduce a balance between the opposing rights. Contemporary terrorism, at the world level, seems also to be strongly influenced by religious extremism and fanaticism.[2]

Against this background I shall try to summarize what the international community has achieved, mainly since the 1940s, in an attempt to introduce some systematic order to this sensitive area, and to identify some of the religious rights challenges that will confront the international community in the next century.

## RELIGIOUS HUMAN RIGHTS LITERATURE

Many experts have argued that religious human rights, as compared with other basic rights, have been largely neglected by the world community. Similarly, many experts agree that human rights literature has generally failed to address adequately the issues of religious rights.[3]

There seems to be a reverse trend afoot in the 1990s. Several international conferences on religious freedom have taken place. For example, the two-volume set *Religious Human Rights in Global Perspective,* edited by Johan D. van der Vyver and John Witte Jr., was the impressive outcome of an international conference at Emory University in Atlanta in 1996. This was followed in 1998 by a special issue of the *Emory International Law Review* dedicated to ground-breaking analysis of the problem of proselytism in Russia.[4] Malcolm D. Evans, in addition to publishing several books generally dealing with European human rights and the jurisprudence of the European Court of Human Rights, recently published an important book devoted specifically to religious rights in Europe.[5] The Center for the Study of Human Rights at Columbia University in New York recently produced a collection of basic documents addressing religious rights.[6] This collection contains selected international texts directly concerning religious rights, and it includes documents on the rights of minorities and the relationship between the state and religious institutions. A world report on religion, published in 1997 by the University of Essex, provides a factual analysis of religious rights in individual countries.[7] A 600-page doctoral thesis by Bahiyyih G. Tahzib, which addresses international protection of freedom of religion or belief, also warrants mention.[8]

I hope that this book will also serve to reverse the trend of ignoring religious rights. I have tried to focus on the big picture presented by the relevant international texts. My approach is broadly gauged. Among the themes discussed are the following: the legal nature of religiously based congregations or communities; the differences between individual rights, collective rights, and group rights; the rights of religious minorities, a controversial area in international law; the effect of new religions, cults, and sects on international norms; the interaction between freedom of conscience and freedom of expression of religious feelings and their respective translation into worship and forms of cult; the status of religious sites; proselytism and conversion, a burgeoning issue in international jurisprudence; limitations and derogation of rights related to religion; the clash between the protection of these rights and other freedoms, such as freedom of expression and association, including the issue of group libel; religion and criminal law; and particular arrangements made between some states and international or national religious entities. These themes will be addressed in connection with the provisions incorporated into global and regional instruments—provisions that are intended to prevent discrimination or persecutions in religiously related areas, such as education, family law, or incitement to religious hatred.

I am aware of the relationship between international and municipal protection of human rights. While constitutional law and domestic legislation and jurisprudence are beyond the scope of this volume, it will be necessary in some cases to compare international provisions with similar ones in the domestic sphere, as well as judicial or quasi-judicial (in the case of monitoring bodies) decisions at the international level and corresponding domestic case law. It will also be useful to consider particular developments in individual states that are likely to have global implications.

## THE LEGAL MEANING OF RELIGION AND BELIEF

Modern human rights law has sought to avoid much philosophical controversy by asserting that the terms *religion* and *belief* are meant to refer to both theistic views of the universe, as well as atheistic, agnostic, rationalistic, and other convictions where religion and belief are absent. Because religion, in general, has been too hard to define, the United Nations has adopted instead a catalog of rights in the sphere of religion, under the heading of freedom of thought, conscience, and religion. The same approach has been followed in regional human rights instruments. None of the international and regional instruments addressing the freedom of rights of religion has attempted to define religion.[9]

### RELIGION

Some legal dictionaries have attempted to define the term religion more precisely. *Stroud's Judicial Dictionary,* for example, provides the following description: "The essential elements of religion are belief in and worship of God." Here, the distinction between religion and belief is absent. Stroud's further asserts that "religion and ethical principles must not be confused, for religion is concerned with man's relation to God, ethics with man's relation to man."[10] By comparison, *Black's Law Dictionary* defines religion as "a [human's] relation to Divinity, to reverence, worship, obedience, and submission to mandates and precepts of supernatural or superior beings. In its broadest sense [religion] includes all forms of belief in the existence of superior beings exercising power over human beings by volition, imposing rules of conduct, with future rewards and punishments."[11]

These and similar dictionary definitions of religion contain several common elements. All incorporate the recognition of the existence of a Supreme Being, usually called God. The nature and power of this being differ from one religion to another. For all religions God has a normative function, and believers are expected to follow God's teachings and rules of conduct. This may include a duty to propagate these teachings and rules among others in order to persuade them to accept the teaching as true. Believers are also expected to express their religious convictions in varying forms of worship or cult. Generally, though not always, a church or other institution is established to organize the cult or worship.

A number of courts, particularly in the United States, have also attempted to define the outer limits of religion for constitutional purposes. In its early years the United States Supreme Court stressed the need for a relationship of humans to some Supreme Being. More than one hundred years ago the Court defined *religion* as a term that "has reference to one's views of his relations to his Creator, and to the obligations they impose of reverence for his being and character, and of obedience to his will. It is often confounded with the cultus or form of worship of a particular sect, but is distinguishable from the latter."[12]

In *Torcaso v. Watkins* (1961), the Court gave wider scope to the legal term *religion*—now including Buddhism, Taoism, Ethical, Cultural, and Secular Humanism among protected religious beliefs.[13] This trend, however, has its limits. As the Court asserted in *Wisconsin v. Yoder* (1972): "Ordered liberty precludes allowing every person to make his own standards on matters of conduct in which society as a whole has important interests."[14] In *United States v. Seeger* (1965) and *Welsh v. United States* (1970), the Supreme Court affirmed this broad approach regarding religious diversity and plurality.[15] Specifically, the Court determined that the First Amendment religion clause forbade the legal distinction between "religions based on a belief in the existence of God as against those religions founded on different beliefs."[16] In subsequent years the Court "moved in the direction of a functional definition of religion, stressing the ultimate concern of individuals. . . . The resulting bifurcated definition of religion fairly accommodates the individual's liberty of belief within the confines of the affirmative secular state."[17]

In *Malnak v. Yogi* (1979) the United States Court of Appeals for the Third Circuit asserted that in order to meet the definition of religion, a belief must (1) address fundamental and ultimate questions; (2) be comprehensive in nature and not an isolated teaching; and (3) present formal and external signs analogous to recognized religions, such as services, ceremonies, clergy, organizational structure, efforts at propagation, observation of holidays, and manifestations similar to those of traditional religions.[18] The existence of these conditions would permit a distinction between generally accepted religions and some beliefs or sets of ideas that may claim to be religious but fall short.

The nature and scope of each religious tradition determine the emphasis it places on certain aspects of existence and human behavior. All religions prescribe norms by which their adherents should conduct their personal, familial, and social lives. In some cases the norms imply a profound identification between the individual and the creed and preclude an easy change of religion.

## BELIEF

Belief is a broader concept than religion. It includes religion but is not limited to its traditional meaning. *Belief* has been defined legally as a "conviction of the truth of a proposition, existing subjectively in the mind, and induced by argument, persuasion, or proof addressed to the judgment."[19] In certain United Nations instruments, the term *belief* has been adopted to cover the rights of nonreligious persons such as atheists, agnostics, rationalists, and others. The debate that accompanied the inclusion of the word *belief* in such documents is instructive in identifying the underlying political motivations. U.N. Special Rapporteur Arcot Krishnaswami, in order to limit controversy, considered the phrase *religion or belief* to include various theistic creeds and beliefs such as "agnosticism, free thought, atheism and rationalism."[20]

There are political, philosophical, social, and many other kinds of beliefs. Nevertheless, the term is frequently used in connection with religion or the absence of religion. For example, there may be totalitarian regimes that require full submission of the individual and of the individual's social group to the beliefs of the system. Nazism, for instance, expected the German individual to identify fully with the Nazi creed in almost religious terms—despite Nazism's nonreligious, antireligious character.[21] Communist and other totalitarian regimes also attempt to control the beliefs of their respective peoples.

Human rights law has thus far avoided a definition of religion, except to ensure that it includes the concept of belief. As John Witte Jr. has noted, "This capacious definition of religion in international law has left it largely to individual states and individual claimants to define the boundaries of the regime of religious rights." Unfortunately, individual legislatures "embrace a bewildering array of definitions of religion."[22]

## THE U.N. SYSTEM

As shown in the following pages, the system of the Universal Declaration of Human Rights has been adopted by other legal texts. It refers to the three basic freedoms: thought, conscience, and religion. Instead of a specific definition, positive human rights law contains a catalog of rights and duties and ways of protecting them. It determines the reach and limits of rights related to religion and belief, and it formulates rules to regulate relations among religions, churches, the state, and individuals. Much is left to the discretion of each constitutional and legal system and to particularized judicial interpretation and legal thought.

The three basic freedoms are mentioned in all the relevant human rights instruments, both globally and regionally. Nevertheless, these freedoms do not have identical weight as legal notions.[23] Freedom of thought and freedom of conscience[24] can be considered more philosophical than legalistic. Both freedoms emanate from the most internal and intimate sphere of human existence. Freedom of conscience can sometimes be legally violated or restricted. Freedom of thought, on the other hand, can only be violated or affected by complicated and sophisticated means of acting upon the human mind.

Freedom of religion in a strict sense includes freedom of belief and freedom from religion, which can be understood as the right not to be coerced into accepting religious norms or behavior. These and related freedoms—including the freedoms of expression, association, teaching, and so forth—must be interpreted in light of the attempt to define religion, an attempt that has not yet produced a consensus.

Once we agree that a legal definition of religion is difficult to achieve, we can appreciate the importance of setting a catalog of rights and duties in clarifying the notion of religion. The elaboration of such a catalog requires a delineation among the three manifestations of such rights. In other words, we must ask whether we are dealing with individual rights, collective rights, or rights of the religious group, community, or congregation. We must also ask whether these rights—individual, collective, and group—warrant protection by domestic and international law.

Positive replies to these questions are vital. Freedom of religion—no matter how religion is defined—is undoubtedly a basic right of each human being, irrespective of group membership. It seems proper to locate this right high on the list of basic rights. Nevertheless, individual religious rights cannot be viewed in isolation, as certain religious practices require group participation. For example, there may be a need for a minimum quorum in order to pray. There may be a need for a leader or priest. There may be a need for the use of religious articles that cannot be provided by the believers themselves—a special installation such as a church, synagogue, or mosque, special furniture, prayer books, and the like that can only be produced or acquired collectively or by an organized institution. In other words, religion is a right belonging to individuals, several persons jointly, or an established group. Sometimes these rights are complementary. Sometimes they conflict. When this happens, individual religious rights may be compromised and require further legal protection.[25]

A catalog of religious rights is therefore essential. United Nations instruments provide such a catalog on a global level, as illustrated by Article 18 of the 1948 Universal Declaration of Human Rights; Articles 18, 20, 26, and 27 of the 1966 International Covenant on Civil and Political Rights; Article 6 of the 1981 Declaration on Intolerance and Discrimination Based on Religion or Belief; and concurring articles in other global and regional texts. Constitutional law may qualify or even modify such provisions. The pertinent international law will be discussed in the following chapters.

## SECTS OR NEW RELIGIOUS MOVEMENTS

The fact that international human rights instruments provide no definition of religion has created confusion regarding the concepts of sect and new religious movements.[26] Special Rapporteur Amor observes that although the denotation of *sect* was originally neutral and meant a community of individuals constituting a minority within a religion that decided to split from that religion, "it often now has a pejorative connotation so that it is frequently regarded as synonymous with danger, and sometimes a non-religious dimension when it is identified with a commercial enterprise."[27] Professor Amor has recommended further study of the problem with the hope that the terms *religions, new religious movements,* and *commercial enterprise* can be better clarified.

In his report on a visit to Germany in 1997, during which he had consultations with the Bundestag Study Commission on sects and psycho-groups, as well as with associations of victims of sects, Professor Amor noted the competition between traditional religions and "a multitude of new groups and communities claiming the status of religions."[28] Reports on the abusive exploitation of followers of such sects, he observed, created a public alarm, especially when the public learned of those cases involving collective suicides. Such developments provoked state intervention, including the establishment of parliamentary commissions in Germany, Belgium, France, and other countries. The Church of Scientology, described as both a sect and a commercial enterprise, received special mention in commission reports. The special rapporteur made a distinction between "sects" and "psycho-groups." Some sects, he observed, are propagators of a religion, while others are not. In order to avoid intolerance, he therefore advised caution when criticizing such groups. Religious organizations, in fact, have complained about the risk of being equated with sects. This has been a particular problem in Germany since the mid-1970s. In response, the German government, concerned that its youth was prone to antisocial behavior and dependency, launched an information and education campaign. Victims of sects created associations that were aimed at trying to avoid the abuses of the freedom of religion and belief, while acknowledging "the need to regulate the psychotherapy market, where financial motives were often concealed under a religious label."[29] Representatives of the Church of Scientology claimed that its group was a religion and fell within the international definition formulated in United Nations studies. Furthermore, the Church of Scientology claimed that it, in fact, was the victim of discrimination and persecution.[30]

In his conclusion, Professor Amor referred to the highly emotional international debate on sects or new religious movements and to a total confusion in which all groups and communities in the field of religion and belief are generally considered to be dangerous and using religion for other ends, whether financial or criminal. Nevertheless, most religious communities in Germany consider themselves to be free to exercise their religious rights. The special rapporteur still recommended a campaign to develop awareness among the media, which he believes distort stories involving religion and belief. He also proposed legislation that would make punishable any writings or statements that foment hatred.[31]

While this book was being written, the French government passed a decree establishing an Interministerial Commission for the Fight against Sects. The goal of this decree is to analyze the phenomenon of sects and encourage additional research about sects. The decree also encourages the public to improve its self-awareness and take necessary measures to counteract any actions by sects that would threaten public order.[32] Other European governments have been examining similar measures that would contain the influence of sects without endangering freedom of belief. Debates have taken place throughout Europe, and the judiciary branches of some countries have been asked to make legal determinations about certain sects. Outside Europe, mainly in the United States, a similar debate involving legal scholars and theologians has been taking place.[33]

The debate involving sects, cults, or new religions is obviously a delicate matter. It has already caused considerable confusion and in some cases has generated a climate of suspicion or even manifest or latent intolerance within society.[34] Measures taken against the Church of Scientology in Germany have been compared with the measures taken against Jewish people in Nazi Germany. The raising of such emotions, if nothing else, may create a good reason to renew the discussion on what is a workable and universal legal definition of religion and belief. Until such time, sects remain prone to regulation, even though such regulation is difficult to effectuate.[35]

The Council of Europe took note of such difficulty in a recent recommendation under the title "Illegal Activities of Sects." The Parliamentary Assembly of the council considered that "major legislation on sects was undesirable" and might "interfere with the freedom of conscience and religion" as well as "harm traditional religions."[36]

# 1.

# RELIGIOUS HUMAN RIGHTS
## UNDER THE UNITED NATIONS

————◆————

During the United Nations era four major instruments have responded globally to human rights issues related to religion and belief: (1) the 1948 Universal Declaration of Human Rights; (2) the 1959 Arcot Krishnaswami Study; (3) the 1966 International Covenants on Human Rights; and (4) the 1981 Declaration on the Elimination of All Forms of Intolerance and Discrimination Based on Religion or Belief. In addition, there have been several general texts and related instruments prohibiting discrimination. This chapter will analyze the religious human rights provisions in these instruments, with some reference to domestic legislation and jurisprudence. The most important of these provisions are reproduced in the Appendix hereto.

## THE UNIVERSAL DECLARATION OF HUMAN RIGHTS

The Universal Declaration of Human Rights, adopted by General Assembly Resolution 217 A (III) of 10 December 1948, has a number of provisions relevant to religious human rights. Article 2 forbids distinctions of any kind, including religion, in the enjoyment of the rights and freedoms set forth in the Declaration. Article 26 refers to religious groups and covers the right of education. Article 29, which addresses the limitations in the exercise of the proclaimed rights, is also relevant to those interested in protecting religious rights.

The most crucial provision of the Universal Declaration on religious rights is Article 18, which states:

> Everyone has the right to freedom of thought, conscience and religion; this right includes freedom to change his religion or belief, and freedom, either alone or in community with others and in public or private, to manifest his religion or belief in teaching, practice, worship and observance.

9

Article 18 greatly influenced the texts incorporated in the 1966 Covenants, and was influential in regional treaties and the 1981 Declaration, which will be discussed below. Nehemiah Robinson, in his classic commentary on the declaration, divided Article 18 into two parts: the first clause guarantees the right to freedom of thought, conscience, and religion; the second enumerates the specific rights included therein. This second part is not exhaustive. It only contains those rights that the United Nations thought essential to include because their observance might not be universal at present.[1]

Robinson understood that freedom of thought is a broad category. In his interpretation, it included the right to profess a religion or to profess none—in other words, the right to believe or not to believe. To Robinson, the freedom of thought included two other freedoms: freedom of conscience and freedom of religion, which were explicitly mentioned "in order to leave no doubts" in the minds of the peoples of the world, as it may be deduced from the *travaux préparatoires*. Freedom of conscience was not seen at the time as a strictly legal concept, and there was some opposition to its inclusion. On the other hand, the sacred and inviolable character of freedom of thought, in the words of René Cassin, allowed it to be understood as part of the vernacular of different legal systems.[2]

The term *belief* has a particular meaning in the declaration. Its inclusion in Article 18, and in similar articles in other instruments, should be interpreted strictly in connection with the term *religion*. It does not refer to beliefs of another character—whether political, cultural, scientific, or economic—all of which deserve protection according to law but do not belong to the sphere normally described as religion. The term *belief* was incorporated into the declaration to protect nonreligious convictions, such as atheism or agnosticism, and its meaning was clarified during the discussions on subsequent instruments dealing with religious rights.

Another difficult problem in the drafting of the Universal Declaration was the recognition of the right to change one's religion, a right that was denied by some religions and countries. The clause received opposition but, nevertheless, was adopted by a vote of 27 to 5, with 12 abstentions. The acceptance was earned, according to Robinson, on the understanding that the declaration must be universal and that this clause did not represent a specific right but was the consequence of freedom of religion and thought. The drafters of the declaration were aware that there were many controversial issues involved, including apostasy; missionary activities; coercion and enticement; proselytism and its limits; the status of new or young religious movements struggling for recognition; and the social dangers inherent in the practices of certain sects using all kinds of manipulations to attract adherents. In chapter 4 I shall deal with these controversies in more detail, especially as many of them continue to demand public and professional attention in many parts of the world.

Article 18 makes a mild concession to the rights of religious groups. It refers to everyone's right to manifest his religion or belief "alone or in community with others." The words "in community" do not involve a clear reference to religious bodies or institutions; such reference would have been outside the spirit prevailing in the United Nations at that time. Yet, these words suggest that religious rights are more than a strictly individual issue. A right to be exercised in community with others must therefore refer to something more than simply the collection of rights of individuals.

The critical role of the Universal Declaration in the development of the legal and political philosophy of the second part of the twentieth century is beyond question. It is one of the most important single legal documents of our time, and most of its contents can now be seen as customary international law. Its impact on domestic law, in the West at least, remains powerful.

## FIRST SPECIFIC STEPS:
## THE KRISHNASWAMI STUDY (1959)

It has been rightly asserted that the subject of religious human rights was shunned and neglected more than any other similar subject, perhaps as a consequence of the generally acknowledged fact that no topic has divided humankind more.[3] The Subcommission on Prevention of Discrimination and Protection of Minorities decided that one of the first studies ordered by the subcommission should deal with this subject, including a program of action to eradicate religious discrimination. To that end, the subcommission appointed in 1956 a special rapporteur, Arcot Krishnaswami from India. He submitted in 1959 a careful and comprehensive report.[4]

The study was based on information that appeared in eighty-two country studies analyzed by the author. Krishnaswami was aware of the difficulties involved with such a comprehensive study of religious rights and emphasized that differential treatment meted out to individuals and groups is not always synonymous with discrimination. Sometimes discriminatory practices are to be found in countries where efforts have been made to eradicate discrimination.

Conscious of the difficulty in defining religion, Krishnaswami intended the phrase religion or belief to include various theistic creeds, as well as agnosticism, free thought, atheism, and rationalism. After recognizing freedom of thought, conscience, and religion as a legal right, he distinguished between the freedom to maintain (or change) religion or belief and the freedom to manifest religion or belief. It is the latter that engenders most of the legal problems.

Krishnaswami anticipated some of the problems emanating from the freedom to manifest religion or belief, and he therefore addressed permissible limitations upon the right, the individual and collective aspects of this right, and the public and private need to express this right. While the freedom to maintain (or change) a religion or belief is less prone to restriction, the right to manifest it is often the subject of state regulation and limitations.

Krishnaswami stressed that the followers of most religions and beliefs are members of some form of organization, church, or religious community.

Therefore, compulsion to join such bodies (or prevention from leaving) may become an infringement of the right to freedom of thought, conscience, and religion. Prescribed religious procedures or formalities do not necessarily involve such infringement. Nevertheless, Article 18 of the Universal Declaration attempts to guard against coercion. While sanctions against apostasy are rare today, some legal systems adopt the law of a particular religion, and this often leads to delicate legal questions.

Freedom to manifest religion or belief, Krishnaswami argued, includes protection of a religion's words, teachings, practice, worship, and observance. To be legitimate, such manifestations of religion must satisfy the criteria established in Article 29 of the Universal Declaration, should be respectful of religious minorities, and should work to ensure a greater measure of freedom for society as a whole.[5]

Krishnaswami concluded that the collective aspect of the freedom to manifest religion or belief in the form of freedom of assembly or the freedom of association and organization was especially important, as it was prone to state intervention and regulation. Minorities were, of course, vulnerable, especially when those minorities had religious affinities with those outside the state.

The Krishnaswami study included a detailed list of components of the freedom to manifest religion or belief. Some of these could be subject to permissible limitations, as in the case of human sacrifice, self-immolation, mutilation, slavery, prostitution, subversive activities, polygamy, and other practices that may clash with the requirements mentioned in Article 29 of the Universal Declaration. In such cases domestic legislation may only preempt norms adopted in international instruments when the minimum standard rule is not affected. The remaining list of freedoms related to the manifestations of religion or belief included worship, processions, pilgrimages, equipment and symbols, funeral arrangements, holidays and days of rest, dietary practices, marriage and divorce, dissemination of religion or belief, and training of personnel. Manifestation of religion or belief also included the freedom to forgo acts incompatible with prescriptions of a religion or belief, such as oaths, military service, participation in religious ceremonies, confession, and compulsory medical treatment.[6]

Krishnaswami devoted a short chapter to showing the possible relationships of a religion to the state. This category included states with either an established church or a state religion; states that recognize several religions; and states that mandate a separation of state and religion. Within this context Krishnaswami discussed the management of religious affairs; the financial relationship between the state and religion; and the duties of public authorities. This is also an area in which local constitutional law may prevail over international rules and where the relationship between the state and religion is profoundly influenced by cultural traditions.[7]

The study ended with a chapter on trends and conclusions that reflected the circumstances of the period in which it was prepared. In a final footnote Krishnaswami commented on the manifestations of antisemitism and other forms of racial prejudice and intolerance that have become the immediate cause of further measures adopted by the international community. He ended his report by enunciating sixteen rules he believed should be approved by the United Nations.[8] These rules were the basis of the Draft Principles on Freedom and Non-Discrimination in the Matter of Religious Rights and Practices. This draft was prepared by the subcommission.[9] It may be useful to summarize the contents herein.

The draft principles are divided into four parts that follow a preamble which proclaims the overall goal of promoting the freedom of thought, conscience, and religion (and eradicating discrimination on the ground of religion or belief). The principles follow very closely the text of the basic rules, with minor modifications.

Part I reaffirms: (1) the right of everyone to adhere, or not to adhere, to a religion or belief, in accordance with the dictates of his conscience; (2) the prior rights of parents or legal guardians to decide the religion or belief in which their child should be brought up—the best interests of the child serving as the guiding principle; and (3) that no one should be subjected to material or moral coercion to impair his freedom to maintain or to change his religion or belief. The wording of these three principles is slightly different from the wording used by Krishnaswami in his first rule, and it incorporates a fourth principle, the banning of any discrimination based on religion or belief.

Part II applies thirteen principles, which serve as a catalog of rights to be ensured to all. According to Part II, each person should be free to comply with the prescriptions of his religion or belief and free from performing acts incompatible with them, particularly as it concerns worship, places of worship, and objects necessary for the performance of rites. The thirteen principles reflecting these basic rules include the following rights:

1. to worship, with equal protection to be accorded to all forms of worship, places of worship, and objects necessary for the performance of rites;
2. to journey to sacred places;
3. to observe dietary practices prescribed by the religion or belief;
4. to acquire or produce materials and objects necessary for the prescribed practices, including dietary practices; when the government controls the means of production and distribution, it shall make those materials or objects available to the members of the religion or belief concerned;
5. to have marriage rites performed in accordance with his religion or belief and not to be compelled to undergo a religious marriage ceremony not in accordance with his convictions; and the right to seek marital dissolution and obtain it solely in accordance with the applicable law, without any discrimination;
6. to have the prescriptions of the religion or belief of a deceased person followed in all matters affecting burial, cremation, or other methods of disposal of the dead, particularly concerning places, symbols, and rites, with equal protection against desecration and interference by outsiders;

7. to have due account taken of the prescriptions of each religion or belief relating to holidays and days of rest;
8. to teach or disseminate his religion or belief, in public or in private; and to be free from being compelled to take religious or atheistic instruction, contrary to his convictions or, in the case of children, to those of their parents or legal guardians;
9. to train personnel or bring teachers from abroad, and to be free from permanent limitations on training abroad;
10. to exemption from compulsory oath-swearing of a religious nature contrary to his convictions;
11. to exemption for genuine objectors to military service, where it is recognized, to be granted in such a manner that no adverse distinction based upon religion or belief may result;
12. to exemption on similar grounds from participation in certain public ceremonies; and
13. to exemption for priests or ministers of religion from having to divulge information received in confidence in the performance of their religious duties.

Part III addresses restrictions. The principles proclaimed in Part I and principles 10 and 13 of Part II shall not be subject to any restrictions. Other freedoms and rights shall be subject only to limitations prescribed by law solely for the purpose of securing the rights and freedoms of others or required by morality, health, public order, and the general welfare in a democratic society. These should be consistent with the principles of the United Nations.

According to Part IV, public authorities shall refrain from making distinctions with respect to the right to freedom of thought, conscience, and religion, and prevent individuals or groups from doing so. When there is a conflict between the demands of two or more religions or beliefs, public authorities should try to find solutions reconciling those demands in a manner ensuring the greatest measure of freedom to the whole society. No adverse distinctions should be made in the granting of subsidies or tax exemptions. But the state may impose general taxes to cover the cost of arrangements compensating the taking of property or of the preservation of religious monuments of historic or artistic value.

As pointed out, the rules prepared by Krishnaswami and the Principles drafted by the subcommission do not differ in substance and, in some cases, are identical. Rule 16, on the duties of public authorities, is more detailed than Part IV of the Principles, but generally is the same.

Many of the Krishnaswami principles have been incorporated into the 1981 U.N. Declaration and in the 1965 Draft Convention still pending before the United Nations. Without a doubt the Krishnaswami study was an important stage in the United Nations work on religious rights and was the first specific step to correct the neglect of religion by the international community. The study will be mentioned frequently in the following pages.

## THE 1966 COVENANTS ON HUMAN RIGHTS

The International Covenant on Economic, Social, and Cultural Rights (ICESCR) and the International Covenant on Civil and Political Rights (ICCPR) were adopted by the U.N. General Assembly on December 16, 1966, by resolution 2200 A (XXI). They became effective on January 3, 1976, and March 23, 1976, respectively.[10] Despite the amount of time that passed between the adoption of the Universal Declaration and the covenants, the 1966 instruments reflect the thinking that inspired the declaration. The legal thought that predominated in the development of group rights in the 1965 Convention on Racial Discrimination, on the other hand, did not influence the covenants, probably because of the modalities of the drafting process.

The most relevant provisions in the ICCPR are Articles 18, 20, and 27. Article 18 has four paragraphs. The first paragraph generally follows, with some minor changes, the wording of Article 18 of the Universal Declaration. The covenant does not refer to the right to change one's religion or belief. Instead it uses milder language, which reflects a compromise. Specifically, it proclaims that the right of everyone to freedom of thought, conscience, and belief shall include freedom to have or to adopt a religion or belief of his choice. There is no doubt, however, that the final text recognizes the right to change one's religion or beliefs or to abandon a religion and adopt a new one. This liberal interpretation is supported by the discussion made during the preparation of the covenant.[11]

Article 18(2) of the ICCPR states that no one shall be subject to coercion that would impair his freedom to follow or to adopt a religion or belief of his choice. The term *coercion* is not defined, but it seems reasonable to infer that it applies to the use of force or threats as well as more subtle forms of illegitimate influence, such as moral pressure or material enticement. Comparatively, the 1981 Declaration contained more detail about the notion of coercion.

Article 18(3) addresses limitations and should be read in conjunction with Article 4 of the covenant, which includes other articles that disallow derogation even in times of public emergency.[12] In addition, Article 18(3) should be compared with Article 29(2) and (3) of the Universal Declaration. Article 18(3) only permits limitations on the freedom to manifest one's religion or belief as are prescribed by law and are necessary to protect public safety, order, health, or morals or the fundamental rights and freedom of others. National security is not listed. Because religion is such a sensitive topic, the text must be interpreted in a restrictive way.

Only manifestations of religion, or religious practices, can be restricted. The freedoms of thought and conscience—and religious ideas not translated into practices—are beyond any restriction. There are virtually no problems regarding the religious practices of the major, well-established religions. Nevertheless, there have been some difficulties with *shehitah*, the slaughtering of animals according to Jewish tradition (and similar practices of the Santerian religion).[13] Also, issues involving the wearing of turbans, skullcaps, or veils or the growth of facial hair have required adjudication. Inevitably, certain religious rites, customs, and rules of behavior clash with public norms, health, or morals, and judicial intervention again becomes necessary. Morality is indisputably the outcome of cultural and historical factors that vary from society to society, and the determination of an international minimum standard may not be equally acceptable to all religions, civilizations, and countries.[14]

Article 18(4) addresses the liberty of parents and legal guardians to ensure that the religious and moral education of their children is in conformity with their own convictions. This is again a highly sensitive area. The United Nations has recognized that the interaction between religion and education is of great importance, but there has still been difficulty in reaching consensus among several international instruments, including the UNESCO Convention against Discrimination in Education, the 1981 Declaration, and the Convention on the Rights of the Child.[15] This area involves issues of both international and constitutional law, and adjudication at the national and international levels frequently has been necessary. For example, the Human Rights Committee in 1978 had to address a complaint submitted by the secretary of the Union of Free Thinkers in Finland against his country. The issue involved teaching history of religion in public schools.[16] The committee took the view that such instruction, if given in a "neutral and objective way" and respecting the convictions of parents and guardians who do not believe in any religion, does not violate Article 18 of the covenant.

Furthermore, Article 20(2) of the ICCPR provides: "Any advocacy of national, racial or religious hatred that constitutes incitement to discrimination, hostility or violence shall be prohibited by law." Article 20 does not require intent. Its wording was criticized, and several states entered reservations about it. The late Professor Partsch, discussing the changes introduced in the different drafts since 1953, stated that the final text abandoned a previous "balanced compromise" reached in the Commission on Human Rights.[17] The Human Rights Committee, on its part, in its General Comment on Article 20, made it clear that states are obliged to adopt the necessary legislative measures prohibiting the actions referred to therein. The prohibitions incorporated into Article 20 are fully compatible with the right of freedom of expression contained in Article 19, the exercise of which carries with it special duties and responsibilities.[18]

Article 20(2), and similar provisions incorporated in regional treaties and other recent instruments, should be compared with Article 4 of the Convention on Racial Discrimination.[19] This provision imposes clear-cut obligations on states to enact anti-incitement legislation, and many states have complied.[20]

A clash between rights may be involved, as some states fear that provisions prohibiting advocacy of racial or religious hatred may jeopardize other rights concerning freedom of speech and association.[21] This fear has manifested itself recently with the issue of hate crimes. The United States Supreme Court, for example, upheld the constitutionality of state legislation on enhancement of punishment for offenses motivated by racial or religious hatred.[22]

## GENERAL COMMENT OF THE HUMAN RIGHTS COMMITTEE

The committee in charge of implementing the Covenant on Civil and Political Rights has also addressed issues related to religious rights. In 1993 the committee summarized its position by issuing a General Comment on Article 18, No. 22 (48).[23]

The committee felt the need to draw to the attention of state parties the fact that the freedoms of thought and conscience are protected equally with the freedom of religion and belief. Article 18 protects theistic, nontheistic, and atheistic beliefs, as well as the right not to profess any religion or belief. The committee stressed that the terms *beliefs* and *religion* are to be broadly construed, rejecting any tendency to discriminate against any religions or beliefs for any reasons, including the fact that they are newly established or represent religious minorities that may be the subject of hostility by a predominant religious community.[24] The committee intended to avoid situations in which well-established religious groups enjoyed a broader legal recognition and protection than newly formed groups. The committee also attempted to address the right to propagate religious ideas that do not enjoy support of the majority, provided that the propagation of these ideas does not exceed the limits imposed by law. Still, it is necessary to ask how broadly the term *belief* may be construed.

The freedoms of thought and conscience, and the freedom to have or adopt a religion or belief of one's choice, are protected unconditionally. No one can be compelled to reveal his or her thoughts or be made to adhere to a religion or belief. In this respect the rights proclaimed in Article 18 should be compared to the right to hold opinions without interference as recognized by Article 19(1) of the covenant. This is not the case with the freedom to manifest religion or belief, whether this freedom is expressed individually or in community with others. This freedom, as mentioned in this provision, encompasses a broad range of acts, including ritual and ceremonial acts and practices integral to such acts, such as the building of places of worship, the use of ritual formulas and objects, the display of symbols, and the observance of holy days and days of rest. It also encompasses dietary regulations, clothing requirements,[25] the use of a particular language, and rituals associated with certain stages in life. This freedom also includes the right to choose religious leaders and teachers, establish seminaries or religious schools, and prepare and distribute religious texts and publications. The committee considered it necessary to list the components of the right to manifest religion or belief following the 1981 Declaration and the Krishnaswami study. The detailed listing was not meant to be exhaustive and should be read in conjunction with the restrictions addressed in Article 18(3).

Paragraph 5 of the General Comment reiterates the notion that the covenant bars any coercion that would impair the right to replace one's current religion with another religion or atheistic views. This right to conversion has burdened all stages of the drafting of international instruments dealing with religion. In defining *coercion* the committee included (1) the use or threat of physical force or penal sanctions, and (2) restrictions on access to education, medical care, employment, or other rights guaranteed by the covenant. The same protection is enjoyed by holders of nonreligious beliefs.

The Human Rights Committee also clarified the reach of Article 18(4) with regard to education. Public school instruction related to the teaching of the general history of religions and ethics is permitted if it is given in a neutral and objective way. Public education that includes instruction in a particular religion or belief, on the other hand, is inconsistent with the covenant—unless a provision is made for nondiscriminatory exemptions or alternatives to those who want them. The guarantee of the freedom to teach a religion or belief includes the liberty of parents or guardians to ensure that their children receive a religious and moral education in conformity with their own convictions.

The 1993 General Comment refers to a former General Comment No. 11(19), which determines that state parties are obligated under Article 20 of the ICCPR to enact laws to prohibit advocacy of national, racial, or religious hatred that constitutes incitement to discrimination, hostility, or violence. The committee emphasized that the prohibition of incitement to religious hatred is fully compatible with other basic freedoms.

The committee also stressed that Article 18(3) should be interpreted strictly: restrictions not specified in the paragraph are disallowed, even if they are utilized to protect other rights. Additionally, limitations may be applied only for their specific purposes and must be directly related and proportionate to the specific need on which they are predicated. They should not be used for discriminatory purposes or be applied in a discriminatory manner. The freedom from coercion and the liberty of parents and guardians to ensure religious and moral education of their children cannot be restricted. Permissible limitations must be established by law and should be interpreted with a view to protect the rights guaranteed under the covenant.[26] Legitimate constraints, such as imprisonment, should not affect religious rights, as far as it is reasonably possible.

In the same paragraph, the committee dealt with the delicate notion of morals, a concept that derives from many social, philosophical, and religious traditions. When the freedom to manifest a religion or belief has the purpose of protecting morals, it must be based on principles not derived exclusively from a single tradition.

The fact that a religion is recognized as an official state religion, or is the religion of the majority of the population, should not result in any impairment of rights for nonbelievers or adherents of other religions, according to the covenant. Privileges for the members of the predominant religion should be regarded as discriminatory. The committee expects state members to report on measures taken to protect the rights of religious minorities under the covenant and its Article 27. States are also required to provide information regarding practices that are punishable as blasphemy. Blasphemy is not mentioned in existing international human rights instruments but has caused controversy in domestic legislation.[27]

Paragraph 11 of the General Comment addresses conscientious objection, a right that is not explicitly mentioned in the covenant. The committee believes that such a right can be derived from Article 18, inasmuch as the use of lethal force may seriously conflict with the freedom of conscience and the right to manifest one's religion or belief. There shall be no discrimination against conscientious objectors on the ground that they have failed to perform military service. The question of conscientious objection in some cases falls outside the scope of religious rights. Pacifism may be considered a belief, but it is generally of a nonreligious nature. *Conscientious* and *religious* may or may not necessarily mean the same thing, as United States and European case law makes clear.[28]

I have dealt in length with the committee's General Comment for three reasons: (1) the comment's intrinsic importance; (2) the authority and influence of the members of the committee who wrote the comment; and (3) the likelihood that the comment will influence the incorporation of religious rights in other modern instruments.[29] In addition, the General Comment will likely play a part in determining the scope of domestic legislation and judicial interpretation. It already has played a part in influencing the Krishnaswami study and the 1981 Declaration.

The International Covenant on Civil and Political Rights is the only global human rights treaty dealing with religion that contains measures of implementation. As of June 1, 1999, 144 states had ratified or acceded to the covenant, and 95 states had become parties to the Optional Protocol on individual communications. The periodic reports submitted by state parties (plus complaints or communications filed by individuals) permitted the Human Rights Committee (which is in charge of implementation) to cover a broad range of human rights issues related to religion. The 1993 General Comment on Article 18 summarized the principal views of the committee in this regard.

The yearly Reports of the Committee—issued as General Assembly Official Records (GAOR), Supplements No. 40—contain salient information on religious rights. When examining the periodic state reports, members of the committee were able to ask questions and require additional information regarding the legislation concerning such rights from representatives of the states. For example, when the second periodic report of Morocco was discussed, members asked questions regarding procedures on the recognition of religious sects, the status of the Bahá'í faith, marriages between members of different religious groups, and the meaning of terms such as *religion of the state, revealed religions,* and *heretical sects*.[30] During the consideration of the second periodic report of Austria, members asked questions regarding the issues of conscientious objectors, status of Jehovah's Witnesses, and criminal-law rules concerning blasphemy.[31] The members also scrutinized Colombia's third periodic report, which provided information on the modifications of the concordat with the Holy See in order to adjust it to the new constitution.[32] The members also discussed blasphemy in the United Kingdom;[33] apostasy and discrimination against religious minorities in Sudan;[34] differences in the treatment of churches in Argentina, Lithuania, and Israel;[35] and restrictions on religious rights in the former USSR.[36] Almost every country that submitted periodic reports was subjected to some scrutiny. When the initial report of Zimbabwe was considered in 1988, the members had to consider the clash between traditional practices and customary law, on one hand, and provisions of the covenant on the other.[37] The committee recommended that practices which were incompatible with the covenant should be prohibited by legislation. A similar discussion took place with regard to Tanzania.[38]

As for individual complaints or communications, the Human Rights Committee addressed relatively few cases involving religious rights, as compared with other rights. Out of 823 communications involving fifty-six states (submitted until 1998), only a few referred to alleged violations of religious human rights. Most of those related to conscientious objection, education, and equality among churches.[39]

The Covenant on Economic, Social, and Cultural Rights refers to religious rights, albeit in a more limited way.[40] Article 13(1) addresses the need to ensure "understanding, tolerance and friendship among all . . . religious groups." Paragraph 3 of the same article refers to the liberty of parents to ensure the religious and moral education of their children in conformity with their own convictions. Article 2(2) forbids discrimination of any kind, including religious discrimination.

The implementation system of the ICESCR has not been effective. Shortly after the creation of the ICESCR in 1976, a Committee on Economic, Social, and Cultural Rights (composed of independent experts) was established and has been meeting periodically to examine the reports submitted by state parties.[41] This committee so far has contributed little to the dialogue on religious rights and the abuse thereof.


## THE UNITED NATIONS DECLARATION ON INTOLERANCE AND DISCRIMINATION BASED ON RELIGION OR BELIEF

The Declaration on the Elimination of All Forms of Intolerance and Discrimination Based on Religion or Belief was proclaimed by the General Assembly of the United Nations by resolution 36/55 of November 25, 1981. It is presently the most important international instrument regarding religious rights and the prohibition of intolerance or discrimination based on religion or belief.[42] The declaration, as well as the draft convention still pending before the United Nations, originated in response to the outburst of antisemitic incidents that occurred in several places in 1959 and 1960. These were called the swastika epidemics, and many feared a revival of Nazism.

The United Nations response to those attacks and the resolutions adopted by the various U.N. organs culminated in the General Assembly resolutions 1780 and 1781 (XVII) of December 8, 1962. These resolutions asked for the preparation of twin but separate declarations and conventions addressing the manifestations of religious and racial discrimination and intolerance. The separation between the two subjects was the result of lobbying by third-world countries who wanted to adopt a document on racism, but were largely indifferent to religious discrimination, and of international politics, the Cold War, the Arab-Israeli conflict, and the issue of antisemitism in the Soviet Union.[43] Some delegates took the view that there was a theoretical difference between religious sentiments, on the one hand, and prejudice, hatred, or discrimination against people of a different race or color, on the other. In any case the result was a speedy preparation of the instruments on race and slow progress on issues of religious discrimination and intolerance.

In 1965 the General Assembly requested that the relevant U.N. bodies try to complete the preparation of both a declaration and convention on religion. Some work was done on both, but in 1972 the General Assembly decided to give priority to the draft declaration. In practice, this meant postponing indefinitely the adoption of a mandatory treaty, despite the fact that a draft, which will be summarized below, was in the process of being developed.

Additional work was slow to develop and consisted mainly of the activities of a working group appointed by the Commission on Human Rights. Finally, in 1981, after tenacious efforts, the Commission on Human Rights completed a draft, which was adopted by a vote of 33 to 0, with 5 abstentions. At the Third Committee of the General Assembly the vote in favor was 45 to 0, again with 5 abstentions. In both cases the abstentions were from the representatives of the Communist members of those bodies. Finally, the General Assembly adopted the draft, without a vote, after two decades of procrastination. The decision was preceded by intensive lobbying and pressure from nongovernmental organizations interested in religious human rights and was supported by several governments. Until the very last moment amendments were submitted, and complicated negotiations took place. This showed the inherent complexity and sensitivity of the issue.

One of the major problems surrounding the drafting of the declaration was the meaning of the term *religion*. Communist spokespersons argued that the use of the word *religion* did not explicitly extend the principle of tolerance to atheistic beliefs. They claimed that it was necessary to ensure full equality of treatment between believers and nonbelievers and that the proposed text was one-sided. On the other hand, Western delegates, in particular the United States representative, took the view that the declaration was intended to protect religious human rights, while the rights of persons without a religion, such as materialists, atheists, or agnostics, could find adequate protection in the text. The face-saving solution, which was rather simplistic, was to insert in the Preamble and in Article 1(1) the word *whatever* before the word *belief*, yielding "whatever belief."

Another difficult issue was the matter of religious conversion, which is addressed in detail in chapter 4. This issue already created difficulties during the preparation of the Universal Declaration and the covenants. Once more, the main opposition came from the Muslim delegations. The Iranian spokesperson rejected the related provision contained in Article 18(2) of the Covenant on Civil and Political Rights. Indonesia insisted on establishing a clear distinction between conversion resulting from persuasion and that which was the consequence of coercion. The matter was settled by way of a double compromise. Explicit references to the right to change one's religion were deleted from the text, both in the Preamble and in Article 1, thus representing a departure from the wording used in the Universal Declaration and the covenant. The result was a weakened text, but this was necessary in order to make the change acceptable to the West and avoid jeopardizing the progress achieved in two decades of protracted and difficult negotiations. As part of the accommodation, a new Article 8 was added. It states that nothing in the declaration shall be construed as restricting or derogating from any right defined in the Universal Declaration of Human Rights and the International Covenants on Human Rights. States that did not ratify the covenants may, after this compromise, claim that the right to change one's religion, although included among the clauses of the Universal Declaration, cannot be afforded the status of customary international law. Nevertheless, there was a great desire to see the draft adopted, and compromise was attainable, especially if it was clear that the right to conversion, although not mentioned explicitly, was not derogated or restricted in the new declaration.

## PROVISIONS OF THE DECLARATION

The difficulties in the drafting of the declaration could already be seen in the discussion about its title. Originally, it was intended to be a Declaration on the Elimination of All Forms of Religious Intolerance, but in 1973 a change was made following an amendment proposed by Morocco in the Third Committee. The purpose of this change was to adjust the title of the draft declaration to that of the draft convention and make it consistent with the wording of the Universal Declaration. The two added words—*discrimination* and *belief*— became significant.

*Discrimination,* the term used in all the anti-discrimination treaties and declarations, has a clear legal meaning. This is not the case with *intolerance,* which is vague and lacks exact legal meaning. *Intolerance* has been used to describe emotional, psychological, philosophical, and religious attitudes that may prompt acts of discrimination or other violations of religious freedoms, as well as manifestations of hate and persecutions against persons or groups of a different religion or belief.[44] Nevertheless, the wording of definitional Article 2(2) of the declaration indicates that the terms *discrimination* and *intolerance* are actually employed as equivalent. This is not the only case of inadequate drafting in the declaration, but it can be explained, if not justified, by the long preparation process, the many amendments, and the search for compromise.

The addition of the word *belief* was intended to satisfy those who wanted to protect the rights of nonbelievers, such as rationalists, freethinkers, atheists, agnostics, and supporters of other nontraditional philosophies. There were also proposals to include explicit references to the right to conduct antireligious propaganda, but this issue was not pursued.

In addition to the change of title many modifications were introduced in the drafts of the Preamble. Many of these modifications were of a semantic nature, but some were meant to address controversial matters of principle and substance. The use of the terms *religion* and *belief* once again dominated the discussions. In response to those who tried to protect nonbelievers, some argued that the original purpose of the document was both to ensure equality among the different religions and to protect religious rights. Those who did not believe in any transcendental or normative religion, it was argued, were already protected by the general freedoms prevailing in a democratic society. There was consensus that coercion against nonbelievers must always be prohibited.

The final text did not include provisions on incitement. Such provisions existed in the preliminary drafts prepared by the Subcommission on Prevention of Discrimination and Protection of Minorities and the Commission on Human Rights, but never made the final cut. Nevertheless, the pending draft convention contains a clause related to incitement.

## THE PROTECTED RIGHTS

Articles 1 and 6 of the declaration contain a catalog of rights that provide a universally agreed-upon minimum standard in the area of religious human rights. Article 1 generally follows the model of Article 18 of the Universal Declaration and the Covenant on Civil and Political Rights—except for the change of religion clause (as amended in the Third Committee) and the saving provision of Article 8 of the declaration. Consequently, authoritative interpretations of the covenant are applicable to the declaration.[45] The declaration uses the term *everyone* in Article 1, meant to protect nationals and aliens, as well as permanent and nonpermanent residents.[46] Paragraph 1 proclaims three fundamental freedoms: the freedoms of thought, conscience, and religion, including whatever belief one chooses. The external manifestations of religion—worship, observance, practice, and teaching—are guaranteed in terms identical to those of the covenant and should be interpreted in conjunction with the rights listed in Article 6 of the declaration.

Article 1(2) prohibits coercion that impairs freedom of religion. But Article 1(3) allows for limitations on the freedom to manifest one's religion or belief, if such limitations are prescribed by law and necessary to protect public safety, order, health or morals, or the fundamental rights of others, as understood in free societies. Serious difficulties may develop when religious rights clash with the notion of morals as interpreted by some countries, and the margin of discretion allowed may differ from country to country. General principles incorporated into human rights law regarding these limitations are also applicable to the declaration.[47] It should be kept in mind that Article 18 of the ICCPR, which is referenced by Article 4 of the covenant, represents one of the rights for which no derogation in time of public emergency is permitted.

Article 6 provides a a concrete list of freedoms of thought, religion, and belief. This list provides a detailed enunciation of the rights that fall within an accepted minimum standard. Some rights are missing, but, on the whole, the list is comprehensive. The list contains the following freedoms:

a. the freedom to worship or assemble in connection with a religion or belief, and to establish and maintain places for these purposes;
b. the freedom to establish and maintain appropriate charitable or humanitarian institutions;
c. the freedom to make, acquire, and use to an adequate extent the necessary articles and materials related to the rites or customs of a religion or belief;
d. the freedom to write, publish, and disseminate relevant publications in these areas;
e. the freedom to teach a religion or belief in places suitable for these purposes;
f. the freedom to solicit and receive voluntary financial and other contributions from individuals and institutions;
g. the freedom to train, appoint, elect, or designate by succession appropriate leaders called for by the requirements and standards of any religion or belief;
h. the freedom to observe days of rest and to celebrate holy days and ceremonies in accordance with the precepts of one's religion or belief;
i. the freedom to establish and maintain communications with individuals and communities in matters of religion and belief at the national and international levels.

All these rights are, of course, subject to the limitations mentioned in Article 1(3). Some of them are tied to the constitutional system of the country and are affected by the nature of the relationship between religion and state in that country.

Article 6 omitted some rights that the Subcommission on the Prevention of Discrimination and Protection of Minorities included in its early drafts. The omitted rights include the right to establish federations, which would complete the right mentioned in Article 6(b); the right to teach and learn the sacred language of each religion (and to bring teachers from abroad), which is not automatically included in Article 6(e); the right to receive state aid when the state controls the means of production and distribution, a right of crucial importance for those religions implementing dietary prescriptions; the right to obtain religious materials and objects; the right to make pilgrimages to religious sites, either inside the country or abroad; the right not to undergo a religious marriage ceremony that is not in conformity with one's convictions; and the right to a burial ceremony in accordance with the religion of the deceased person. The subcommission's draft also included provisions on the legal status of cemeteries, religious oaths, and discrimination by the state when granting subsidies or taxing constituents. Some of the missing rights are listed in the pending draft convention.

Article 6 should be compared with principles 16 and 17 of the Concluding Document of the 1989 Vienna meeting of the Conference on Security and Cooperation in Europe, which includes a few of the omitted provisions.

The original text of the declaration prepared by the subcommission was strongly influenced by Arcot Krishnaswami's principles. The final text was strongly affected by the amendments, compromises, and concessions that resulted from the long drafting process. Political considerations, as always, played a crucial role, and nongovernmental organizations were active lobbyists. In particular, the issues of religious education and the preservation of certain rites and customs (such as blood transfusions) provoked lengthy discussions.

It is important to stress that Article 6 of the declaration addresses individual rights, collective rights, and rights that can only be exercised by a group. Compared to previous instruments, it represents important progress, especially as it anticipates the needs of religious communities or congregations. Many previous U.N. instruments, which focused exclusively on individual rights, failed to address the fact that only groups can establish and maintain places of worship and religious institutions, or appoint religious leaders, or establish federations.

## PROHIBITION OF DISCRIMINATION AND INTOLERANCE

Articles 2 and 3 of the declaration address intolerance and discrimination based on religion and belief. These articles, influenced by the Declaration and Convention on Racial Discrimination, are affected by similar difficulties, particularly in the way in which the terms *discrimination* and *intolerance* are employed. It has already been pointed out that *discrimination* has a precise legal meaning under international and human rights law while *intolerance* does not. This leads to vague and inconsistent drafting. For example, Article 2(1) refers to *discrimination* only. Article 2(2) mentions *intolerance and discrimination*. The term *intolerance* is not used at all in Article 3 or Article 4(1), which address measures to be taken by states. Article 4(2) distinguishes between the need to prohibit discrimination and to combat intolerance, a distinction that tries to differentiate between both forms of behavior. As for the declaration, the Convention on Racial Discrimination again serves as the model for the definition of the two words. Under Article 2(2), *intolerance and discrimination based on religion or belief* means any distinction, exclusion, restriction, or preference based on religion or belief and having as its purpose or as its effect nullification or impairment of the recognition, enjoyment or exercise of human rights and fundamental freedoms on an equal basis. Religious discrimination and intolerance are not limited to public life, as was the case in the Convention on Racial Discrimination.

Overall, the text is deficient, particularly since Article 2(1) prohibits discrimination by the state and by institutions, groups of persons, or persons. As Krishnaswami's study reminds us, however, not every preference based on religion or belief can be considered discriminatory and thus prohibited. For example, a concordat between a state with a predominantly Catholic population and the Holy See may be appropriate. Additionally, many states declare as public holidays the days sacred to the majority of the population; this would not be discriminatory if observance of the holy days of the minorities is duly protected, as far as possible.[48] More difficult is the case of states that permit only members of a given religion to accede to certain public positions, such as president of the state. Some states, in fact, have an established church or even a state religion. When do such situations become discriminatory?[49] As a general rule, no impairment should attach to any person or group in the enjoyment of fundamental freedoms. Otherwise, preferences may constitute discrimination. The given facts and social reality—as well as common sense—are determinative factors.

The prohibition of discrimination by institutions or persons also creates problems. For example, religious institutions should be granted some leeway when hiring personnel, mandating dressing habits, or organizing the observance of particular customs. The granting of privileges to members of one religion in given circumstances does not necessarily curtail the basic human rights of others and would therefore not contradict the declaration.

Another concern is the possibility of a clash between the recognition of religious rights and societal norms. For example, the clash between religious rights and the prohibition of discrimination based on gender may be irresolvable—and, in fact, has resulted in frequent adjudication. In order to guarantee the observance of the rights proclaimed in the declaration, state action is often necessary. According to Article 4 of the declaration, all states shall take effective measures to prevent and eliminate discrimination on grounds of religion or belief in all fields of civil, economic, political, social, and cultural life, enacting or rescinding where necessary legislation to that effect. States should also take all appropriate steps to combat intolerance on the grounds of religion or belief.

Problems arising from the imprecise use of the terms *discrimination* and *intolerance* have already been mentioned. Although the meaning of *to combat* is not explained, it suggests an obligation to adopt criminal law measures against organizations that incite others to practice religious intolerance. Special Rapporteur Elizabeth Odio Benito, in fact, has recommended the adoption of penal laws.[50] This may be contrary to the policies of certain countries that are reluctant to limit in any way the freedoms of speech and association.

Article 7 refers to national legislation that would allow everyone to avail himself or herself of the enunciated rights and freedoms. This article, which has been criticized for its vagueness, has been difficult to apply.

Article 5, which addresses the rights of the child, is among the most controversial provisions in the declaration. There is a close relationship between religion and education, and the attempt of a religion to influence the child may conflict with the attempt of the parents to raise that child. Article 5 is long, and it fails to clarify important points, such as who would qualify as a child. Article 5 does recognize the right of parents (or legal guardians) to organize their families in accordance to their religion or belief. Furthermore, Article 5 promotes the notion that children should have access to religious education in accordance to the wishes of their parents or legal guardians. The "best interest of the child"—an idea that appears in the Declaration on the Rights of the Child and the Convention on the Rights of the Child but is not mentioned in the covenant[51]—should be the guiding principle.

The proviso "best interest of the child" is intended to limit the freedom of action of parents and legal guardians. Nevertheless, the declaration does not deal with the many questions likely to be raised when the wishes of the parents conflict with the best interest of the child. Moreover, in totalitarian or ideological states, the best interest of the child may be interpreted differently by the educational authorities and the parents of the child. Limitations on parental authority have frequently required adjudication at the domestic and international levels.

In general, the child should be protected against religious discrimination. The practices of a religion or belief in which a child is raised should not be injurious to the child's physical or mental health (Articles 5(5)). The limitations mentioned in Article 1(3) of the declaration, namely, public safety, order, health, or morals or the fundamental rights and freedoms of others, should be taken into account.

## EVALUATION OF THE DECLARATION

On the whole the 1981 Declaration was an important breakthrough in the struggle to extend international protection to religion. Of course, a declaration is not a treaty and is therefore not binding. Nevertheless, as a U.N. solemn statement it carries weight and gives expression to prevailing international trends. It does have certain legal effect, and it implies an expectation of obedience by members of the international community to the extent that it may be seen as stating rules of customary international law.[52]

The catalog of rights contained in the declaration is helpful although not complete. The explicit references not only to individual rights or rights to be exercised collectively but also to the rights of the group (or the religious community or congregation) is of monumental importance, especially when compared to other limited international texts. Compromise has been necessary, but Article 8 has made possible the universal acceptance of the declaration. The wording of several articles is unsatisfactory, reflecting the protracted negotiations. Nevertheless, the declaration unquestionably represents progress in a sensitive area of human rights that, in comparison with other rights, had been largely neglected.

## THE NECESSITY OR POSSIBILITY OF A CONVENTION

Some may ask whether the declaration makes unnecessary the preparation of a binding convention on religious human rights. The answer may be inconclusive, particularly if the end result is a treaty that does not fully address substantive rights respecting religion. Nevertheless, concerned nongovernmental organizations have advocated the adoption of a convention. A similar stand was taken by the special rapporteurs, the Subcommission on the Prevention of the Discrimination and Protection of Minorities, and a 1984 Seminar on the Encouragement of Understanding, Tolerance, and Respect in Matters Relating to Freedom of Religion or Belief.[53] The General Assembly of the United Nations, which deals every year with the elimination of all forms of religious intolerance, has not directly addressed the issue of whether there should be a convention. In its last resolutions before this writing, the General Assembly nevertheless urged states to take measures to combat hatred, intolerance, and acts of violence, including those motivated by religious extremism, and to guarantee freedom of thought, conscience, religion, and belief. The General Assembly also welcomed steps to implement the declaration and encouraged the Commission on Human Rights to do the same. Still, there was no reference at all to the question of a convention.[54] The 1993 Vienna Conference on Human Rights also remained silent on this issue.[55]

Theo van Boven, in a working paper prepared at the request of the Subcommission on Prevention of Discrimination and Protection of Minorities, has taken a cautious view on the question of a convention. He recommended that, prior to the drafting of such an instrument, solid preparatory work should be done.[56] Others, such as Yoram Dinstein, have stressed the singular contribution that a convention could make to the promotion of freedom of religion. Dinstein is, however, aware of the fact that the prospects for a convention are unlikely, and that there is very little enthusiasm for a new implementation mechanism.[57]

The draft convention presently pending, as elaborated by the Commission on Human Rights,[58] contains a preamble and twelve articles adopted by the commission. The draft reflects the prevailing mood when it was discussed simultaneously with the draft declaration. The major differences between the substantive articles of the declaration and those of the draft convention are the result of the amendments added in the latter stages of the preparation of the declaration. Also, the draft convention lists some rights not mentioned in the 1981 Declaration. For example, draft Article IX follows the pattern of Article 4 of the Convention on Racial Discrimination and is likely to result in controversy, if work on the draft convention should continue. The measures of implementation are similar to those incorporated into other anti-discrimination instruments, which are based mainly on a reporting system that encompasses individual petitions.

## IMPLEMENTATION OF THE DECLARATION

Since continued work on a convention now seems doubtful, it may be more useful to examine the various ways that the 1981 Declaration has been monitored. (Nongovernmental organizations may collaborate and do their own monitoring.) Because the Human Rights Committee has a duty to follow the relevant articles of the covenant, it has been suggested that working groups be established to make sure that it does so, although no formal proposals have been advanced in this regard. In any case, the principles listed in the declaration should provide governments with guidance to adjust their own legislation to the international minimum standard.

Both the Commission on Human Rights and the Subcommission on Prevention of Discrimination and Protection of Minorities appointed special rapporteurs to conduct studies and submit reports related to the implementation of the declaration. The special rapporteur of the commission, Angelo Vidal d'Almeida Ribeiro, was appointed in 1986 and submitted seven reports.[59] A new special rapporteur, Abdelfattah Amor, was appointed in 1993. The special rapporteur of the subcommission, Elizabeth Odio Benito, was appointed in 1983, and her task was to undertake a comprehensive study of the scope of the problems related to intolerance on grounds of religion or belief. Odio Benito, using the declaration as a term of reference, was able to update the findings of the Krishnaswami study.[60]

The reports submitted by the special rapporteurs provide a global perspective on the state of religious rights. The special rapporteurs circulated questionnaires among many states and based their reports on the responses. In addition, they analyzed the present state of affairs in the various countries, commented on issues reflected in the individual responses, and formulated recommendations based on their conclusions.

In her study Odio Benito concluded that the phrase *intolerance and discrimination based on religion or belief* encompassed not only discrimination, but also included acts intended to stir up hatred against or persecution of persons or groups. She stressed the uniformity of the Universal Declaration, the Covenant on Civil and Political Rights, and the 1981 Declaration regarding the right to change one's religion or to remain without any at all. According to Odio Benito, full realization of all other human rights is closely linked to freedoms of thought, conscience, religion, and belief. Violations of religious rights frequently involve violation of many other basic rights, including the right to life. A listing of such violations, region by region, is included in the study, which also examined various church-state relationships. The author of the study did not draw a firm conclusion as to whether, and to what extent, any of the existing constitutional arrangements give rise, per se or in practice, to religious intolerance. She did, however, point out when, on the whole, the existing situation falls below the standards in the 1981 Declaration.

Furthermore, Odio Benito recommended that the international community continue its efforts to adopt a convention. This is consistent with the conclusions reached by the 1984 United Nations Seminar on the Encouragement of Understanding, Tolerance, and Respect in Matters Relating to Freedom of Religion or Belief. Odio Benito also suggested that several studies should be made concerning the following subjects: discrimination against women within churches and within religions; discrimination against centuries-old religions that do not belong to the group of major religions; and the emergence of new religions and practices of sects. Until the adoption of a convention containing implementation measures, these kinds of studies are critical in helping the appropriate bodies determine what human rights issues are most salient. In order to make these kinds of determinations, human rights bodies may resort to arrangements that the ECOSOC (Economic and Social Council) can make under Article 64 of the U.N. Charter.

Angelo Vidal d'Almeida Ribeiro, the former special rapporteur of the Commission on Human Rights, also filed reports addressing allegations against certain governments whose practices may have departed from the provisions of the declaration. He transmitted these allegations to the respective governments in seven detailed and documented reports. These reports also contained comments formulated by the affected governments. The special rapporteur aimed to identify factors that might impede the implementation of the declaration and the collection of specific information. He circulated questionnaires to the governments and established communication with them based on their replies. He also directly approached those governments against which allegations had been made. The reports contained information from nongovernmental sources, including religious groups and organizations.

The reported cases covered a wide range of situations involving persons of various religions under different legal and political systems. These cases came from most regions of the world. The special rapporteur highlighted the fact that the majority of allegations involved the right of religious choice; the right to change one's religion; the right to worship in public and in private; and the right not to be subjected to discrimination on any grounds. Violations of the declaration's provisions have also been a reflection and cause of violations concerning other fundamental freedoms and rights. Violence has frequently accompanied these violations. Sometimes this violence has erupted on a massive scale, as has been the case in the former Yugoslavia.

Special Rapporteur d'Almeida Ribeiro noted some positive developments and stressed the importance of interfaith dialogue. In particular, he favored the preparation of a binding instrument, especially in the light of the recommendations submitted by Theo van Boven to the Subcommission on Prevention of Discrimination and Protection of Minorities.

Following the resignation of Angelo Vidal d'Almeida Ribeiro, the chairman of the Commission on Human Rights appointed Abdelfattah Amor as special rapporteur. Professor Amor has submitted reports since 1994.[61] In particular, he sent summaries of allegations made against certain countries (concerning religious rights) to those countries against which those allegations were made. Such allegations concerned various forms of harassment, arrest, torture, or ill-treatment of victims of religious intolerance. Some of the reports referred to the desecration or destruction of religious sanctuaries or cemeteries. The special rapporteur, in order to support his views and observations, has also made visits *in situ* and has drawn on governmental and nongovernmental sources, taking into account any information received from religious groups. He also sent questionnaires to governments regarding the subject of his mandate and responded to urgent appeals made by Bangladesh, Iran, Iraq, Pakistan, and Saudi Arabia.

While conducting his work, Amor found and addressed numerous examples of religiously oriented persecution and discrimination. These include murders carried out by armed groups of Islamic militants; discrimination against groups such as the Church of Scientology in Germany; imprisonment due to expression of religious beliefs; discrimination against religious minorities, particularly Christians and Shi'ite Muslims in Saudi Arabia; restrictions against Jehovah's Witnesses in Austria; persecution against writer Taslima Nassrin, and other acts of religious intolerance against the Hindu, Christian, and Buddhist minorities in Bangladesh; restrictions upon Protestant organizations in Belarus; persecution against Christians and Christian missionaries in Bhutan, where Buddhism and Hinduism are the only recognized religions; prohibition and persecution (including acts of physical violence) of many sects in Bulgaria; violation of the right to conscientious objection in Cyprus; restrictions on religious activities and attacks on the freedom of religion of Jehovah's Witnesses, Seventh-day Adventists, and Baptists in Cuba; violence, including assassinations, by Islamic fundamentalist groups in Egypt; violations of religious freedom in Ethiopia; restrictive legislation in the Russian Federation; imprisonment of conscientious objectors and harassment of religious groups in Greece; religiously oriented killings and violence in India; persecutions against Bahá'ís, Jews, and Christians in Iran; persecutions against Shi'ite Muslims in Iraq; incidents in the territories occupied by Israel, Kenya, Lebanon, and Liberia; anti-conversion laws in Malaysia and Morocco; anti-Protestant incidents in Mexico; discrimination against Christians in Mongolia; persecution against Christian and Muslim religious communities in Myanmar; persecution of religious minorities in Pakistan; killing of Christians in the Philippines; intolerance in Romania; massacres of clergymen in Rwanda; severe violations and violence in Sudan and Sri Lanka; violation of the rights of religious minorities in Turkey, Vietnam, Yemen, and Zimbabwe.[62]

In order to achieve as complete a picture as possible, Special Rapporteur Amor visited numerous countries, including China, Pakistan, Iran, India,

Greece, Sudan, Australia, and Germany. Based on these visits, he submitted reports with conclusions and recommendations.[63]

As part of his work, Special Rapporteur Amor requested clarifications from the respective governments and suggested approaches that would address discrimination within the framework of the particular government. Amor took the view that the achievement of religious tolerance and nondiscrimination must go together with the achievement of human rights as a whole. He believed his goal of curbing religious extremism and terrorism could be achieved through education. He acknowledged that in certain cases it is difficult to establish a clear distinction between religious and ethnic conflicts, and between such conflicts and political persecution. Still, he devoted special attention to conversion and proselytism, blasphemy, attacks on places of worship and religious sites, and problems related to sects and conscientious objection. He also addressed in his conclusions and recommendations the issue of ethnic cleansing in former Yugoslavia and ethnically related events in Algeria. Along with addressing particular problems, Amor also invited the states he investigated to share legal texts related to the freedom of belief; his hope was to build a compendium of national enactments related to that freedom.

In his 1996 report[64] Amor divided the violations of religious rights into six categories. These categories, based on the communications he received, included (1) violations of the principle of nondiscrimination in religion and belief; (2) violations of the principle of tolerance, a category that reflected the concern about religious extremism; (3) violations of the freedom of thought, conscience, and religion or belief, including the freedom to change religion; (4) violations of the freedom to manifest one's religion or belief; (5) violations of the freedom to dispose religious property; and (6) attacks on the right to life, physical integrity, and security of person. He concluded that the elaboration of an international convention on the elimination of religious intolerance and discrimination was a necessary but premature step, given the present circumstances.[65]

In his 1998 report Amor paid special attention to the development of a culture of tolerance and stressed the role of education as an essential and priority means of combating intolerance and discrimination.[66] He surveyed the replies received from seventy-seven states to a questionnaire on problems relating to freedom of religion and belief from the standpoint of the curricula and textbooks of elementary and secondary schools. Among his preliminary findings Amor noted a marked difference between states based on secular principles and those based on a theocracy or official state religion. In particular, he highlighted the problems related to the compulsory nature of religious instruction; the imposing of a particular kind of religious instruction on members of another faith without giving them the right to be excused; the difficulties created when minority religions have no private religious institutions; and the limited teaching of comparative religion. In response, the rapporteur recommended further study of religious extremism, proselytism, freedom of religion and poverty, and sects and new religious movements.

## THE UNITED NATIONS DECLARATION ON MINORITIES

Religious rights include (1) individual rights; (2) collective rights (exercised by several persons jointly as prescribed by Article 27 of the Covenant on Civil and Political Rights); and (3) rights of the religious group or community. The last category contains the rights of what is usually described as a religious minority. It is difficult to analyze this subject because there is no generally accepted definition of *religious minority*. Many definitions have been proposed, and one enjoying support is that of Professor Francesco Capotorti, U.N. special rapporteur on minorities. According to Capotorti,

> a minority is a group which is numerically inferior to the rest of the population of a state and in a non-dominant position, whose members possess ethnic, religious or linguistic characteristics which differ from those of the rest of the population and who, if only implicitly, maintain a sense of solidarity, directed towards preserving their culture, traditions, religion or language.[67]

There are as many definitions of *minority* as there are proposals to replace the term.[68] Self-perception and the perception of the surrounding society are of great importance, particularly in the case of religious minorities or groups. In general, states have been less reluctant to recognize the rights of an organized religious group or minority, believing that there will be few consequences of such recognition—except in the case of territorial concentration or political tension. Many states understand that it is virtually impossible to respect freedom of religion or belief without (1) permitting believers to organize their representative institutions; (2) granting them some authority to deal with the individual members of the faith; and (3) allowing them to maintain contact freely with similar organized groups outside the state. Much, of course, depends on the constitutional regime of the state, and there have been instances of special arrangements between states and certain churches or religions, a subject to which we shall return in the next chapter.

When analyzing the evolution of the status of religious minorities and other minorities, we need to consider four major stages: (1) an early period of nonsystematic protection of religious groups through the incorporation of special protective clauses in international treaties and through humanitarian intervention of influential powers; (2) the protective system under the League of Nations, based on special treaties, special clauses in general treaties, or unilateral undertakings; (3) the pattern followed by the United Nations as expressed in Article 27 of the Political Covenant (and slightly less so in the 1992 declaration on minorities), implying an almost total shift from group protection to a guarantee of individual rights and freedoms; and (4) modern trends, which acknowledge the necessity of harmonizing individual freedoms, the rights of the state, and the needs of organized religious groups.

The early treaties granted protection to certain religious minorities, frequently as a consequence of territorial changes. Usually, the treaties were based on the link between one of the parties and a sector of the population of the other state. It was only after the Vienna Congress in 1815 that the scope of such treaties was expanded.[69] Humanitarian intervention produced positive results in some cases, but, without an articulated scheme, these treaties had obvious limitations.

The League of Nations system for the protection of religious and other minorities was far from perfect. Nevertheless, its failure was not the consequence of intrinsic defects but was due to the political turmoil in Europe after World War I, especially the assault by the Nazi and Fascist regimes against democracy and the rule of law. The League's Covenant did not incorporate any general article about minorities, and attempts to include a comprehensive article on religious persecution did not succeed. States that signed treaties or made declarations about minorities included Poland; Austria; Czechoslovakia; the Kingdom of the Serbs, Croats, and Slovenes; Bulgaria; Romania; Hungary; Greece; Turkey; Albania; Lithuania; Latvia; Estonia; and Iraq. Provisions on minority rights were also incorporated in treaties concerning Danzig, the Aland Islands, Upper Silesia, and Memel.[70]

Under the League of Nations system many rights were guaranteed. These included the free exercise (in public and private) of any creed, religion, or belief; equality of treatment in law and in fact, with a prohibition against discrimination; equal access to public employment and professions; the use of minority languages in religious ceremonies or activities; the right to establish institutions and schools; and the right to have public funds allocated to religious, educational, and charitable needs. Such guarantees could not be derogated by domestic legislation without the approval of the Council of the League. The Council was entitled to consider violations and take appropriate action. Disputes were to be submitted to the Permanent Court of International Justice, which had compulsory jurisdiction. A mechanism for petitions by individuals or associations acting on behalf of a minority was established, and the Council could make recommendations based on the respective case. For example, under the Bernheim petition in 1933, which was based on the convention between Germany and Poland of 1922 regarding Upper Silesia, the Nazis were prevented for some time from implementing measures against Jews, who were considered a religious, ethnic, and linguistic minority.[71]

The Permanent Court of International Justice dealt on several occasions with issues related to minorities. Its *Advisory Opinion on Minority Schools in Albania*, although referring primarily to the linguistic rights of the Greek minority in Albania, became universally respected as it acknowledged the need for all minorities (especially religious minorities) to have suitable means for the preservation of their traditions and characteristics.[72]

In the United Nations period the prevailing opinion asserted that individual rights and the principle of nondiscrimination were the appropriate means of protecting everyone, including members of minorities. There was an overall reluctance to recognize any type of group rights, mainly for historical and political reasons. In fact, the Charter does not refer to minorities at all. A proposed inclusion of an article on minorities in the Universal Declaration of Human Rights was not accepted. Article 26 does refer to the promotion of understanding, tolerance, and friendship among racial or religious groups, but this reference is vague. The Subcommission on the Prevention of Discrimination and the Protection of Minorities introduced Article 27 of the Covenant on Civil and Political Rights, a controversial and highly criticized article that nevertheless serves as the basis of the United Nations approach to the issue. Article 27 refers to religious and other minorities, members of which should not be denied the right, in community with other members of their group, to profess and practice their own religion.[73] The criticism of Article 27 exposed the shortcomings of the covenant's approach to minority rights and led to the 1992 United Nations Declaration on the Rights of Persons Belonging to National or Ethnic, Religious, and Linguistic Minorities, which represented some progress in the acceptance of minority rights.[74]

As its title indicates, the declaration embraces national or ethnic, religious, and linguistic minorities. But these terms are hard to define. The term *national minority* frequently includes minorities that represent a part of some other nation, or what some describe as a parent state.[75] (This same kind of definition may apply to religious groups, too.) But in the declaration the term *national minorities* is equivalent to ethnic, religious, and linguistic minorities. While the preamble of the declaration promotes the principles mentioned in the Declaration on Intolerance and Discrimination Based on Religion or Belief, parts of the declaration require clarification.

Article 1 of the 1992 declaration urges states to take measures to protect the existence and identity of religious minorities. There is an implicit acknowledgment of group rights, or rights that go beyond the scope of individual rights. Article 2 grants to persons belonging to minorities the right to profess and practice their own religion and to participate effectively in religious life. These persons are entitled to establish and maintain their own associations and to establish and maintain free and peaceful contacts with other members of their group, including those who reside in other states. Otherwise, the relationship of the U.N. declaration on minorities to religious human rights is limited. Nevertheless, the declaration represents progress (with regard to freedom of religion and belief) from the development of the Political Covenant.

## RELIGIOUS RIGHTS IN OTHER RELEVANT INSTRUMENTS

Several legal texts adopted separately during the United Nations era contain provisions on religious rights. Humanitarian law—consolidated in the four widely ratified Geneva conventions of 1949—contains provisions prohibiting any adverse distinctions founded on religion or faith.[76] The Convention on Prisoners of War also addressed religiously oriented issues, such as the exercise of religious duties, attendance of services, the role of chaplains and ministers of religion, and the use of facilities for the performance of their duties. In particular, the Fourth Convention urged respect for the religious convictions and practices of the protected persons. This convention also referred to the work of ministers of religion, the use of books and articles for religious needs, and the need for adequate premises for the religious services.

The 1979 Convention on the Elimination of All Forms of Discrimination against Women contained provisions that clashed with practices of some religious traditions that were incorporated into general legislation.[77] Several states expressed reservations about the clauses that were perceived to conflict with religious traditions. Both the Human Rights Committee under the Political Covenant and the Committee on the Elimination of Discrimination against Women (CEDAW) addressed the issue of equality for women, especially in matters concerning family law. Judicial or quasi-judicial intervention has been required, most notably in Europe. In order to gain a full perspective, this clash between gender-oriented law and law that is grounded on religious traditions should be seen in the wider context of the discussion on the universality of human rights.

Because religious rights and education are closely related, international instruments addressing education are relevant for the analysis of religious rights. The freedom to teach one's religion (and ensure that parents' wishes for the religious education of their children are respected) and the degree to which the state supports religious instruction raise complicated issues that can only be resolved by careful balancing among differing human rights. The UNESCO Convention against Discrimination in Education, adopted in 1960 and in force since 1962, was one measure that tried to prohibit discrimination based on religion.[78] Under this measure separate educational systems for religious purposes were permitted, provided that participation in such systems was optional and conformed to authorized standards (Article 2). Overall, education was meant to promote understanding and tolerance among religious groups. Yet, it was important that religious and moral education was imparted in conformity with the convictions of the children, meaning that nobody should be compelled to receive religious instruction inconsistent with his or her convictions (Article 5).

In order to gain a full understanding of the relationship between education and religion, the provisions of the UNESCO Convention against Discrimination in Education should be read in conjunction with the relevant articles of the 1948 Universal Declaration of Human Rights and the 1966 Covenant on Social, Cultural, and Economic Rights. In addition, the Declaration on the Rights of the Child and the Convention on the Rights of the Child, which contain provisions related to religion and education, should be considered. These provisions also emphasize the need to give primary consideration to the best interest of the child.[79] Despite the attempt to provide a suitable framework for addressing issues pertaining to education and religion, however, the relationship between these issues is by no means straightforward and has provoked judicial intervention at the municipal, regional, and international levels.[80]

The International Labor Organization (ILO), which in 1958 adopted the Convention (No. 111) concerning Discrimination in Respect of Employment and Occupation (in force since 1960), attempted to prohibit discrimination on the basis of religion.[81] Specifically, the ILO organized bodies that addressed employee complaints that were based on denial of equality because of religion. These complaints often resulted when religious duties conflicted with working conditions, especially in regard to days of rest and holidays. There have also been many instances of judicial intervention.[82]

Another important ILO treaty addressing religious rights has been the 1989 Convention No. 169, concerning Indigenous and Tribal Populations and Peoples. This is a partial revision of the 1957 convention on this subject. The new convention is more group-oriented and recognizes the aspirations of indigenous peoples to maintain and develop their identities and religions, ensuring protection for their religious and spiritual values and practices. The United Nations has also addressed this subject and proclaimed 1993 as the International Year for the World's Indigenous Peoples. General Assembly Resolution 45/164 (1990) made reference to cultural identity and restrictions on religious customs.[83]

International instruments related to the condition of migrant workers have also considered their cultural and religious needs. The 1990 U.N. Convention on the Protection of the Rights of Migrant Workers and Their Families contained provisions guaranteeing the religious rights of such migrants. Article 12 of the convention was clearly inspired by Article 18 of the Political Covenant.[84]

## CONCLUSIONS

Based on the foregoing, the following conclusions can be reached.

First, United Nations instruments dealing with religious human rights do not define the term *religion*. This is the result of a general trend to avoid ideological or philosophical definitions that may cause controversy and make it more difficult to reach agreement between states in such a delicate area of human behavior. It is, however, indisputable that, in United Nations law and in modern human rights law, the term *religion,* usually followed by the word *belief*, means theistic convictions, involving a transcendental view of the universe and a normative code of behavior, as well as atheistic, agnostic, rationalistic, and other views in which both elements may be absent.

Second, the United Nations system for the protection of religious human rights does not presently include any specific obligatory treaty regarding religious human rights. Article 18 of the 1966 International Covenant on Civil and Political Rights, and provisions related to religious issues in the covenant and in treaties prepared by the United Nations and other international bodies, are, of course, mandatory for those states that ratified such instruments. A significant number of those provisions are seen today as reflecting customary international law, and some, such as the prohibition of discrimination on religious grounds or the outlawing of genocide against religious groups, belong to the restricted category of *jus cogens*. Freedom of religion is one of the fundamental rights that cannot be derogated in states of emergency. The General Comment on Article 18 formulated by the Human Rights Committee constitutes an authoritative source for the interpretation of the covenant clauses.

Third, the discussion on the need and/or convenience of a mandatory treaty on religious rights and freedoms is inconclusive. The main argument in favor of a convention is, of course, the general desire to grant religious rights a protection similar to that extended to other basic rights. The example of the widely ratified Convention on Racial Discrimination, incorporating a relatively effective system of monitoring and implementation, is pointed out as justifying the treaty-oriented approach. Arguments against a treaty, neither new nor exclusive to the sphere of religion, are the risk of having to compromise on a very low common denominator of protection and the possible reluctance on the part of some states to ratify an instrument that may clash with long-established systems of law, mainly in the area of family law, personal status, and conversion.

Given this inconclusive debate over a mandatory instrument, the existence of a monitoring system, in the form of reports or studies by special rapporteurs appointed by U.N. organs, provides a modest degree of protection of religious rights, naturally not equivalent to conventional obligations assumed by states. There have been proposals, mainly from nongovernmental organizations, aimed at improving that system. These include suggestions to establish national bodies to monitor religious rights, in the spirit of the 1981 Declaration, the submission of periodic reports from member states to ECOSOC, and similar measures not implying a mandatory treaty.

Fourth, the 1981 Declaration on the Elimination of All Forms of Intolerance and Discrimination Based on Religion or Belief was a powerful step forward in the search for a system of protection of religious human rights. The declaration, which incorporated many—though not all—of the principles enunciated in the seminal study by Arcot Krishnaswami, includes a comprehensive and detailed catalog of rights related to freedom of conscience, religion, and belief, and their exercise in practice. The declaration progresses beyond the purely individualistic approach of the covenants and is nearer to some recent instruments that acknowledge the group dimension of religious human rights. Such rights cannot be adequately protected unless the rights of religious organizations, communities, and congregations as such are recognized and ensured beyond the purely individualistic freedoms. This may be of great importance for collectivities and communities of a religious origin in which the religious element may appear combined with ethnic and cultural characteristics.

Fifth, there are some particularly complicated problems that continue to arouse controversy. Examples of such problems include matters of conversion, "opting out" from some religions or recognized religious communities, blasphemy, rights of women and children, and conscientious objection (which is not always a religious matter). A major controversy—not exclusively affecting religious rights—relates to the question of striking a balance between the prohibition of incitement against religious groups, as enunciated in Article 20 of the ICCPR, and the freedoms of speech or association. There have been different answers to this question, depending on the constitutional systems of the respective countries. The precedent of the Convention on Racial Discrimination and trends presently prevailing in connection with religious rights seem to indicate a growing understanding of the need to protect substantive social values against abuses of the freedoms of speech and association.

Sixth, in the 1990s tragic events affecting the life and welfare of millions of persons have taken place, involving population sectors defined by religion as well as ethnic identity. The need to ensure the protection of religious, ethnic, and cultural groups, irrespective of the nature of the group, was acknowledged by the judiciary of several countries. The shocking practices of "ethnic cleansing" in the former Yugoslavia and Rwanda have added urgency to the recognition of that need.

The protection of religious human rights during the United Nations era is thus quite limited. Provisions of a positive character do exist and have exercised a considerable influence on domestic legislation. The claim that they are not enough, particularly at times of high international and intra-national tension, seems to be supported by current events. Religious human rights deserve more than to remain a neglected chapter in the universal endeavors to ensure observance of and respect for human rights.

# 2.

# REGIONAL PROTECTION
# OF RELIGIOUS HUMAN RIGHTS

◆

Chapter 1 analyzed the protection of religious human rights under the United Nations. This chapter addresses the protection extended to rights related to religion by the main regional systems of human rights. Regional affinities are an important element in the development of such systems. It is therefore not surprising that the most satisfactory protection is that prevailing in Europe. The European Commission and Court of Human Rights dealt frequently with issues pertaining to this area, and some of their decisions are also discussed elsewhere in this book. The European institutional arrangements concerning monitoring of human rights are now undergoing a basic change, which, it is hoped, will improve protection. In addition, the Organization for Security and Cooperation in Europe (OSCE)—formerly the Conference for Security and Cooperation in Europe (CSCE)—has recently developed important principles in the area of religious freedoms.

In America, monitoring and judicial activity in respect of religious human rights has been scarce, and the Inter-American Court has had no opportunity to issue any important judgment in this respect. As to Africa, the African Commission on Human and Peoples' Rights has not been too creative. Although not a regional system in a geographical sense, the approach of Islam to religious human rights will also be summarily referred to. So will some special bilateral and sectorial arrangements.

The main regional provisions on religious human rights are included in the appendix hereto.

## EUROPE

The literature on the European system for the protection of human rights, including religious rights, is vast.[1] Several books deal specifically with the activities of the European Court and Commission of Human Rights.[2] The court's decisions on issues of proselytism have provoked considerable interest, as we shall see in chapter 4. Some of these works refer specifically to religious rights.[3]

The major European human rights documents follow in general the orientation of the 1948 Universal Declaration of Human Rights and the 1966 International Covenants. The basic provisions of these documents recur with some variations and expansions in (1) the 1950 European Convention for the Protection of Human Rights and Fundamental Freedoms;[4] (2) the 1975 Final Act of the Helsinki Conference on Security and Cooperation in Europe (Principle VII); (3) the Concluding Document of the Vienna Meeting of 1989 (particularly Principles 16 and 17); (4) the 1990 Document of the Copenhagen Meeting of the CSCE Conference on the Human Dimension; and (5) the 1990 Paris Charter for a New Europe.[5]

The basic guarantee is set out in Article 9 of the 1950 European Convention. Paragraph 1 is identical to Article 18 of the Universal Declaration of Human Rights. Paragraph 2, to be compared with Article 18, paragraph 3 of the International Covenant on Civil and Political Rights, states:

> Freedom to manifest one's religion or beliefs shall be subject only to such limitations as are prescribed by law and are necessary in a democratic society in the interests of public safety, for the protection of public order, health or morals, or for the protection of the rights and freedoms of others.

The words "necessary in a democratic society" are absent from the covenant. They were inserted in the European text instead of a reference to limitations in the interests of national security in an earlier draft. The European Convention did not incorporate a provision intended to preserve national rules restricting the rights of certain religions.[6]

Other provisions of the Convention deal with privacy, family life, freedom of expression and its limits, freedom of association and assembly and their limits, marriage, and prohibition of discrimination on religious grounds.

Article 2 of the First Protocol to the Convention, adopted in 1952, proclaims the need to respect the rights of parents to ensure education and teaching in conformity with their own religious and philosophical convictions. This Article caused controversy and some states entered reservations to it.[7]

As to the OSCE, Principle VII of the 1975 Final Act of the Helsinki Conference on Security and Cooperation in Europe refers to the promise of the participating states to respect human rights and fundamental freedoms—including the freedoms of thought, conscience, and religion and belief—for all, without distinction as to race, sex, language, or religion.

The Concluding Document of the Vienna Meeting of 1989 (CSCE) contains two important principles (16 and 17) related to religious human rights. In order to ensure freedom to profess and practice religion or belief, the participating states will take effective measures to prevent and eliminate discrimination against individuals or communities on grounds of religion or belief and ensure the effective equality between believers and nonbelievers (16a). They will foster a climate of mutual tolerance and respect between believers of different communities as well as between believers and nonbelievers (16b). Religious communities have the right to establish and maintain places of worship and assembly, to organize themselves according to their own hierarchical and institutional structure, to freely appoint and replace their personnel, and to solicit and receive financial and other contributions (16d). Participating states should engage in consultations with religious faiths, institutions, and organizations in order to understand their requirements (16e). The right to give and receive religious education in the language of one's choice and parental rights regarding the religious and moral education of their children are recognized (16f and 16g). Provisions on the training of religious personnel, and on books and publications are also included in Principle 16.

Principle 17 solidifies the rights espoused in Principle 16 by asserting that the exercise of the mentioned rights may be subject only to limitations established by law and consistent with international law. According to Principle 17, domestic laws and regulations must ensure the full and effective implementation of the freedoms of thought, conscience, and religion or belief.[8]

The Concluding Document of the Vienna Meeting of 1989 was adopted on June 29, 1990, by the Copenhagen Meeting of the CSCE Conference on the Human Dimension. It proclaims in Article 9.4 everyone's right to freedom of thought, conscience, and religion, including the right to change and manifest one's religion or belief. Article 18 addresses conscientious objection. Articles 24 and 25 address limitations and derogations. Article 40 condemns totalitarianism, racial and ethnic hatred, antisemitism, xenophobia, and persecution on religious grounds. Article 40.1 urges states to adopt laws "to provide protection against . . . incitement to violence against persons or groups based on national, racial, ethnic, or religious discrimination, hostility or hatred, including anti-Semitism."

The monitoring of human rights by the Council of Europe, the OSCE, and the European Union has produced significant case law with regard to religious rights. Some cases directly addressed the issue of religion, while others dealt with related matters such as education, the exercise and manifestation of religious rights, freedom of expression, conscientious objections, medical issues, parental rights, and employment.[9] Several decisions are mentioned in different chapters of this work. European case law is not always consistent, and there have been differences of opinion between the European Commission and the European Court on Human Rights.

It is beyond the scope of this book to deal in detail with the numerous cases considered by the European Human Rights Commission and Court. Nevertheless, some cases are notable and deserve mention, especially as they suggest a prevailing trend. The two leading cases related to proselytism are *Kokkinakis* and *Larissis*, and these are discussed in chapter 4. Other cases have addressed the meaning of salient terms including: *religion and belief; coercion; necessary in a democratic society; margin of appreciation;* and *practice and manifestation of belief.* Other cases have also addressed important concepts such as parental rights and convictions, and freedom of expression and religion. In sum, the monitoring of human rights by the European system was instrumental in clarifying the scope of religious rights and freedoms.

One of the most notable cases is *Arrowsmith v. UK*, in which the European Commission on Human Rights decided that the right to manifest beliefs included beliefs of a nonreligious nature, such as pacifism.[10] Not all ideas or views are to be considered beliefs for the purposes of Article 9 of the 1950 European Convention, the commission held. The term *belief* connotes the expression of spiritual or philosophical convictions that, while not necessarily organized as a religion, have an identifiable formal content. According to *Arrowsmith*, the distribution of leaflets with pacifist views may amount to a manifestation within the meaning of Article 9(1) of the convention.

In *Campbell and Cosans v. UK*, the European Court held that the term *belief* means views that attain a certain level of cogency, seriousness, cohesion, and importance.[11] Therefore, not all opinions or ideas are beliefs in the context of Article 2 of the First Protocol. A belief of a nonreligious nature may be considered within the scope of Article 9 of the European Convention if it relates to a well-established school of thought, such as atheism or pacifism. According to Malcolm Evans, the mainstream religious traditions, such as Christianity, Judaism, Islam, Hinduism, Sikhism, and Buddhism, are clearly embraced, while the beliefs of Jehovah's Witnesses, the Church of Scientology, and the Unification Church (the "Moonies") have been mostly acknowledged.[12] In *Chappel v. UK*, the commission avoided deciding whether Druidism was a religion for the purposes of Article 9, but justified restrictions imposed under Article 9(2).[13] An association of physicians espousing anti-abortionist views was considered to be within the scope of Article 9, while a group of political prisoners opposed to wearing prison uniforms was deemed to be outside the protection of Article 9.

In *Otto Preminger Institute v. Austria*, the commission and the court reached different conclusions regarding the questions of freedom of expression, blasphemy, and respect for the religious beliefs of others.[14] The commission decided that the forfeiture and seizure of a film that it considered merely satirical violated Article 10 of the convention. The court, on the other hand, decided that the right to express controversial views had to be weighed against the rights of other persons in not being exposed to those views.[15]

After some initial hesitancy the benefits of Article 9 have been made available to churches and other legal entities who have been able to submit applications directly and on behalf of their members. A church body is capable of possessing and exercising the rights contained in Article 9(1) in its own capacity as a representative of its members, according to the commission. Nevertheless, such a right belongs only to entities with religious and philosophical aims and not to economic enterprises. There may be some borderline cases, such as when a limited liability company owned by an association of freethinkers acts for the separation of church and state. It therefore has become necessary to make a distinction between freedom of religion, which can be exercised by an association, and freedom of conscience, which cannot. This distinction has been criticized.[16] Some authorities believe that only the rights of individuals—as opposed to the rights and *locus standi* of religious groups and minorities—should be recognized. This view was recently expressed in documents such as the 1992 United Nations Declaration on the Rights of Persons belonging to National or Ethnic, Religious, and Linguistic Minorities and the 1995 Framework Convention for the Protection of National Minorities of the Council of Europe, as well as CSCE texts.

The relationship between religious rights and education has also been the subject of many decisions by the European tribunals. In *Kjeldsen, Busk Madsen and Pedersen v. Denmark*, for example, the European Court held that the state is forbidden to pursue an aim of indoctrination that might be considered as not respecting parents' religious and philosophical convictions.[17] The commission decided that requiring children to attend classes in society and morality was not a form of indoctrination.[18]

When individuals protest acts mandated by the authorities in areas such as taxation, pension schemes, and elections, the European Commission has generally followed the rule that if the individuals are able to continue in their beliefs, the *forum internum* remains untouched and there is no breach of Article 9.[19] In *Darby v. Sweden*, however, the commission, in deciding the case of a non-Lutheran Finnish citizen who was requested to pay a tax to the Swedish Lutheran Church, declared that Article 9(1) forbids an authority from involving a person in religious activities against his will when he is not a member of the respective religious community.[20]

In summary, the European system, in its attempt to protect human rights, has fostered the development and clarification of the law concerning religion and belief. Despite a lack of overall consistency and criticism regarding its views on sects, cults, and new religions, the commission and the court have produced a body of notable jurisprudence.

In order to complete the overview of the European system for the protection of religious human rights, it is necessary to mention the European Framework Convention for the Protection of National Minorities adopted by the Council of Europe's Committee of Ministers on November 10, 1994.[21] Despite its restrictive title, the Framework Convention urged the universal respect for "the religious identity of each person belonging to a national minority," as well as the creation of "appropriate conditions enabling [minorities] to express, preserve and develop this identity." This implies the right to full and effective equality, the prohibition of discrimination, and the "right of persons belonging to national minorities . . . to maintain and develop . . . the essential elements of their identity, namely their religion, language, traditions and cultural heritage" (Article 5). Although forced assimilation was proscribed, the convention's dictates were not group oriented, and the convention did not recognize collective rights. This reflected the compromises necessary for the convention to create the first legally binding multilateral instrument devoted to the protection of national minorities in general. In fact, twelve ratifications were required. Beyond the indicated references, religious rights of minorities were not specified.

Another document worthy of mention is the text elaborated by the CSCE Meeting of Experts on National Minorities that took place in Geneva in July 1991. The term *national minorities* was adopted for the bearers of religious identity. According to the text, such identity should be protected and promoted, as minorities are seen as "a factor of enrichment of each respective State and society." Furthermore, the text emphasized that issues regarding minorities are matters of "legitimate international concern and consequently do not exclusively constitute an internal affair of the respective State." The CSCE document refers to institutional arrangements, including territorial autonomy and self-administration by minorities with regard to those aspects concerning their identity where territorial autonomy does not apply. This provision of self-administration is especially important for religious minorities not concentrated in specific areas and affects the relations between the religious minority and the state, on the one hand, and the relations between the group and its individual members, on the other.

## THE AMERICAS

The regional American system for the protection of human rights is based on the obligations emanating from the 1960 Convention on Human Rights.[22] The 1948 Charter of the Organization of American States contains few requirements for human rights. The American Declaration of the Rights of Man, proclaimed the same year, did not form part of the charter, and was not seen as positive law.

Freedom of conscience and religion is proclaimed in Article 12 of the 1960 Convention on Human Rights, while freedom of thought and expression is the subject of Article 13. Specifically, Article 12(1) provides that everyone has the right to freedom of conscience and religion, including the freedom "to maintain or to change one's religion or beliefs." According to Article 12(2), no one "shall be subject to restrictions that might impair the freedom to maintain or to change his religion or beliefs." Article 13(1) includes the freedom to impart information and ideas through any medium. This article was broadly interpreted by the Inter-American Court of Human Rights, which stressed that the expression and dissemination of ideas are indivisible concepts.[23]

The Inter-American Commission on Human Rights, which started its work in 1960, has played an important role in the development of human rights, even though the commission has had different functions in both the charter and the convention. Since 1970 the Inter-American Commission on Human Rights has performed its duties on behalf of the Organization of American States (OAS). Its statute was incorporated into the 1948 Charter of the Organization of American States.

Few cases concerning religious rights have come to the attention of the monitoring institutions, even in the face of massive and widespread violations of basic rights. This can be explained by the fact that American institutions have been preoccupied with questions of fact and the proof of fact relating to breaches of human rights rather than with the content of these norms.[24] As a result, most cases have involved killings, disappearances, torture, arbitrary detention, denial of due process, and other major attacks upon fundamental rights.

Several cases have addressed issues involving Jehovah's Witnesses, a sect that as a group has been subject to restrictions while its individual members have been subject to criminal procedures and penalties. For example, the Argentine government in 1976 prohibited the activities of the Jehovah's Witnesses, and the army closed their offices and shops and arrested members of the sect. Children of Jehovah's Witnesses were expelled from school, based on the claim that they refused to sing the national anthem. The treatment of the sect was denounced, and a case involving Jehovah's Witnesses subsequently came before the Inter-American Commission. The commission declared that the government of Argentina violated several rights, including freedom of religion, and ordered it to reestablish respect for religious freedom. In response, the Argentine authorities denied the religious nature of the Jehovah's Witnesses. After considering the annual report of the commission, the General Assembly of the OAS urged the Argentine government to acknowledge the right of Jehovah's Witnesses to freedom of religion.[25] A similar case involving the denial of rights to Jehovah's Witnesses in Paraguay was also considered by the commission.[26]

Sometimes issues are raised by religious groups, whose members can be concerned with personal rather than religious rights. For example, the issue of abortion has been raised in a petition filed against the United States by an organization called Catholics for Christian Political Action. The group did not focus on the religious aspect of abortion, but rather on the right to life and when it begins. Ultimately, the Inter-American Commission decided that there had been no violation of the American Declaration of the Rights of Man.[27] In addition, the Inter-American monitoring system also considered allegations of persecutions of priests and the Catholic Church in Guatemala.[28]

## AFRICA

The African Charter on Human and Peoples' Rights is an important source when determining the human and religious rights of Africans.[29] Article 8 of the African Charter, which guarantees freedom of conscience and the free practice of religion, is particularly important. Article 9, which proclaims a general right to disseminate opinions, is also relevant. Significantly, the charter does not contain any specific provision on change of religion.

Despite the charter, the African Commission on Human Rights has not determined clearly what constitutes a violation of the freedom of religion and conscience. Also, the commission has failed to define a savings clause, whose language (subject to law and order) may limit the reach of the charter. The commission did consider a few cases addressing religious rights, such as *Amnesty International v. Sudan* (involving prisoners of conscience) and *Association of Member Episcopal Conferences v. Sudan* (involving the alleged persecution of Christians in Sudan). The commission consolidated the cases with previous ones and asked permission from the Sudanese government to conduct investigations.[30] (It was alleged that missionaries were expelled from the town of Juba, priests were arrested, and churches were destroyed.) The commission also asked permission to visit Zaire, Malawi, Chad, Senegal, Mauritania, and Nigeria. In 1995 Algeria invited the commission to conduct an on-the-spot investigation on human rights.[31]

Evelyn Ankumah, a Ghanaian jurist who has studied the work of the commission, has called upon the commission to make "a clear and reasoned determination as to what constitutes violation of freedom of religion." Ankumah believes that the suppression of freedom of religion in one state is likely to threaten the security of a neighboring state. In particular, she has singled out the need to address the issue of a change of religion.[32]

## ISLAM

Islam is a world religion and not a regional entity. Nevertheless, it is worthy of mention because of the consolidated interests of Muslim states. These interests have been formalized through the Organization of the Islamic Conference, which was formed in 1972 when the Third Islamic Conference of Foreign Ministers adopted its charter. Membership is open to every Muslim state, including states where Islam is the official state religion and other states where the majority of the population is Muslim.[33]

For Islamic states, the Cairo Declaration on Human Rights (1990) is seen as the authoritative document reflecting the Islamic approach to international human rights. Particularly noteworthy is Article 10 of the declaration, which prohibits "any form of compulsion on man or to exploit his poverty or ignorance in order to convert him to another religion or to atheism." Article 22, which allows freedom of expression in a manner "as would not be contrary to the principles of the Shari'a," is also salient.[34]

Juliane Kokott has addressed the apparent dichotomy between the traditional notions of Islam and the rules governing modern human rights.[35] Kokott asserts that Islam is compatible with universal human rights, but Islamic law, the *shari'a*, as interpreted more than a millennium ago, contains rules that seem to contradict modern human rights formulations, particularly in the area of freedom of religion and apostasy. Kokott believes that the Cairo

Declaration "tends to Islamize human rights at the cost of their universality."[36] In general, Islamic nations seem to have difficulty in finding conformity between the *shari'a* and internationally recognized human rights standards.[37] Abdullahi Ahmed An-Na'im asserts that although the Islamic theory of the freedom of belief "was comparatively superior to those of other state-religions in the past and the practice was generally better than the theory, both are no longer acceptable from a modern human rights point of view."[38] Donna E. Arzt refers to the "tortuous" relationship between Islamic law and international law.[39]

## SPECIAL AND BILATERAL ARRANGEMENTS

Although they are not properly forms of regional protection of religious human rights, some bilateral or special arrangements between several states and the Holy See of the Roman Catholic Church (or between several states and religious institutions or communities of religious origin) are worthy of mention. It is beyond the scope of this work to deal with the constitutional and administrative provisions regarding religious entities or activities or with legislation concerning religious rights. This would encompass an analysis covering a wide range of legal, economic, educational, and political issues. Nevertheless, the Holy See, because of its special nature and its international importance, plays a crucial role in addressing and determining religious human rights.

Neither the Holy See nor Vatican City is a member of the United Nations; their status in international law is not absolutely clear. Nevertheless, the Holy See has signed many treaties and has entered into bilateral agreements, in some cases called concordats, with a number of states. In addition, the Holy See has participated in numerous intergovernmental conferences, and it conducts full-scale diplomatic activity in which it is represented by the papal nuncios. (Of course, the Catholic Church and the pope play an instrumental role in the worldwide Catholic faith community.) In recent years the Holy See has been active and has signed new agreements with several states, and in some cases the new agreements have replaced former ones.[40]

The 1993 Fundamental Agreement between the Holy See and the State of Israel (included in the appendix hereto) is particularly noteworthy. This agreement was made in preparation for the establishment of diplomatic relations between the Holy See and Israel. It also incorporated diverse provisions on religious rights.[41] But this document has a significance that goes beyond its specific diplomatic purpose: it demonstrates the commitment by two religiously influential entities to uphold the human right to freedom of religion and conscience as set forth in the Universal Declaration of Human Rights. Amending some of the controversial declarations of the Second Vatican Council, the Holy See reiterated its condemnation of hatred, persecution, racism, and all other manifestations of antisemitism and religious intolerance. In return, Israel recognized the right of the Catholic Church to carry out its religious, moral, educational, and charitable aims and to allow the church to control its institutions in Israel. The "status quo" in the Christian Holy Places will be maintained, and the freedom of Catholic worship is guaranteed. The agreement also addressed specific topics such as pilgrimages, schools and institutes of study, cultural exchanges, access to historical documents, charitable functions, property rights, fiscal matters, and commitment to the peaceful resolution of conflicts.

Silvio Ferrari underscores the historical significance of this agreement, which he labels "the first real Concordat to be concluded with a non-Christian and non-Western country (at least non-fully Western)."[42] It also has the potential to become a model for future concordats with non-Catholic countries. The agreement was followed by the establishment of full diplomatic relations between the parties.

Spain provides a good example of how special bilateral arrangements with religious communities can be productively used. Spain replaced a concordat signed with the Holy See in 1953 with several agreements. These included a basic agreement, which was reached in 1976. Spain also signed separate agreements in 1992 with other Spanish-based religious groups, including the Federation of Evangelical Religious Institutions, the Federation of Jewish Communities, and the Islamic Commission. These agreements were reached under the Spanish Constitution of 1978 and the 1980 Religious Liberty Law. This law allows for agreements of cooperation with religious groups that have achieved notorious influence in Spanish society. The agreements refer to a wide range of subjects including freedom of religion and worship; the status of the respective religious communities, their buildings and premises, cemeteries, personnel, and fiscal issues; religious ceremonies regarding marriages; religious services; assistance to military personnel in prisons, hospitals, community and educational establishments; tax exemptions; holy days and festivities; matters concerning religious and cultural heritage; and dietary practices, including animal slaughter.[43]

Another country that has been active in modifying its concordat with the Holy See is Colombia, which recently signed an agreement to ensure full religious freedom to all churches and sects.[44] Also, Italy and the Holy See signed an agreement in 1984.[45]

It would be fitting to end this chapter by mentioning unilateral statements or declarations that have greatly influenced religious human rights. One of the most notable declarations is the *Declaration on the Relationship of the Church to Non-Christian Religions (Nostra Aetate),* adopted on October 28, 1965, by the Second Vatican Council.[46] In this declaration the church repudiated all persecutions against any person, including hatred, discrimination, and displays of antisemitism. Another notable declaration, "Guidelines and Suggestions for Implementing the Conciliar Declaration *Nostra Aetate*," was adopted by the church's Commission for Religious Relations with the Jews in 1974. This recalls the condemnation by the council of antisemitism and all other discrimination. It also makes concrete suggestions regarding liturgy, education, and common social action in the search for social justice and peace.[47]

The World Council of Churches adopted in 1948 the "Declaration on Religious Liberty," which stresses the indispensability of freedom of religion for the international order. According to this declaration the right to such freedom should be recognized and observed without distinctions. The declaration further asserts that all persons have the right to determine their own faith and creed; change their belief; express their religious beliefs in worship, teaching, and practice; and form religious organizations. The declaration also acknowledges the rights of parents concerning the religious education of their children and promotes limitations prescribed by law that are necessary to protect order and welfare, morals, and the rights and freedoms of others.[48]

The legal effect of the above-mentioned declarations is limited because of their unilateral character. Nevertheless, they represent significant steps in attempting to achieve a worldwide system of protection of religious rights.

# 3.

# PROTECTING RELIGIOUS GROUPS FROM PERSECUTION AND INCITEMENT

———————◆———————

International law after World War II was not group oriented. The general conception that prevailed in modern human rights law centered on the respect for individual rights and the prohibition of discrimination. Little attention was devoted to the protection of groups as such, or of their members as belonging to a group. An early and major exception was the Convention on Genocide, specifically aimed at protecting the physical existence of religious and other collective entities or groups.[1] This convention will be discussed separately below.

Other manifestations of group hatred, incitement, or defamation are only indirectly dealt with in general instruments on human rights. In this chapter I intend to discuss how international law presently approaches the question of curbing incitement and persecution against collectivities. Religious communities are particularly exposed to such attacks and to severe expressions of intolerance that may become illegal, endangering their victims as well as social peace, even when they do not involve violence. Defamation of groups, group libel, or defamation of persons belonging to a certain group, may affect the rights of the individual and the social standing of the entire group to which the individual belongs. Justice Frankfurter stressed that relationship four decades ago. He stated: "A man's job and his educational opportunities and the dignity accorded him may depend as much on the reputation of the racial and religious group to which he willy-nilly belongs as on his own merits."[2]

The need to protect religious groups from discrimination and persecution is strongly felt today.[3] Discrimination, at least when it is based on racial grounds, is adequately addressed by international law, although the issue of implementation has not been satisfactorily resolved. Discrimination is a well-defined legal notion.[4] The prohibition of racial discrimination has become a peremptory norm of international law (*jus cogens*),[5] and the trend is to accord the same status to discrimination on religious grounds.[6] Incitement to discrimination, a subsidiary aspect of the prevention of discrimination, is also clearly

51

forbidden. Hatred and intolerance are less precise terms. Incitement to hatred, or to intolerance and other related evils, is mentioned in some provisions, but international law is still struggling with the need to ensure coordination between basic rights such as freedom of speech or freedom of association, and the right of collective entities, or their members because of membership in such entities, not to be subjected to libel, defamation, hostility, intolerance, or incitement to hatred.

The 1966 International Covenant on Civil and Political Rights contains several relevant provisions.[7] Article 19 authorizes limitations on freedom of expression to protect the right and reputation of "others." Article 20 prohibits advocacy of national, racial, or religious hatred that constitutes incitement to discrimination, hostility, or violence. Articles 10(2) and 11(2) of the 1950 European Convention for the Protection of Human Rights and Fundamental Freedoms[8] restrict freedom of expression, assembly and association when necessary in a democratic society in the interests of the "prevention of disorder" and "protection of the reputation or rights of others." The American Convention on Human Rights refers to everyone's right to have "his honor respected and his dignity recognized"; to liability to ensure the "reputation of others"; and to penalizing "advocacy of national, racial or religious hatred that constitute incitement to lawless violence or any other similar illegal action against any person or group of persons on any grounds including those of race, color, religion, language, or national origin."[9]

The U.N. Declaration on the Elimination of All Forms of Intolerance and of Discrimination Based on Religion or Belief (1981) calls upon states to take "all appropriate measures to combat intolerance on the grounds of religion or other beliefs."[10] The 1978 UNESCO Declaration on Race and Racial Prejudice, in Article 5(3), urges the "mass media and all organized groups within national communities" to refrain from presenting "a stereotyped, partial, unilateral or tendentious picture of individuals and of various human groups."[11] According to Article 6, states should take steps "to prohibit and eradicate racism [and] racist propaganda" and should "combat racial prejudice." The Paris Charter for a New Europe, adopted on November 21, 1990, at the Paris Summit of the Conference on Security and Cooperation in Europe, states the determination of the thirty-four participating states from Europe, the United States, and Canada "to combat all forms of racial and ethnic hatred, anti-Semitism, xenophobia, and discrimination against anyone, as well as persecution on religious and ideological grounds."[12]

## RELEVANCE OF THE CONVENTION
## ON RACIAL DISCRIMINATION

The above-mentioned declarations, obviously of great moral and political significance, are not positive international law, although they may certainly influence domestic legislation. But the main obligatory provisions concerning incitement against groups, communities, or collective entities are those contained in the U.N. Convention on the Elimination of All Forms of Racial Discrimination, ratified, as of August 1999, by 155 states.[13] They are obviously relevant to the area of religion, although the convention avoids references to that area.

Article 4 of the convention, quoted in full in the appendix hereto, contains provisions concerning incitement, hatred, or hostility against persons and collectivities. It is a controversial article and was subjected to criticism and formal reservations. However, Article 4 has become an important guideline for states, and several have enacted domestic legislation in the spirit of its provisions.[14] The article is of obvious relevance to the religious area. Article 4 provides, in its pertinent part:

> States Parties condemn all propaganda and all organizations which are based on ideas or theories of superiority of one race or group of persons of one colour or ethnic origin, or which attempt to justify or promote racial hatred and discrimination in any form, and undertake to adopt immediate and positive measures designed to eradicate all incitement to, or acts of, such discrimination, and to this end, with due regard to the principles embodied in the Universal Declaration of Human Rights and the rights expressly set forth in Article 5 of this Convention, inter alia:
>
> (a) Shall declare an offence punishable by law all dissemination of ideas based on racial superiority or hatred, incitement to racial discrimination, as well as all acts of violence or incitement to such acts against any race or group of persons of another colour or ethnic origin, and also the provision of any assistance to racist activities, including the financing thereof;
>
> (b) Shall declare illegal and prohibit organizations, and also organized and all other propaganda activities, which promote and incite racial discrimination and shall recognize participation in such organizations or activities as an offence punishable by law;
>
> (c) Shall not permit public authorities or public institutions, national or local, to promote or incite racial discrimination.

The text of Article 4 is a compromise. During the entire drafting process, including its last stages in the General Assembly, numerous amendments were submitted.[15] In order to achieve agreement, it was necessary to bridge the radical differences between those who saw in Article 4 the "key article" of the convention and those who considered it a threat to the basic freedoms of speech and association. Jose D. Ingles, the special rapporteur designated by the Committee on the Elimination of Racial Discrimination (CERD) to submit a study on the interpretation of Article 4, pointed out that the final text "afforded a compromise between those who wished the enactment of positive legislation to penalize not only 'incitement to discrimination' but also the 'dissemination of ideas based on racial superiority or hatred,' and those who did not wish to see freedom of speech or assembly impaired."[16] As a consequence of the search for compromise, the text adopted is not entirely satisfactory and contains some shortcomings. With these limitations, the text may be seen as a guideline to interpret in a similar spirit the provisions on incitement in the instruments on religious rights.

## CLASH BETWEEN RIGHTS

The difficulties of some states to go along with the text of Article 4 should not be underestimated. Similar difficulties may be expected if a mandatory convention is drafted with regard to religious incitement. They refer to issues that are central to the nature of the respective legal systems, although the objections raised by some representatives did not always reflect a real respect for fundamental freedoms or exaggerated the risks involved in the text. The representative of Colombia, for instance, stated that the Parliament of his country would be unable to ratify "a pact contrary to the political constitution of the country and contrary to the norms of public life." In his view, Article 4 was a throwback to the past, since "punishing ideas, whatever they may be, is to aid and abet tyranny, and leads to the abuse of power. . . . As far as we are concerned and as far as democracy is concerned, ideas should be fought with ideas and reasons; theories must be refuted by arguments and not by the scaffold, prison, exile, confiscation or fines."[17]

This apocalyptic appraisal of the dangers inherent in Article 4 seems far away from the support that many democratic countries have given to Article 4 by incorporating its provisions in their internal legislation. But it was impossible to ignore the objections raised by some Western states that were eager to avoid a clash between their legal systems and the convention, and expressed this apprehension in their reservations. For example, when President Carter sent the convention to the U.S. Senate for ratification in 1978, the United States government recommended a reservation stating that nothing in the convention "shall be deemed to require or to authorize legislation or other action . . . which would restrict the right of free speech. . . . " The United States also recommended a declaration indicating the nonexecuting nature of Article 4, among others.[18] Italy stated that Article 4 must not "jeopardize the right to freedom of opinion and expression and the right to freedom of peaceful assembly and association. . . . "[19]

Declarations or reservations were made upon signature or upon ratification by several states parties. The United Kingdom interpreted Article 4 as requiring the adoption of legislation "only in so far as it may consider with due regard to the principles embodied in the Universal Declaration of Human Rights and the rights expressly set forth in Article 5 of the Convention" that legislative additions to, or variation of, existing law and practice are necessary to attain the purposes of Article 4.[20] In March 1991, at a meeting of CERD, clarification was requested concerning the interpretative statement of the United Kingdom "and its possible adverse implications for the full implementation of Article 4(b) in the context of the non-prohibition of the British National Party."[21]

The interpretation by CERD of the nature of the obligations assumed by states parties to the convention leaves no room for doubt. General Recommendation I of the committee, adopted in 1972, says clearly that the implementation by states parties of the provisions envisaged in Article 4 is obligatory, and, if domestic legislation is not sufficient, it should be supplemented by adequate additional measures.[22]

As stated by Judge Ingles in the conclusions and recommendations of his study, approved by CERD, Article 4 is not self-executing. However, the "clearcut and unambiguous" provisions of paragraphs (a) and (b) "are not discretionary, but mandatory."[23] States parties are bound to enact implementing legislation in accordance with Article 4, "even if they allege that racial discrimination is unknown or that there are no racist organizations" in their jurisdictions.[24] The article has a preventive role, and a reservation retaining the discretion to determine if and when it is necessary to enact adequate legislation would be "incompatible with the object and purpose of the Convention."[25] The rights of free speech and free association are not absolute and are subject to limitations, in accordance with Article 29 of the Universal Declaration and Articles 19 and 21 of the International Covenant on Civil and Political Rights. Some states may be confronted with serious constitutional problems. In pointing out the difficulties the United States may encounter in criminalizing speech and association on the basis of racist content as a result of the content-neutral protection afforded by the First Amendment of the U.S. Constitution, Professor Meron indicates that what may be overly broad for one legal and social system is not so for another. This does not necessarily mean making a value judgment as to which system is superior.[26] It may be argued, however, that the convention and CERD did in fact make such a value judgment by opting for the system definitely incorporated into Article 4.

For these reasons, constitutional provisions alone, without implementing legislation, are not enough. Article 4 imposes the duty to declare certain acts or activities as offenses punishable by law, and the same applies to participation in organizations that engage in prohibited acts. The imposition of civil liability alone would be insufficient. But the needs of states should be taken into consideration. The adoption of legislation "is a slow process," and states parties are entitled to complete the process of adjusting their legislation within a reasonable time, subject to the principle that treaties should be observed in good faith.[27]

The text of Article 4 was adopted by the Third Committee of the U.N. General Assembly after many amendments were submitted. It was necessary to take several separate votes, including on the words "with due regard to the principles embodied in the Universal Declaration of Human Rights and the rights expressly set forth in Article 5 of the Convention" in the introductory paragraph. Separate votes were also taken on the phrases "all dissemination of ideas based on racial superiority or hatred" and "also the provision of any assistance to racist activities, including the financing thereof," both in paragraph (a). These formulations were ultimately retained, without any votes against and with five abstentions.[28]

When the draft was submitted to the General Assembly, a new attempt was made to delete the terms "dissemination of ideas based on racial discrimination or hatred." An amendment submitted to that effect by five Latin American states was defeated by a vote of 54 against, 25 in favor, and 23 abstentions. This demonstrates the extent to which the question of incitement was considered a difficult one, mainly because of the word *hatred*. It was recalled that Article 9 of the Declaration on the Elimination of All Forms of Racial Discrimination did not incorporate the term *hatred* and only condemns propaganda and organizations based on ideas or theories of the superiority of one race or group of persons of one color or ethnic origin with a view to justifying or promoting racial discrimination.

The introduction of the term *hatred* was considered problematic. Is it possible to incriminate the dissemination of ideas based on hatred? Hatred is a feeling, a state of mind, and not a clearly established legal interest, as is the case of discrimination. As to the dissemination of ideas intended to cause racial or religious discrimination or hatred, the question of possible restrictions on scientific research was raised. The lessons of the Nazi regime, prolific in the production of publications apparently scientific in their form but undoubtedly racist in content, were taken into consideration. Today, restrictions imposed upon individuals who argue that the Holocaust never took place or was not of the magnitude asserted by historians—and so accepted even in judicial decisions—are related to the aims of Article 4. They draw a distinction between legitimate scientific research and the dissemination of ideas and theories intended to provoke racial or religious hatred.[29]

Article 4 does not require criminal intent. It is the "mere act of dissemination" that is penalized, irrespective of intent or consequences.[30]

## THE "WITH DUE REGARD" CLAUSE

In order to avoid interpretations that states might consider incompatible with their constitutional systems, the sentence beginning with the words "with due regard" was introduced in the opening paragraph of Article 4. This sentence was interpreted as meaning that Article 4 does not impose on states parties any obligation to take measures that "are not fully consistent with its constitutional guarantees of freedom, including freedom of speech and association," as pointed out by a United States spokesman.[31] This interpretation was shared by other states that believed that the "with due regard" formula was sufficient to permit them to sign and ratify the convention. The question is, however, to what extent the "with due regard" clause can be seen as implying neutrality in a clash between the prohibition of incitement to racial (or religious) hatred, on the one hand, and unrestricted freedom of speech and association, on the other.

As already indicated, the general spirit of the convention, the wide international support expressed in the large number of ratifications, and state practice as translated in legislation based on the convention, may support the view that neutrality was not intended. States are free to ratify or not to ratify the convention. They may also ratify it with reservations, unless the reservations are considered incompatible with the object and purpose of the convention, as interpreted by two-thirds of the states parties. This was a controversial provision, incorporated at the last moment by the General Assembly.[32] The special rapporteur on Article 4 pointed out that a reservation allowing the respective states the discretion to determine if and when it is necessary to enact legislation in accordance with the mandatory provision of Article 4 may be considered as incompatible with the object and purpose of the convention and therefore cannot be permitted under Article 20(2). This seems to be the approach followed by CERD.[33]

The need to achieve a compromise in order to make the convention acceptable to all states again led to vague language that left a majority of states or, in the last instance, the International Court, with the decision on the legality of a reservation. When a state ratifies the convention without expressing reservations to Article 4, the "with due regard" clause cannot be seen as relieving that state from the duty to implement Article 4 and the corresponding duty to adopt legislation to that effect. For many states the new clause facilitated the vote in favor of the convention. But it did not solve the difficult question of a clash between rights. To claim that it permits states to ratify the treaty without adopting domestic legislation aimed at implementing Article 4 would deprive the convention of one of its major aims. CERD stated: "It could not have been the intention of the drafters of the Convention to enable states parties to construe the phrase . . . as cancelling the obligations relating to the prohibition of the racist activities concerned. . . . "[34]

The Human Rights Committee took a similar approach in its General Comment II on Article 20 of the International Covenant on Civil and Political Rights,[35] applicable both to racial and religious hatred and considered by the committee as fully compatible with freedom of expression. The committee believes that states parties which have not yet done so should take the necessary measures and sanctions in case of violation.

## CONTENTS OF ARTICLE 4

The wording of the opening paragraph of Article 4 is rather unsatisfactory and must be read in conjunction with the definition of racial discrimination in Article 1 of the convention. The phrase "race or group of persons of one colour or ethnic origin" should be broadly interpreted. There is no definition in the convention of the terms *race* and *ethnic*, but it seems reasonable to assume that the intention of the drafters was to protect every group that has a defined collective identity.[36] In their interpretation of the notion of *racial discrimination,* domestic tribunals in different countries have taken the view that what is important is the fact that the group sees itself as a distinctive collective entity and is so perceived by the surrounding population.[37] The convention does not refer to religious groups, although frequently religion is combined with other group characteristics. Jews, Arabs, Sikhs, Kurds, and Armenians are examples of such complex identities. There is no doubt that the convention protects such groups. CERD gave some attention to the issue of religion, and members of the committee took different views on the question of whether attacks against religious groups were to be dealt with under the Convention on Racial Discrimination.[38]

The opening paragraph of Article 4 condemns "propaganda," while operative paragraph (c) refers to "organized and all other propaganda activities." It seems reasonable to conclude that the purpose was to cover intentional dissemination of racist ideas in an organized way and not to deal with casual, isolated expressions. In some cases, however, the distinction is difficult. One person's persistent campaign of racist manifestations addressed to the public should be considered "organized propaganda" despite the fact that no organization is involved. The various media employed—radio, television, press, and wide distribution by mail or Internet of inciting material—are a decisive consideration in determining organized propaganda. A treaty cannot be casuistic, and the differences in wording should not be construed in a way that clashes with the obvious intentions of the drafters.

The opening paragraph contains a reference to "racial hatred." However, as already indicated, it is difficult to define *hatred,* which is a feeling or sentiment that may not express itself in deeds. In the same paragraph states parties undertake to adopt measures designed "to eradicate all incitement to, or acts of, such discrimination." The absence of a reference to incitement to racial hatred should be regarded only as a drafting deficiency, since in operative paragraph (a) states parties are asked to "declare an offence punishable by law all dissemination of ideas based on racial superiority or hatred." It is not only incitement to discrimination that must be eradicated but also incitement to hatred.

States are called upon to adopt various kinds of measures, always with due regard to the principles embodied in the Universal Declaration of Human Rights and the rights expressly set forth in Article 5. The compromise-building formula, which helped to accelerate the preparation of the convention, as we have seen, does not solve the critical problem of clashes between rights. The spirit of the convention is not to permit freedom of speech or association to take precedence over the right to be free from discrimination or incitement. States parties will have to find ways to accommodate their domestic legislation to the undertakings contained in the convention.

Article 4(a), (b), and (c) lists, though not exhaustively, the duties imposed upon states. States shall declare the following to be offenses punishable by law:

### 1. All Dissemination of Ideas Based on Racial Superiority or Hatred

The problems involved in the use of the term "ideas" have already been discussed. While Article 4 does not restrict scientific research, it aims to avoid racism hidden under the name of scientific research. Domestic criminal law will have to solve the problems involved in accordance with each country's definition of what constitutes a criminal act. The UNESCO Declaration on Race and Racial Prejudice, in order to cope with this problem, calls upon specialists in natural and social sciences and cultural studies, as well as scientific organizations and associations, to ensure that "their research findings are not misinterpreted."[39]

The convention does not define ideas based on hatred. The difficulties in arriving at such a definition may be even greater when dealing with feelings originated in religion.

### 2. Incitement to Racial Discrimination

The word *incitement* created difficulties during the drafting of the convention. It must be interpreted in conjunction with the full text of Article 4 and in light of the difficulties that were supposedly resolved with the "with due regard . . . " sentence.

### 3. Acts of Violence, or Incitement to Such Acts against Any Race or Group of Persons of Another Color or Ethnic Origin

Acts of violence are always punishable, except when explicitly permitted by law. As to incitement, the remarks in item 2 are also applicable here, though it would have been preferable to use a more general term when referring to the victims of such acts.

### 4. Provision of Any Assistance to Racist Activities, Including the Financing Thereof

In this connection the question was asked whether buying a propaganda booklet of a racist organization could be considered a crime. The British representative in the Third Committee stated that Great Britain could not agree to punish by law anyone who had only paid a subscription toward membership in a fascist organization.[40] Once the law declares that a fascist organization, as defined by law, is illegal, membership in it becomes an offense. But still there may be borderline cases, where states implementing the convention and adopting legal measures to that effect will have to define the differences between legal and illicit acts. The word *assistance*, not defined in the convention, also requires clarification in domestic law.

The purpose of paragraph (b) is to outlaw racist organizations. There is no definition of the term *organization*, although legal status, program, and size are relevant features. The main substantive problem is the possible clash between that purpose and freedom of association. At what stage of their existence should hate organizations be declared illegal and disbanded? Do they have to engage in actual activities in order to be declared illegal, or is it enough that their program or articles of association reflect their intention? What is the meaning of "promote and incite racial discrimination"?

The *travaux préparatoires* are helpful in this respect. Racist organizations should not be allowed to become a danger to peace and should be declared illegal as soon as it becomes clear that they intend to engage in the promotion of and incitement to discrimination. It would appear that there is no need to wait for a "clear and present danger" to society. However, legal systems in which criminal intention alone is not sufficient to outlaw an organization before it translates that intention into criminal acts may face difficulties in implementing preventive steps against racist incitement or organization.

An interesting case in this regard was decided in Israel in 1987. The High Court of Justice was asked to determine whether the Israel Broadcasting Authority was entitled to refuse to broadcast utterances containing undisputed racial incitement. The issue was freedom of speech rather than freedom of association, but the question of "clear and present danger" was raised. Justice Bach took the view that clear racial incitement was sufficient to justify restrictions, even when there was no "near certainty" of harm to the social order. He stated that there was no need in Israel, with the tragic and traumatic background of the Jewish people, to emphasize "the utterly destructive influence of incitement to racial hatred."[41]

The reference to "organized and all other propaganda activities" was not casual. "All other propaganda activities are those carried on not by organized associations but by groups that do not possess the status of organizations, or by individuals." The words "all other" should be clarified by domestic legislation. They indicate, however, a trend toward a broad interpretation.

With regard to "promote and incite," it should be noted that the Declaration on the Elimination of All Forms of Intolerance and of Discrimination Based on Religion or Belief refers to "promote or incite."[42] The difference between the verbs *promote* and *incite* is not clear. Neither is it clear if both activities are necessary to justify the prohibition. The explanation for the use of both terms was that *promotion* presented a "lower degree" of motivation and may be present even in the absence of an intention to *incite*. Incitement, on the other hand, is a conscious and motivated act. Incitement may cause hatred, and the fact of creating "an atmosphere of racial hatred" would inevitably lead indirectly to racial discrimination.[43]

The final part of Article 4 is unrelated to the area of criminal law. While states parties should certainly "not permit public authorities or public institutions, national or local, to promote or incite racial discrimination," a better place for this provision might have been in Article 2, which deals with obligations of states parties. The prohibition should be interpreted as covering activities and statements of all organs of the state, including autonomous bodies and spokesmen of the state in international forums.

Article 4 is undoubtedly one of the important articles of the Convention on Racial Discrimination, if not the most important. Even with the compromise of the "with due regard" clause, the article takes a stand on the conflict between rights, in favor of the prohibition of racial discrimination and incitement. It would appear that in case of a clash of rights, the orientation of Article 4 is that freedom of speech or association cannot be invoked to prevent a state party from taking legal measures, inclusive of a penal nature, against violations of the convention.

Article 4 is not self-executing, and therefore actions of the state to implement its provisions are indispensable. A state that ratifies the convention but does not adopt legislation in the spirit of Article 4 is not fulfilling its obligations under the convention. This may dissuade states from ratifying the convention, but the text, despite the weaknesses in its drafting, does not leave any doubt in this respect. International practice, as expressed in the legislation adopted by many states parties, shows that Article 4 did not deter ratification.

Article 4 is an ambitious provision. It is presently the most articulate provision in international law intended to fight not only racial discrimination but also related evils such as racial hatred, racist propaganda, and association with racist purposes. It is applicable to the interpretation of similar texts dealing with religion.

Its shortcomings are rather in the area of good legislative technique and drafting. The preparation of a draft model law covering its provisions may provide the clarifications required in the present text. The secretary-general of the United Nations has prepared such a draft on model legislation intended to ensure "adequate protection to the victims of racism and racial discrimination, through legislative guarantees, criminalization of racist acts, the development of recourse procedures and the establishment of independent national bodies to monitor implementation."[44] It may be difficult to achieve general agreement to such a model, and it remains to be seen to what extent national legislatures will adopt the model. But, as correctly asserted by members of CERD, the international convention, rather than imperfect national laws, should serve as the basis for the model legislation.[45] In this respect Article 4 is crucial. It is also of evident relevance to the subject of discrimination and incitement on grounds of religion.


## GROUP LIBEL

From time to time the question of group libel—or group defamation—and the measures to be taken to curb it is revived in certain countries. The controversy in regard to this legal dilemma began in the 1940s under the influence of the lessons of World War II. Since then, many states, including Western democracies, have enacted legislation outlawing group libel. As to international law, some instruments have incorporated provisions on the matter.

Group libel involves general problems related to human rights law, such as the balance between freedoms, the admissibility of derogations and limitations of basic rights, and procedural difficulties concerning the victim, or victims, of this particular offense. Manifestations of religious intolerance, disregard for the collective aspirations of ethnic and religious groups, and the humiliation or persecution of entire communities are frequently interwoven with organized campaigns of defamation.

Lawyers are divided on the question. Strict civil libertarians, particularly in the United States, are against any measures likely to restrict freedom of speech and related liberties, however serious the social dangers involved in the abuse of those freedoms may be. In their view, group libel is protected by the prohibition on restricting free speech. Others take a more flexible view: freedom of speech, as other liberties, can be subjected to limitations when it is likely to cause serious breaches of the peace or of public order. Other jurists claim that there should be no freedom of speech to defame, insult, hurt, or ridicule an entire group, and that, in such cases, the group is entitled to a legal remedy. For them, the content of the speech is sufficient to invoke the operation of the law.[46]

I have mentioned already the ruling of the Israeli High Court of Justice in the *Israel Broadcasting Authority* case, which was rather indecisive regarding the question of when group defamation can be restricted, although all the judges expressed revulsion regarding racism. Justice Barak considered that restriction of freedom of expression must be the last resort. Although Israeli law does not require a "clear and present danger" of damage, as is the rule in the United States, a theoretical possibility is not sufficient, and freedom of speech can be limited only where there is a "near certainty" of real harm to the social order.

Justice Bach took a different position with regard to incitement to racial hatred: "No other form of expression can so effectively create violence, stir the lowest and most vile instincts in human beings, and lead to the degradation of sections of the population against whom the propaganda is directed." He therefore considered that the Broadcasting Authority was entitled to refuse to broadcast utterances containing clear incitement, even when there was not a "near certainty" of harm to the social order. Moreover, Justice Bach indicated support for measures aimed at curbing group libel.[47]

## THE MEANING OF GROUP LIBEL

The term *group libel* needs clarification. The meaning of *libel* is well known: malicious defamation, slander, vilification of a person exposing him or her to hatred, contempt, or ridicule. Most modern legal systems curb individual libel. *Group libel* involves a more complicated situation. It is, of course, libel, but it is addressed not against a specified individual or several identified individuals but against a whole group.

In cases of ordinary libel, everyone recognizes that the victim or target of the defamatory utterance, the individual or individuals affected, is entitled to protection by the law. When someone says, "The black men John Adams and Joseph Smith are rapists," or "The Jews Haim Rabinovich and Salomon Cohen are traitors," the named individuals have, subject to some conditions, the right to take legal action against the slanderers.

But what about the expressions "blacks are rapists" or "Jews are traitors"— when a whole racial, religious, or ethnic group rather than identified individuals is defamed, insulted, or hurt? Do John Adams and Joseph Smith, or Haim Rabinovich and Salomon Cohen, or other members of their respective groups, have the right and the possibility to invoke the legal process to prevent group libel, to punish the perpetrators, and to receive compensation for the harm they sustained? Can blacks as a group, or Catholics, Muslims, or Jews, as a group, or organizations representing them, take legal steps asking for redress? More difficult still, how and when may group defamation be prevented? Only when an interference with public order may follow, or when, despite the fact that no incidents may be expected, the expression is of such a nature that it profoundly hurts a specific sector of the public? Illustrations of this latter aspect include the famous *Skokie* case in the United States or attempted marches or demonstrations by racist gangs in Arab villages in the Galilee that caused considerable debate in Israel.

The law of group libel varies from country to country, and occasionally from time to time. In some countries domestic legislation does not authorize civil actions for group libel unless the plaintiff can prove that he is personally included in the defamatory statement. In some countries prosecution in cases of group libel is only possible with the consent of the attorney general or a similar public authority.[48] In others, group libel is actionable when defamation is on racial grounds but not when the slander is of a religious nature.

In cases of group libel not only an individual but a community as a whole suffers. Such libelous expressions are essentially directed against the group more than against its individual members. In the same way that the intention of genocide is to destroy the group rather than a few or many of its individual members, so the intention of hate insults or defamation is to hurt the whole group rather than this or that individual member. When bigots say or write that "blacks are rapists," or "Jews are exploiters and traitors," or "Muslims are terrorists," or "Burakumin are inferior," or "Indians are drunkards," they imply that all blacks, Jews, Muslims, Burakumin, or Indians possess the despicable characteristics attributed to them, that no distinction as to individuals is worth the effort, that the negative, dangerous quality is to be attributed automatically to the entire community. That entire group should therefore be suspected, feared, and treated in such a way as to make it impossible for its members to harm society.

In the cases of both individual and group libel damage is done. It would appear that the social harm is much more serious in the case of group libel, when no individuals are named. Yet group libel is more difficult to combat through the courts than the simple case of libel against an individual. Having stressed the social dangers involved in group libel, one should not ignore the problems that make it difficult to combat it with the help of the law.

## CURBING GROUP LIBEL

The general principles regarding derogations and limitations in the field of human rights and basic liberties—such as those emanating from Articles 29 and 30 of the Universal Declaration on Human Rights and Article 5 of the International Covenant on Civil and Political Rights—are, of course, applicable. Also relevant is the discussion on the legal meaning of a series of terms frequently employed in this context, such as *freedom of speech, incitement, fighting words, public order, public health, public morality, provocation, clear and present danger, captive audience, criminal intention, breach of the peace, political comment,* and many others. Because of the attempts to disguise group defamation as political comment or scientific argumentation, the precise use of such terms is sometimes of crucial importance. Legal semantics are relevant here. As Kenneth Lasson puts it: "To suggest that the law cannot distinguish between political comment and racial defamation is akin to equating Michelangelo's nudes with those in a 42nd Street pornographic bookstore."[49]

Because of all these difficulties, the effort to outlaw group libel was confronted by many objections, some strictly of a legal nature, others more practical. It has been argued that group libel legislation is of no use, and that Nazi or similar organizations will not be stopped by such laws; that instead it may provide bigots with a forum for the dissemination of their views; that oppressed groups may themselves become victims of such legislation. Those voicing such arguments come up with the already well-known formula: Education is the only effective way of dealing with bigotry and religion and race defamation, not legislation.

The objections should not be ignored, but they are not convincing. The law, particularly criminal law, is the most effective means of education and enlightenment. The law sets standards of behavior to which human beings must conform. The purpose of law, particularly criminal law, is to prevent crime rather than to punish it. Declaring that specific acts are criminal and forbidden is undoubtedly an educational and preventive measure. Of course, preventive measures may not always be feasible or adequate. It is virtually impossible, in a democratic society, to prevent someone having access to the communications media from engaging in defamatory statements. It is possible, and justifiable, to prevent individuals and organizations devoted to propagating group defamation from obtaining access to such media when they belong to the state or to other public organs. Democratic countries where freedom of speech is a respected value have outlawed bigoted organizations through domestic legislation and relevant international agreements. The *Skokie* case would become impossible if the organizations engaged in the planning and implementation of such and similar provocations were to be banned by law. Jews, frequent victims of group libel, have advocated such legal steps for years in many places, although some Jewish-American groups did not feel comfortable with them.

When prevention is impossible or inadequate, the main problem is the question of limitations on free speech. Should society remain idle, hoping that reason will overcome bigotry, or should the law declare that some defamatory expressions are a punishable crime? The latter approach may be technically difficult, but, as we shall see, many legal systems have attempted it. Democratic societies anxious to safeguard freedom of expression and related liberties have found it necessary to limit their use in cases of conflict with basic social ideals and interests. When free speech corrupts, when it seriously offends religious beliefs, when it jeopardizes public order and national security, it is legitimate to limit it. When free speech is used to harm those whose good repute society is obligated to protect, it is legitimate to suppress it and provide redress for the victims.

The Supreme Court of a country with a free-speech tradition, the United States, has declared that free speech must be accommodated to other equally basic needs of society. Libelous utterances "are of such slight social value . . . that any benefit that may be derived from them is clearly outweighted by the social interest in order and morality."[50]

It is up to each system of criminal law to define when a criminal offense is being committed and when and how it should be punished. It is up to each general system of law to establish what redress should be available to the victims.

Domestic legislation and international law contain provisions against group libel. Those provisions, particularly domestic legislation, differ from place to place. In general, European countries have promulgated more specific legislation banning group libel, undoubtedly as a consequence of the tragic lessons of recent history. It was already noted that there are different degrees of severity in the approach to group libel. Some countries require proof of interference with public order and peace; some establish the need to prove intention or motive in addition to the objective result; some authorize prosecution only with the acquiescence of the state; and some go as far as to prohibit the activities of, membership in, and financing of hate organizations.

As an example of domestic legislation, the Consultative Assembly of the Council of Europe drafted model legislation in 1966 making it an offense publicly to call for or incite to hatred, intolerance, discrimination, or violence against persons or groups of persons distinguished by color, race, ethnic or national origin, or religion, or insulting such groups by holding them in contempt or slandering them on account of their distinguishing particularities. The model law also calls for the prosecution and/or prohibition of organizations whose aims or activities fall within the above mentioned activities.[51] A recommendation, contained in the same resolution, to prepare a European convention on a uniform law against incitement to hatred has not as yet been implemented.

Some domestic provisions deserve special mention. In France, Act No. 72/546 of July 1, 1972, defines racial defamation and insult. It excludes the need of deliberate intention and grants standing to organizations and individuals. So does a Belgian law of 1981 on the suppression of certain acts prompted by racism or xenophobia. The Scandinavian countries of Denmark, Iceland, Norway, and Sweden have legislation against any person who, by mockery, slander, insult, threat, or other means, attacks a group of persons on the ground of their nationality, color, race, or religion. The Dutch Penal Code penalizes defamatory or other expressions offensive to a group. The Czech Penal Code punishes vituperation against any nation, its language, or race, or a group of inhabitants for its confession or lack of religious conviction. Hungary outlaws abusive language or incitement to hatred with regard to national minorities. Polish legislation deals with those who publicly insult, deride, or humiliate a group of the population, or offend religious feelings. The former USSR and Romania took measures to combat incitement to national or religious enmity and discord, and propaganda to that effect. Australia, Guinea, India, and several Latin American countries have similar legislation. The Philippines and Spain incorporated Article 4 of the Convention on Racial Discrimination into their internal criminal legislation. Austria, the Federal Republic of Germany, Greece, and Italy prohibit the existence of racist organizations.[52]

The classic case in the United States—where some states have incorporated group libel statutes in their criminal codes—was *Beauharnais v. Illinois*. There the United States Supreme Court decided, by five to four, in favor of the constitutionality of a state law prohibiting any publication "which portrays depravity, criminality, unchastity, or lack of virtue of a class of citizens, of any race, color, creed, or religion which . . . exposes the citizens . . . to contempt, derision, obloquy or which is productive of breach of the peace or riots. . . ." Protections of the First Amendment free-speech clause were invoked, but eight of the nine justices—the split was on marginal matters—considered that group libel laws are constitutional in the United States. The dangers involved were eloquently stated by Justice Douglas: "Hitler and his Nazis," he said, "showed how evil a conspiracy could be which was aimed at destroying a race by exposing it to contempt, derision, and obloquy." Justice Frankfurter pointed out that "the lewd and obscene, the profane," "libelous utterances," and "the insulting or 'fighting' words" are not within the area of constitutionally protected speech.[53] The question whether the *Beauharnais* doctrine is still valid remains open, and new proposed group libel legislation was resisted.

In the famous but not well understood *Skokie* case,[54] a Nazi group applied for authorization to demonstrate in a Chicago suburb heavily populated by Jews, many of them Holocaust survivors. The Village of Skokie tried to prevent the march, but the United States Supreme Court upheld the right of the Nazis—represented, to the chagrin of many, by the American Civil Liberties Union—to demonstrate. The case was not, however, a real test case on the merits of group libel. As Lasson points out, the Skokie citizens did not attack the demonstration on its merits but on context-related exceptions. "Had they properly framed the issue, that might have restrained the Nazis within constitutional bounds," Lasson concludes.[55]

In Israel the prevailing trend does not support a liberal approach to group libel. According to Article 4 of the Defamation Law of 1965, defamation of any group shall be treated in like manner as the defamation of a body corporate, "provided that it shall not be a ground for a civil action or private complaint."[56] The law on racism requires the written consent of the attorney general in order to initiate criminal proceedings. The legal establishment took a restrictive line in this respect. As stated by Justice Izhak Zamir, while he was still in office as attorney general, prosecution would only be undertaken "in extreme cases, which create a clear and immediate danger for public peace." Zamir admits the usefulness of private criminal actions in cases of libel but, of course, the problem of standing rights comes up.[57] Proposals to include in the anti-racism law provisions permitting voluntary organizations to initiate criminal proceedings were not successful and were attacked by civil libertarians.

Modern international law has incorporated the tragic lessons of World War II into several instruments. Bigotry outbursts that took place in several countries in the late 1950s prompted international organizations to adopt provisions intended to defend ethnic, religious, and similar groups against hatred and hostility. The 1966 International Covenant on Civil and Political Rights contains several measures related to the subject. Article 17 prohibits attacks on the honor and reputation of a person. Article 19 permits restrictions on freedom of expression to protect the right and reputation of others. Article 20 prohibits advocacy of national, racial or religious hatred that constitutes incitement to discrimination, hostility, or violence. Group libel may be seen as included in the prohibition of advocacy of hatred.

The International Convention on the Elimination of All Forms of Racial Discrimination deals not only with discrimination but also with propaganda and organizations based on ideas or theories of superiority of one race or group or who attempt to justify or promote racial hatred. The convention urges signatory states to declare punishable by law all dissemination of ideas based on racial superiority or hatred, and to outlaw organizations and propaganda that promote and incite to racial discrimination.

The 1978 UNESCO Declaration on Race and Racial Prejudice, aimed at protecting group identity, condemns doctrines of racial inequality and particularly urges the mass media and all organized groups within national communities—with due regard to the principle of freedom of expression as embodied in the Universal Declaration on Human Rights—to refrain "from presenting a stereotyped, partial, unilateral or tendentious picture of individuals and of various human groups."[58]

At the regional level, the American Convention on Human Rights contains provisions on everyone's right to have "his honor respected and his dignity recognized," on liability to ensure the "reputation of others," and on "advocacy of national, racial, or religious hatred that constitute incitement to lawless violence or any other similar illegal action against any person or group of persons on any grounds including those of race, colour, religion, language, or national origin," considering it an offense punishable by law.[59]

The European Convention on Human Rights of 1950 contains provisions restricting freedom of expression, assembly, and association when necessary in a democratic society in the interests, inter alia, of the prevention of disorder or crime and protection of the reputation or rights of others.[60]

The promotion of group hatred and hostility, the humiliation and defamation of groups, the discrimination or persecution that necessarily follows, are the roots of violence, disorder, and resentment that have disrupted coexistence and harmony in many places in the world. Society has not only the right but also the duty to permit ethnic, religious, linguistic, and cultural groups to defend themselves against abuses and insult.

Such defense should include access to legal remedies on behalf of the affected group as such, in addition to individual steps. Legislation against group libel should include the possibility of redress once the offense is committed, as well as the possibility of preventing its commission by means of prohibiting and disbanding organizations established for criminal purposes. That this is not inconsistent with basic liberties is sustained by the fact that international human rights law contains provisions to such an effect and that the domestic law of freedom-loving nations has incorporated similar norms.

## INTERNATIONAL CRIMINAL LAW

### THE GENOCIDE CONVENTION

Postwar international law had to give its answer to the lessons of the most costly conflict of history in terms of human lives. Those responsible for the construction of an international order aimed at the preservation of peace and prevention of horrendous crimes, such as those committed before and during World War II, were conscious of the need to avoid the recurrence of criminal policies directed against some specific religious or other groups.

For this reason, one of the first human rights treaties adopted in the U.N. period was the International Convention on the Prevention and Punishment of the Crime of Genocide (1948).[61] Approved by the General Assembly, by a vote of 55 to 0, on December 9, 1948—one day before the adoption of the Universal Declaration on Human Rights—it entered into force in 1951 and has been widely ratified.[62] As stated by the International Court of Justice, "the Convention was manifestly adopted for a purely humanitarian and civilizing purpose." Its origins show that it was the intention of the U.N. "to condemn and punish genocide as 'a crime under international law' involving a denial of the right of existence of entire human rights groups, a denial which shocks the conscience of mankind and results in great losses to humanity. . . . "[63]

Today, more than five decades after the convention entered into force, it seems apparent that its main significance lies in the assertion by the international community of the universal duty to protect the existence of ethnic and religious groups by declaring genocide to be an international crime, whether committed in time of peace or in time of war. The prohibition of genocide is seen today as part of *jus cogens*.[64] The convention does not contain measures of implementation. It has exercised little influence in preventing clear-cut genocidal situations in various parts of the world during the past few decades. The convention needs updating and, as we shall see, some steps to that effect have been taken. But on the whole it is one of the basic instruments for the protection of ethnic and religious groups, dealing, as it does, with the basic right of groups to maintain their existence.

The literature on genocide (since 1944, when Raphael Lemkin coined this new term for a very old crime[65]) has become very profuse.[66] Nehemiah Robinson and others have analyzed the convention in the light of the preparatory work and have discussed the special problems involved in its application. Two special rapporteurs appointed by the Subcommission on Prevention of Discrimination and Protection of Minorities, Nicodeme Ruhashyankiko and Ben Whitaker, have prepared detailed studies on the convention.[67] Interested nongovernmental organizations have submitted statements dealing with some of the problems related to the convention.[68] We shall therefore refer briefly to the main provisions of the convention that are especially relevant to our subject and try to identify the questions presently under discussion.

The convention consists of a preamble and nineteen articles. The preamble refers to General Assembly Resolution 96 (I) of December 11, 1946, which is seen as broader than the scope of the convention.[69] Article I confirms that genocide, whether committed in time of peace or in time of war, is a crime under international law that states parties undertake to prevent and to punish.[70]

Article II, which is of crucial importance for our purpose, should be interpreted restrictively. The article lists the acts to be defined as genocide, when "committed with intent to destroy, in whole or in part, a national, ethnical, racial or religious group, as such."

The five acts constituting genocide are:

(a) Killing members of the group;
(b) Causing serious bodily or mental harm to members of the group;
(c) Deliberately inflicting on the group conditions of life calculated to bring about its physical destruction in whole or in part;
(d) Imposing measures intended to prevent births within the group;
(e) Forcibly transferring children of the group to another group.

The influence of the tragic events of World War II and of the Nazi extermination policy against Jews, Gypsies, and others on the convention is indisputable.

What typifies the crime as genocide is the intent to destroy the group. Since a group consists of individuals, its destruction can only be achieved by steps taken against individuals. But the object of the crime of genocide is the group; not every group, but only national, ethnic, racial, or religious groups are protected. Proposals also to include "political" groups were finally disregarded in the Sixth Committee on the grounds that such groups were not permanent and their inclusion in the convention might prevent states from ratifying the convention.[71] Economic groups were also excluded.

The crime of genocide exists when there is an intent to destroy the group "as such." As shown by the history of the convention, the words "as such," introduced by a Venezuelan amendment, aimed at avoiding the possibility of the culprits claiming that the crime was not committed because of hatred toward the group itself but for other reasons, such as destruction during war, robbery, profiteering, or the like. Controversy on those words broke out during the discussion of the text as well as after the adoption of the convention. In some cases where governments were accused of genocidal acts, the absence of intent was invoked to deny the existence of genocide.[72]

The intention must not necessarily imply the destruction of the entire group. The words "in part" were introduced to eliminate any doubt:

> The intent to destroy a multitude of persons of the same group because of their belonging to this group, must be classified as genocide even if these persons constitute only part of a group either within a country or within a region or within a single community, provided the number is substantial; the Convention is intended to deal with action against large numbers, not individuals even if they happen to possess the same group characteristics. It will be up to the courts to decide in each case whether the number was sufficiently large.[73]

As mentioned, the list of acts involving genocide is restricted. But many problems arise in the interpretation of each one of those acts. The final text of the convention does not include any reference to "cultural genocide"—also called "ethnocide"—as originally proposed in early drafts. During the preparation of the convention the decision not to have a reference to cultural genocide—mentioned in General Assembly Resolution 96 (I)—was, and still is, controversial. Those favoring the exclusion of cultural genocide pointed out the lack of precision of that term and the obvious and great differences between massive extermination and the deprivation of cultural rights. It is claimed, however, that in the light of contemporary experience, the convention should be amended to include a reference to cultural genocide, so as to extend the scope of the definition of genocide beyond the concept of physical destruction of persons.[74]

In addition to genocide, Article III of the convention declares punishable other acts when related to genocide, such as conspiracy, incitement, attempt, and complicity. The final text did not incorporate, as proposed, the outlawing of public propaganda to provoke genocide or proposals providing for the disbanding of organizations whose aim is the commission of genocide. Recent developments, such as the attempts to deny the magnitude of the genocide during World War II or to defend those who committed it, raise the question if, in any revision of the convention, special attention should not be paid to these aspects of the problem.

Article IV deals with the punishment of persons committing genocide, whether they are "constitutionally responsible rulers, public officials or private individuals." The final text did not include proposals for making the plea of obedience to superior orders nonadmissible. Opinions have been voiced in favor of including such a provision in case the convention is revised. It is beyond the scope of these pages to deal with general questions of criminal responsibility, superior orders, state responsibility, and other related issues.

Under Article V, states parties undertake to enact legislation making effective the provisions of the convention, particularly through the imposition of effective penalties on persons guilty of genocide or other prohibited acts.[75] According to Article VI, such persons shall be tried by a competent tribunal of the state in the territory in which the act was committed, "or by such international penal tribunal as may have jurisdiction with respect to those contracting parties which shall have accepted its jurisdiction." Article VI caused much difficulty during the preparation of the convention and has been criticized as being inadequate. The matters of universal jurisdiction and the establishment of an international penal court are involved here.

Article VII provides that genocide and related crimes shall not be considered political crimes for the purpose of extradition. This article was also subjected to criticism. A provision based on the principle *aut dedere aut punire* ("to extradite or to punish") would be pertinent here. Such principle was included in the more recent Convention on Torture.[76] Article VIII—considered by some to be superfluous and of no practical value—permits states parties to call upon the competent organs of the U.N. to take action for "the prevention and suppression" of acts of genocide. Still, this is the only article relating to the prevention of genocide.

Article IX deals with the role of the International Court of Justice, establishing its compulsory jurisdiction in all disputes relating to the convention. It raised controversy, and several states submitted reservations to it. The following articles include the usual final clauses.

The convention does not contain provisions on reservations.[77] At the request of the General Assembly, the International Court of Justice gave an advisory opinion on reservations by states parties ratifying the convention. According to the court, a state that has made a reservation can be regarded as being a party to the convention if the reservation "is compatible with the object and purpose of the Convention." If a state party objects to a reservation it can in fact consider that the reserving state is not a party to the treaty.

Despite the shortcomings of the convention regarding implementation, its significance in the aftermath of World War II and the Nuremberg judgment can certainly not be overstated. Nor can its influence be overstated on the preparation of the Code of Offenses against the Peace and Security of Mankind and on the discussions concerning the establishment of an international criminal jurisdiction.[78] The Convention on the Non-Applicability of Statutory Limitations to War Crimes and Crimes against Humanity[79] specifically includes the crime of genocide, thereby stressing its role as a crucial step in outlawing attacks on the existence of national, ethnic, or religious groups either in wartime or in peacetime. Suggestions on the possibility of establishing an international criminal jurisdiction, or an international body entrusted with carrying out investigations and taking steps to prevent genocide, as well as on the preparation of an additional protocol to the convention on universal jurisdiction in cases of genocide have not been successful.[80]

Five decades after the adoption of the Convention on Genocide the subject, unfortunately, continues to require international consideration. Millions of persons have been exterminated since World War II, with indisputable genocidal intentions according to the definition of the convention. The right to the life of the group is an essential condition for the enjoyment of all other rights, and its preservation should be kept permanently on the international agenda.

## "ETHNIC CLEANSING"

The shocking term *ethnic cleansing* is used in connection with various and severe breaches of international and human rights law—breaches that have resulted in hundreds of thousands of victims and millions of refugees. The religious affiliation of the victims was in many cases the motivation behind the crimes.

*Ethnic cleansing* may refer to one or more of four specific crimes: (1) forms of genocide; (2) war crimes; (3) crimes against humanity; and (4) hate crimes. It refers also to the motivation that induces perpetrators to commit any of the offenses pertaining to those areas of international criminal law. In the case of genocide, the intent is the physical annihilation of a certain group as such. In the case of ethnic cleansing, the intent is to rid a given territory of populations that do not belong to a particular ethnic, religious, or linguistic group.

*Ethnic cleansing* has been used mainly to describe the recent tragic events in former Yugoslavia. A large body of documents, literature, and decisions, including those of the International Court of Justice, already exists dealing with the events in this context.[81] However, the term has also been applied in other instances. In Sukhumi, Georgia, former Soviet Union, Abkhazian insurgents have been accused of having carried out mass ethnic cleansing, and 200,000 Georgians are thought to have been uprooted.[82] The same terminology— *vycisteni*—was used with regard to the situation of the Gypsies in the Czech Republic.[83] The press has attributed ethnic and racist motivations to situations affecting Indian populations in some parts of Latin America, such as the massacre of the Yanomami tribe in the state of Roraima, Brazil, described by the federal attorney general as "genocide."[84] Hundreds of thousands were killed or fled from Rwanda-Burundi as a consequence of ethnic confrontations between the Tutsi and the Hutu. In response, on November 8, 1994, the Security Council created the International Criminal Tribunal for Rwanda by Resolution 955.

The issue is wider than purely ethnic in a strict sense, as was pointed out in a comment by Angelo Vidal d'Almeida Ribeiro, a former special rapporteur of the Commission on Human Rights on the implementation of the 1981 Declaration on the Elimination of All Forms of Intolerance and of Discrimination Based on Religion or Belief. In his seventh report (1993)—after stating that the conflict in the former Yugoslavia is not a religious one but opposes different national and ethnic groups—the special rapporteur referred to the serious damage suffered by religious and cultural monuments and sites of Muslims, Orthodox Christians, and Catholics alike. The special rapporteur wrote: "Such wanton destruction appears to be part of the policy of certain groups aimed at eradicating the religious and cultural base of ethnic communities living in a given area in order to encourage their departure and prevent their eventual return."[85] Ethnic and religious hatred may be intermingled in this case, as in many others, and it would be unjustified to disregard religious animosity or hatred as an important ingredient in the conflict usually described as ethnic.

The relationship between religious identity and the horrible notion of "cleansing" was also raised in the same area years ago. In 1942 a Chetnik military commander, attending a Chetnik assembly in Tebinje, stated that "the Serbian lands must be cleansed from Catholics and Muslims. They will be populated by Serbs only." The same phraseology goes back to a 1941 proclamation by General Draza Mihajlovic, the leader of the Royal Chetniks, who included among their war aims the "creation of a Great Yugoslavia with the Greater Serbia which ought to be ethnically pure" as well as "cleansing of the state territory of all national minorities and non-national elements."[86]

The expression *ethnic cleansing* entered U.N. terminology when the Commission on Human Rights, in its special session on the situation in former Yugoslavia (August 13-15, 1992), and the Subcommission on Prevention of Discrimination and Protection of Minorities, at its forty-fourth session, condemned "ethnic cleansing" policies.[87] The Security Council issued a similar condemnation in Resolution 771 (1992).[88] The General Assembly did so on several occasions, such as in Resolution 46/242 of August 25, 1992; Resolution 47/80 of December 16, 1992; and Resolution 47/121 of December 18, 1992.[89] The words *ethnic cleansing* appear in many later official documents, sometimes with explanatory remarks and sometimes without any details.

Following Security Council Resolution 780, adopted on October 6, 1992, a commission of experts to deal with the issue of "ethnic cleansing" was established.[90] The aims of the commission were to investigate ethnic cleansing, to study all available reports on ethnic cleansing, and to determine the most effective way to approach the problem.[91] The commission elaborated a definition of the expression *ethnic cleansing*—which it described as relatively new—strictly in the context of the conflicts in the former Yugoslavia. According to that definition, *ethnic cleansing* means "rendering an area ethnically homoge-neous by using force or intimidation to remove persons or given groups from the area" (paragraph 55 of the interim report).

Based on the many reports describing the policy and practices conducted in the former Yugoslavia, the commission, notwithstanding its own definition, enumerated a series of acts falling under the heading of "ethnic cleansing." These are, per paragraph 56, murder; torture; arbitrary arrest and detention; extrajudicial executions, rape, and sexual assault; confinement of civilian popu-lation in ghetto areas; forcible removal, displacement, and deportation of ci-vilian population; deliberate military attacks or threats of attacks on civilians and civilian areas; and wanton destruction of property.

The commission stressed in its interim report that the above-mentioned practices constitute crimes against humanity and can be assimilated to specific war crimes, and in some cases they could also "fall within the meaning of the Genocide Convention." Despite the reference to "relevant human rights," the commission of experts spoke of ethnic cleansing practices as crimes against humanity and as war crimes. It also considered them exclusively in the context of the conflicts in the former Yugoslavia.

Thus, the explanation by the commission of the meaning of *ethnic cleans-ing* seems to be at the same time too broad and too limited. It includes several major offenses already defined as such by international law and sanctioned by the respective international instruments. From this angle, ethnic cleansing would be the purpose, the motivation behind such crimes. On the other hand, by limiting the term to the conflict in former Yugoslavia, the commission avoided a more theoretical and universal approach. In addition, by allowing alterna-tive interpretations the commission may have opened the way to view ethnic cleansing as an aggravating circumstance justifying a more severe treatment of the offense.

The list of acts considered by the commission of experts as leading to ethnic cleansing could be enlarged. Professor Meron, for instance, explicitly men-tions acts of harassment, discrimination, beatings, intimidation, siege, and cutting off supplies, which are not listed by the commission.[92] Were such a broad view taken, almost every act of coercion or violence that violates hu-manitarian law would involve ethnic cleansing, if committed with specific in-tent. Some authors, however, take a restrictive view. McCoubrey describes the "outrage of ethnic cleansing" as meaning "forced displacement of non-Serb people from Bosnian-Serb occupied territory." However, he also states that it may be equated with genocide.[93]

Eli Lauterpacht—who was a judge ad hoc in the case concerning applica-tion of the Convention on the Prevention and Punishment of the Crime of Genocide (Requests for Provisional Measures) that came up twice before the International Court of Justice, both times in connection with the situation in Yugoslavia—referred to "the forced migration of civilians, more commonly known as 'ethnic cleansing,'" committed as "part of a deliberate campaign by the Serbs to eliminate Muslim control of, and presence in, substantial parts of

Bosnia Herzegovina."[94] Lauterpacht also considered the Serbian acts as acts of genocide that fall within several of the categories under Article 2 of the Convention on Genocide, being "clearly directed against an ethnical or religious group as such," and being "intended to destroy that group, if not in whole, certainly in part."[95]

The General Assembly in Resolution 47/121 states that ethnic cleansing is "a form of genocide" but also takes note of the statement of the special rapporteur of the Commission on Human Rights that "ethnic cleansing did not appear to be the consequence of the war, but rather its goal."[96] The special rapporteur himself, Polish statesman Tadeusz Mazowiecki, appointed in February 1993, traces "the first wave of ethnic cleansing in Eastern Bosnia and Herzegovina" by the Serb forces to April/May 1992. Yet the special rapporteur does not attempt to define the term. However, in his second periodic report he describes it as "the forced displacement and detention of civilians, arbitrary executions, attacks on towns as well as the destruction of villages and religious sites, as part of a deliberate and systematic policy. . . ."[97]

An international tribunal was established under Security Council Resolution 808 of February 22, 1993, "for the prosecution of persons responsible for serious violations of international humanitarian law committed in the territory of the former Yugoslavia since 1991." Among them, "mass killings and the continuance of the practice of 'ethnic cleansing'" are explicitly mentioned.[98]

The tribunal was established by the Security Council by means of a Chapter VII decision in light of the existence of a threat to peace, for reasons of expedience, and in order to create an effective and binding obligation to take whatever action is required. The tribunal has to apply existing international humanitarian law in accordance with the principle *nullum crime sine lege* (no crime without a law). Such law does not refer explicitly to ethnic cleansing, although most of the violations to be dealt with obviously are covered by it. In his report, the U.N. secretary-general specifically refers to ethnic cleansing as a form of crime against humanity.[99] So does Security Council Resolution 827 (1993), establishing the tribunal, referring to the "continuance of the practice of 'ethnic cleansing,' including for the acquisition and the holding of territory."[100]

The tribunal, the statute of which was adopted by the Security Council on May 29, 1993, is an ad hoc tribunal established to prosecute crimes in the former Yugoslavia. It is not a permanent institution, and as such it has no power to adjudicate crimes committed outside the indicated context. It is the first international criminal court established since the Nuremberg and Tokyo trials. While the normal process for the creation of such a tribunal should have been an international treaty, it became clear that this would be impossible under the circumstances. The Security Council acted thus, moved by considerations of urgency and expediency, as in the case of Rwanda in November 1994.

The tribunal started its work on November 17, 1993, after overcoming great practical difficulties. This is not the place to deal with the prospects of the tribunal becoming an effective instrument of international criminal law. It seems to be a step forward, until a permanent international criminal court of a universal character is established. The creation of such a permanent international criminal court was the purpose of the international conference that met in Rome in the summer of 1998 and prepared a treaty to that effect, adopted by a vote of 120 in favor, 7 against, and 21 abstentions. The crime of genocide, "persecution against any identifiable group or collectivity" on religious and other grounds and "by reason of the identity of the group or collectivity," as crimes against humanity, and "attacks against buildings dedicated to religion," as war crimes, are listed among the crimes within the jurisdiction of the court.

## THE MEANING OF "ETHNIC CLEANSING"

In the case of genocide the act must be directed toward the destruction of a group *as such*. A similar approach may be applied to the issue of ethnic cleansing. The acts considered illegal must be directed toward the elimination from a given territory of people who do not belong to a particular ethnic or religious or linguistic group. Such acts are in any case violations of international law; they shall be described as "ethnic cleansing" when, irrespective of result, they lead toward such a "cleansing," or deportation, or forced homogeneity of the population of a given area. "Ethnic cleansing" would not be considered a new or a different crime. It would be the intention, the motivation, or the objective to induce the commitment of some offenses. It could also be seen as an aggravating circumstance, justifying harsher penalties in some cases as provided in some legislation with regard to so-called hate crimes.

In Resolution 47/80 of December 16, 1992,[101] the U.N. General Assembly relates the notion of "ethnic cleansing" to that of racial hatred—both offenses "totally incompatible with universally recognized human rights and fundamental freedoms." Both humanitarian law and human rights law are relevant to this "abhorrent practice," which violates the prohibitions of both protective systems. It seems reasonable to interpret the words "racial hatred" broadly, as meaning group hatred in general. The resolution refers to "grounds of race, color, religion or ethnic origin" and notes the importance of respecting the rights of persons belonging to national, ethnic, religious, and linguistic minorities. The victim or target of hatred may belong to a group identified by race, color, religion, or other natural unifying factor. What is significant is that the victim is hated because of his or her membership in a specific group, whatever its nature, and therefore the group becomes the target of the offense. What is important is that the individuals or the group regard themselves, and are regarded by others, as having a particular historical identity in terms of ethnicity, religion, or culture.

The title of General Assembly Resolution 47/80 is helpful, since it stresses the relationship between the result desired by the offenders—"ethnic cleansing"—and the criminal motive of "racist hatred" in a broad sense that has led to the commission of the criminal act. "Ethnic cleansing" is, thus, an area of convergence of violations of both humanitarian law and human rights law in the area of discrimination and incitement to group hatred.

In Resolution 47/80 the General Assembly recalls and reaffirms previous instruments on racism and discrimination on grounds of race, color, religion, or ethnic origin, and points out their negative impact on peace and security. The resolution explicitly reiterates former Resolution 46/242, of August 25, 1992, which also regards "ethnic cleansing" as a grave violation of international humanitarian law and declares "ethnic cleansing" and racial hatred as practices "totally incompatible" with human rights, the perpetrators of which are individually responsible and should be brought to justice.

The Security Council took a different approach on the several occasions in which it dealt with the issue. In Resolution 808 (1993), confirming previous Resolution 713 (1991), and subsequent relevant resolutions, particularly Resolutions 764, 771, and 780, all in 1992,[102] the Security Council does not refer to racial hatred or discrimination. The council expresses its grave alarm at the widespread violations of international humanitarian law, mass killings, and the practice of "ethnic cleansing." Again, in Resolution 836 of June 14, 1993, the council declares "unlawful and totally unacceptable . . . any taking of territory by force or any practice of 'ethnic cleansing.'"

The differences between the resolutions of the General Assembly and the Security Council can, of course, be explained by their respective tasks, but the lack of clarity in the definition of the condemned practice may also have played a role. While the Security Council emphasizes the security aspect and the violations of war and humanitarian law, the General Assembly, in Resolution 47/80, pays attention to the combination of that practice and the notion of group hatred, stressing the discriminatory intention. The fact that General Assembly Resolution 47/80 originated in the Third Committee in relation to the racial issue is naturally relevant in this respect, since other General Assembly resolutions do not relate "ethnic cleansing" to racial hatred in particular. The differences in the wording used by both principal U.N. bodies do not involve contradictions, given their respective functions. They are not helpful, however, in achieving a generally accepted definition of the offense in question.

The U.N. World Conference on Human Rights that took place in Vienna in 1993 dealt with the issue of "ethnic cleansing" in its Final Outcome.[103] It did not define the meaning of the words but expressed its "dismay" at massive violations of human rights, especially in the form of "genocide, 'ethnic cleansing' and systematic rape of women in war situations creating mass exodus of refugees and displaced persons." Strongly condemning such abhorrent practices, the conference reiterated "the call that perpetrators of such crimes be punished and such practices immediately stopped." Part II of the document, under the heading "Equality, Dignity, and Tolerance," Chapter A, "Racism, Racial Discrimination, Xenophobia, and Other Forms of Intolerance," outlines the relationship with general human rights.

The two principal human rights implementation bodies, the Human Rights Committee and the Committee on the Elimination of Racial Discrimination, dealt with "ethnic cleansing." The Human Rights Committee, at its forty-eighth session, in July 1993, acting under Article 40, paragraph 1(b) of the 1966 International Covenant on Civil and Political Rights, found that the new states within the boundaries of the former Yugoslavia took upon themselves the obligations of the former Yugoslavia under the covenant and requested the governments of Bosnia and Herzegovina, Croatia, and Serbia and Montenegro (Federal Republic of Yugoslavia) to submit reports on the events in former Yugoslavia. The committee discussed those reports, focusing on the issue of "ethnic cleansing" as part of the war objectives. Bosnia claimed that the Serbian policy "was based on the principle that persons of different religions and ethnic origins could not live side by side, and the concept of ethnic cleansing was a corollary of that concept."[104] The Human Rights Committee requested the governments involved to take measures to prevent and combat the policy of "ethnic cleansing" and to combat advocacy of national, racial, or religious hatred constituting incitement to discrimination, hostility, and violence, in relation to Article 20 of the covenant.[105]

The Committee on the Elimination of Racial Discrimination, for its part, related the issue of "ethnic cleansing" to the need to incorporate into the Penal Codes Article 4 of the Convention on Racial Discrimination, which prohibits incitement. It mentioned separately the "massive, gross and systematic human rights violations occurring in the territory of Bosnia Herzegovina," and the practices of "ethnic cleansing," "including forced population transfers, torture, rape, summary executions, the blockading of international humanitarian aid and the commission of atrocities for the purpose of instilling terror among the civilian population."[106]

General Assembly Resolution 47/80, already analyzed, links the issue of "ethnic cleansing," a "grave and serious violation of international humanitarian law," with the issues of hatred and discrimination. Both are seen as "totally incompatible with universally recognized human rights and freedoms," and states are called upon "to cooperate in eliminating all forms of 'ethnic cleansing' and racial hatred."

Hatred is, of course, a sentiment or state of mind that may or may not express itself in violence or other illegal acts. When it does, it should be assimilated to intent or motive. The result of such intent and acts is considered under some legislations as a specific offense, called "hate crimes." For instance, several laws authorize a judge to increase the penalties if the perpetrator "intentionally selects" the victim or targeted property because of some qualities of the person, or owner or occupant of the property, such as race, color, religion, national origin, or ancestry.

This issue originated controversy at the public and judicial levels, and in the United States it was argued that such attitudes violate the First Amendment by punishing offensive thought. In June 1993 the United States Supreme Court, in the *Wisconsin v. Mitchell* case, unanimously ruled that states may impose harsher sentences on criminals who choose their victims on the basis of race, religion, or other similar characteristics.[107] The Court decided that, under the indicated state statutes, motive plays the same role as in anti-discrimination laws. In the words of Chief Justice Rehnquist, while "a defendant's abstract beliefs, however obnoxious to most people, may not be taken into consideration by a sentencing judge, . . . the belief is no longer abstract once it provides the motive" for the illegal act. The defendant's motive for committing the offense is an important factor, which may constitute an aggravating circumstance. The Wisconsin statute in question singles out for enhancement bias-inspired conduct because this conduct is thought to inflict greater individual and societal harm: "[B]ias motivated crimes are more likely to provoke retaliatory crimes, inflict distinct emotional harm on their victims, and incite community unrest." Racial hatred is an aggravating factor when murder is committed and the judge must take into account racial animus, said the Court.[108]

There are, of course, enormous differences between organized brutal crimes in a situation of armed conflict, on the one hand, and isolated hate crimes in a stable society, on the other. However, between motives leading people to commit grave massive crimes and motives that induce them, as in the above-mentioned case for instance, to beat a person of a different color, or race, or religion, the difference is mainly a quantitative one. Rape is always a crime. If committed with the intent of "ethnically cleansing" an area, the penalty should be enhanced. This connects the issue of "ethnic cleansing" to that of hate crimes. Racial or religious hatred or bias is behind "ethnic cleansing," as it may be behind genocide.

The Security Council placed emphasis on the dangers involved in acts described as "ethnic cleansing" in situations of armed conflict. The General Assembly related "ethnic cleansing" to racial hatred and discrimination, and therefore followed a more general approach. The description of "ethnic cleansing" used by the commission of experts appointed by the United Nations is more in line, although not completely, with the limited interpretation, and aims at establishing a well-defined, restrictively described offense.

As to the target or victim, it seems that the word *ethnic* should be interpreted liberally, as meaning a distinct group of a given ethnic, racial, religious, or cultural character. This interpretation appears to be in line with the approaches of the General Assembly and Human Rights Committee and was also adopted by the special rapporteur on the implementation of the 1981 Declaration on the Elimination of All Forms of Intolerance and of Discrimination Based on Religion or Belief. It is also sustained by some manifestations of the interested parties. In all cases, undoubtedly, racial or religious hatred is involved, and thus hate crimes are being committed whatever the results deriving from the indicated motive.

# 4.

# PROSELYTISM AND CHANGE
# OF RELIGION

◆

Issues related to change of religion—conversion, apostasy, proselytism, evangelization, and missionary activities—have caused considerable controversy during the preparation of human rights instruments concerning religious rights. In fact, during the drafting of the Universal Declaration on Human Rights in 1948 representatives of some states argued against any reference to an individual's right to change religion. The controversy resurfaced in 1966 during the preparation of both the International Covenant on Civil and Political Rights (ICCPR) and the International Covenant on Economic, Social, and Cultural Rights (ICESCR). In 1981, when the penultimate draft of the Declaration on the Elimination of All Forms of Intolerance and Discrimination Based on Religion or Belief was presented to the General Assembly of the United Nations, opposition to such a reference could have prevented the unanimous acceptance of the declaration had a compromise not been accepted. However, the issues related to change of religion have not been resolved, and they are likely to continue to cause great difficulties if a draft convention on religious rights is considered.

The situation is not surprising. Some religions do not accept the right to abandon and adopt another religion or the right to remain without a religion. In some cases apostasy or heresy are considered crimes and are severely punished. Additionally, some states demand that individuals follow formal steps in order to change their membership in a recognized religious community or congregation and even criminalize attempts to induce other persons to change their religion or join a different religious group.

Moreover, these issues are part of the larger controversy between the universal character of modern human rights and cultural relativism. Advocates for cultural relativism argue that human rights law is strictly a Western institution and, therefore, not applicable to other cultures or societies. Accordingly, they contend that particular cultures or religions have to be protected against external intrusions likely to disadvantage indigenous cultural or religious identity.

80

This approach, however, clashes with the view expressed by most scholars, which stresses the universal validity of human rights.

The controversy over proselytism, conversion, teaching or dissemination of religious views, missionary activities, and related situations has recently come to the fore as a consequence of changes in international life. In Central Europe, Eastern Europe, and Africa conflicts have arisen between indigenous churches and foreign religions promoting missionary programs. In certain cases governments have been involved in such confrontations. For example, in Latin America the visit of Pope John Paul II in early 1996 highlighted the Catholic resentment toward evangelical prosperity.[1] Additionally, in several countries, such as Russia, conflicts among churches have given rise to legal action, including penal measures. International judiciaries have intervened in a few instances, while in some countries the full power of the state has been mobilized to prevent foreign churches from attempting to attract converts from the local population.

In 1993 the Human Rights Committee issued an important General Comment specifically on the question of conversion and proselytism. The committee observed that the freedom to have or to adopt a religion or belief necessarily entails the freedom to choose a religion or belief, including, inter alia, the right to replace one's current religion or belief with another or to adopt atheistic views, as well as the right to retain one's religion or belief.[2]

The Human Rights Committee also pointed out that Article 18(2) of the ICCPR bars coercion that would impair the right to have, or to adopt, a religion or belief. Impermissible impairment includes the use (or threat) of physical force or penal sanctions to compel believers or nonbelievers (1) to adhere to their current religious beliefs and congregations; (2) to recant their religion or belief; or (3) to convert. The committee identified some particular policies and practices, such as those that restrict access to education, medical care, employment, or the rights to vote or participate in the conduct of public affairs guaranteed in the ICCPR as examples of illegitimate practices. We shall come back to this General Comment.

In October 1995 the Human Rights Committee, dealing with the third periodic report submitted by Morocco, expressed concern at the obstacles to the right to change one's religion. In its report on Libya the committee pointed out restrictions on an individual's right to change religion.[3] When the Committee on the Elimination of Racial Discrimination (CERD) discussed the periodic report submitted by Cyprus, questions were asked regarding the genuine equality enjoyed by minority religions such as the Muslim community.[4] United Nations special rapporteurs also addressed the issue when considering individual state reports.

In 1996 a seminar organized by the Office for Democratic Institutions and Human Rights of the Organization for Security and Cooperation in Europe (OSCE) on constitutional, legal, and administrative aspects of the freedom of religion devoted considerable attention to the issue of change of religion or belief.[5] As alluded to above, the international community cannot avoid formulating a coherent position on this subject, even if opponents argue that this has been settled during the evolution of international human rights and relations.

## PROSELYTISM *VS.* RELIGIOUS IDENTITY AND PRIVACY

No single human right can be considered in isolation; all human rights are interconnected. There may be tensions among various human rights. For instance, the right to proselytize, with respect to freedom of expression, might interfere with other rights equally deserving of protection. The rights proclaimed in Article 18 of the Universal Declaration of Human Rights,[6] Article 18 of the ICCPR,[7] and Articles 1 and 6 of the 1981 Declaration on the Elimination of All Forms of Intolerance and Discrimination Based on Religion or Belief[8] may be affected by coercion or through religious persons being subjected to preaching that harms their beliefs. The provisions of Article 19(1) of the ICCPR, concerning the right to hold opinions without interference, are certainly applicable to religious opinions. Religious persons may not wish to be exposed to any type of indoctrination in any form, whether oral or written. In some instances states in which one religion prevails may grant the members of that religion certain privileges and advantages—including limitations on the proselytizing rights of other religions.[9]

In addition to infringing on the right to hold opinions without interference, proselytism and indoctrination also implicate the right to privacy as proclaimed in Article 12 of the Universal Declaration and Article 17 of the ICCPR. The need to reconcile these conflicting rights to disseminate religious teaching, on the one hand, and to protect a religious group's privacy, intimacy, isolation, or strong desire to defend its religious identity against any intrusion, on the other, constitutes an important consideration when attempting to establish the scope and limits of the right to proselytism.

Fernando Volio has stated that the zone of privacy is a zone of freedom, a zone of isolation, a legal cloister for those qualities, wishes, projects, and lifestyles that each individual man, woman, or child wishes to enjoy or experience. Privacy includes not only the security of those areas protected by Article 17 of the covenant—home, correspondence, family, honor, reputation—but also rights listed in other articles, including, "for example, the freedom of thought, conscience, and religion" and "the right to determine the moral and religious education of one's children."[10]

Sometimes proselytism, protected under Article 19 of the ICCPR as the freedom to impart information and ideas of all kinds, regardless of frontiers, is limited by the rights of others. This is because dissemination of information and ideas may be offensive to the religious feelings of others. For example, the European Commission on Human Rights (ECHR) denied the appeal of a United Kingdom conviction of a poet who depicted Jesus Christ as a homosexual. The commission held that the artist's freedom of expression could be restricted under Article 10(2) of the European Convention to avoid offending the religious sensitivities of others.[11] Also in Britain, an attempt to prosecute Salman Rushdie failed in 1989 when a magistrate declared that legislation on blasphemy protected only Christianity, not Islam. Therefore, the ECHR denied an appeal submitted against the decision.[12] Kevin Boyle criticizes "the continued existence of an offense protecting only the majority Christian faith in Britain . . . and its acceptance by the institutions under the ECHR as compatible with European human rights standards."[13]

In the view of some authors the mere fact that proselytism may annoy the targets of such activity is not a sufficient justification for restricting uninvited speech. They contend that people should be free to disseminate their views on the true religion and should "not be silenced merely because some people would prefer not to hear their views." Among other things, persons should be free to deliver literature door to door.[14] However, in places where people are present by force of law—"where the listeners are a captive audience" (schools, hospitals, prisons, military installations)—the rule may be different. In classrooms, for example, where students are not permitted to leave, teachers and school officials should exert reasonable control. They should essentially try to protect both those who wish to communicate religious views and those who do not want "to be compelled to listen to a sermon."[15]

The problem is similar in the other situations including captive audiences, where exposing the captive audience to proselytizing speech or literature becomes a form of coercion. European jurisprudence has confronted instances involving religious instruction in schools against the wishes of parents who oppose such indoctrination.[16] These captive audience cases, however, do not always involve interfaith proselytism. In fact, sometimes religious instruction may be coercive even when the exposed group is part of the same religion.[17]

Thus, the problem of proselytism is a clash between rights. Which right should prevail in concrete situations cannot be decided in the abstract. A just solution may require striking an elusive balance. The clash between proselytism as equivalent to freedom of expression and the right to defend a group's religious identity (coupled with the right to privacy) is an example of the delicacy of the matters involved. A free society must find ways of accommodating equally valid human rights.

Arcot Krishnaswami, in his *Study of Discrimination in the Matter of Religious Rights and Practices*, accepted the legitimacy of restrictive measures in extreme cases. As such, his Rule 1 prohibits coercion and improper inducements. Principle 3, as elaborated by the Subcommission on Prevention of Discrimination and Protection of Minorities, refers to material or moral coercion.[18] As we shall see, reports of the special rapporteurs (appointed by the Commission on Human Rights and the subcommission) mention penal measures against missionary activity that have been adopted by several states. Some countries levy penalties only against material enticement, namely, giving or promising material benefits as an inducement to change one's religion.[19] In some cases it is difficult to draw the dividing line between legitimate proselytism and improper inducement. Thus, varying degrees of restrictive measures exist that are endorsed by different countries.

## CHANGE OF RELIGION AND PROSELYTISM

In order to understand how international human rights law relates to issues of conversion, apostasy, proselytism, evangelization, and missionary activities, it is necessary to clarify the contexts in which those concepts are used. Essentially, they all turn on three major questions. First, is there a basic human right, of a universal and customary legal character, to change one's religion or belief? Second, is there a right to act so as to convince or induce other persons to change their religion or beliefs? Finally, if so, what are the limits, if any, of such a right?

Compounding the difficulty of answering these questions is the fact that the terms used in these questions have a variety of meanings; which meaning attaches generally depends on the angle of observation. Specifically, what constitutes the sacred duty of evangelization for one group may be viewed by another group as improper proselytizing.[20] Some groups consider a particular act to be a normal exercise of freedom of expression and freedom of teaching or propagating a religion or belief. At the same time, others may view the exact same act as an illegitimate intrusion into their privacy or group identity and a violation of their freedom of conscience. The common denominator, however, is religion, or, more precisely, religion or belief. Therefore, it is necessary to clarify the meaning of the three basic freedoms regarding religion or belief as proclaimed by modern positive human rights law—the freedoms of thought, conscience, and religion.

Proselytism and related issues mainly concern freedom of religion in a strict sense. This freedom clearly includes freedom of *belief*, as something different from a narrow understanding of religion, and freedom *from* religion, understood as the right not to be coerced into accepting religious norms or behavior. The right to proselytize, and related freedoms, including the freedoms of expression, association, and teaching, must be interpreted in light of attempts to define religion. Unfortunately, consensus on the definition of religion does not exist.

The terminology related to change of religion is complicated. Change of religion may be the result of two different states of mind and sets of actions. First, a person may, prompted by reason or emotion, reach the conclusion that his or her religion or belief is wrong, unsatisfactory, or insufficient. The person may then decide to opt out of the religion, adopt another religion or belief, or remain without any religion. This may lead the person to change his or her public or private behavior as well. Second, a change in a person's convictions may translate into, or require, changes in that person's affiliation or membership in a group. This derives from the fact that religious persons are usually not isolated individuals but rather members of a religious group, community, congregation, or church. Such changes in group affiliation or membership are not always purely private and may require special formal measures in some countries and legal systems.

Such changes of religion will not always be spontaneous or merely the consequence of intellectual or emotional causes or inducement. Sometimes external factors will be of great weight, if not decisive. Such factors may be the outcome of the activities of other persons, churches, or institutions. Representatives of such groups usually try to explain their own religious views and influence people through preaching, teaching, propagating, and advocating their religious convictions. Methods of inducement can be dangerous to the mental health of the prospective proselytes, particularly if sects combine religious ideas with disturbing forms of collective or individual behavior. To avoid such results, some states have imposed restrictive legislation on proselytism, often at the initiative of certain dominant religions.

To understand the differences between illegitimate proselytism and legitimate conversion based on individual convictions and without external interference, further terminological clarifications seem necessary. It has been pointed out that "[o]ne group's evangelization is another group's proselytism."[21] A distinction between convert and proselyte is specifically made by some religions. The Spanish word *conversos*, for instance, was used in Christian Spain and Portugal for Moorish or Jewish converts to Christianity, and sometimes for their descendants. Unlike the terms *Marranos, alboraycos*, or *tornadizos*, the term *conversos* had no derogatory implications.[22] The word *proselytism* later acquired a pejorative, and sometimes threatening, meaning. Proselytism has been described as a kind of evangelistic malpractice involving improper activities.[23] Activities are often considered illegal when they include intimidation, coercion, bribery, economic enticement, and similar practices.

As to the present meaning of the aforementioned terms, it seems useful to distinguish between definitions based on religious, legal, and more general sources. General dictionaries reflect these distinctions. *Webster's New Dictionary of Synonyms* states that *convert* and *proselyte* are synonyms.[24] It has also been stated that

> both denote a person who has embraced another creed, opinion, or doctrine than the one he has previously accepted or adhered to. Convert commonly implies a sincere and voluntary change of belief. . . . Proselyte basically denotes a convert to another religion. . . . In general use . . . the term may suggest less a reverent or convicted and voluntary embracing than a yielding to the persuasions and urgings of another, be it an earnest missionary or zealot or someone with less praiseworthy motives.[25]

The term *apostasy* means "abandonment or renunciation of a religious faith."[26] The term *apostasy* is usually applied by members of the deserted faith to the change of one faith for another. An apostate, from the viewpoint of the religion, church, or group that is being abandoned, becomes a proselyte from the perspective of the corresponding religion, church, or group that is being joined. How apostasy and apostate are defined depends on the position of the respective churches or religions as well as on the ways or methods leading to conversion.

The term *evangelization* is identified with Christian efforts to induce non-Christians to join the Christian religion, to accept its gospel *(evangel)*. Sometimes the term is attached to the attempts of some Christian churches to obtain the adhesion of Christians belonging to other Christian churches, inducing them to change their affiliation and embrace the evangelizing group.

The term *mission* refers to "persons commissioned by a . . . religious organization for the purpose of propagating its faith."[27] Missionaries are those sent to do this. In the view of groups exposed to missionary activities and opposed to them, the term *mission* has also acquired a derogatory and even threatening meaning. I have mentioned Catholic resentment regarding evangelical prosperity in Latin America in recent years. Resentment may be too mild a description for the reaction of some religions who see their identity endangered.

Thus, the terminology concerning changes of religion is imprecise at best and is frequently accompanied by a heavy burden of suspicion or prejudice, some of which may well be justified. Even so, the drafters of various human rights instruments desired success in incorporating the aforementioned right into the universal framework for the protection of human rights. Accordingly, they put aside preferences regarding definitions and adopted a more practical approach. On this sensitive topic, though, even this was not enough to avoid confrontations. This becomes particularly apparent in the discussion of those instruments and the history of the *travaux préparatoires* below.

## PROSELYTISM AND CONVERSION IN THE UNITED NATIONS ERA

Article 18 of the Universal Declaration of Human Rights and Article 18 of the 1966 Covenant on Civil and Political Rights are the most important human rights provisions concerning religion. Their relevance to the issues of change of religion, conversion, and proselytism is crucial. These articles refer to three freedoms: thought, conscience, and religion. Freedom of thought is beyond regulation. As Leo Pfeffer properly observed, there is no need for a constitutional guarantee to ensure that freedom "for, as the common-law adage has it, the devil himself knows not the thoughts of man."[28] In general, neither states nor individuals can interfere with thoughts or beliefs, whether religious or antireligious, which are not translated into actions, behavior, or conduct.[29] These thoughts and beliefs belong to the most internal sphere of human life, and there is no way to coerce a human being to continue or abandon specific religious beliefs. Illegal and exceptional methods of acting on the human mind are beyond the scope of this discussion.

Relevant to our subject are the freedoms of conscience and religion as proclaimed in both Articles 18 and related human rights provisions. It was the incorporation of references to the right to change religion that engendered debates and clashes in United Nations bodies. This development is not surprising in light of the approach of classic international law to the issue of change of religion, either imposed or voluntary. I have addressed the historical developments regarding this matter in chapter 1. A short summary may be helpful here to understand recent difficulties.

The rule *cuius regio, eius religio* of the Religious Peace of Augsburg (1555) and its coercive implications was modified by bilateral treaties in the early stages of modern international law, most notably in the Peace of Westphalia (1648). Post-seventeenth-century treaties often incorporated protective clauses for religion on the grounds of reciprocity. Several countries enacted democratic and liberal constitutions containing rules on freedom of religion and belief, and prohibiting forced conversions.

Between the two world wars, an interesting development arose regarding religious rights—the minority treaties. The minority treaties were a scheme for the protection of national, ethnic, cultural, or religious minorities. They also contained numerous provisions concerning religious rights. This system collapsed, along with the League of Nations, at the same time that peace and democracy in Europe collapsed. One cannot assess how these treaties would have evolved had World War II not ended the system.[30] However, the entire system was discredited when the San Francisco Conference met and attempted to build a new international order based on the United Nations. The emphasis was now almost exclusively on *individual* rights and freedoms; group rights were suspect. Religious human rights were considered adequately protected by the general rules regarding the rights of the individual, coupled with the principle of nondiscrimination. Whenever someone's rights were jeopardized or violated because of a group characteristic—race, religion, color, ethnic or national origin, culture, or language—the necessary remedy would result from protecting the rights of the person, on a purely individual basis, mainly by the rule of nondiscrimination.[31]

## THE UNIVERSAL DECLARATION OF HUMAN RIGHTS

The United Nations Charter (1945) and the Universal Declaration of Human Rights (1948) were drafted with this backdrop in mind. The United Nations Charter contains very few references to religious rights and none on change of religion.[32] Article 2 of the 1948 Universal Declaration of Human Rights,[33] however, forbids distinctions of any kind, including religion, in the enjoyment of the rights and freedoms set forth in the Declaration. Article 18, of decisive importance, provides that

[e]veryone has the right to freedom of thought, conscience and religion; this right *includes freedom to change his religion or belief*, and freedom,

either alone or in community with others and in public or private, to manifest his religion or belief in teaching, practice, worship and observance.

Article 26 includes a reference to religious groups. It contains a provision related to the subject at hand: education shall promote understanding, tolerance, and friendship among all religious groups. Article 29, on limitations in the exercise of the proclaimed rights, is also relevant. It states that limitations on individual rights and freedoms are only those determined by law solely for the purpose of securing due recognition and respect for the rights and freedoms of others and of meeting the just requirements of morality, public order, and the general welfare in a democratic society.

The very difficult problem in the drafting of the Universal Declaration— again controversial when the 1966 Covenants and the 1981 Declaration were drafted—was the freedom to change one's religion or belief, a freedom denied by some religions and states. The clause was originally opposed but was finally adopted by a vote of 27 to 5, with 12 abstentions. The authors of the 1948 Universal Declaration were aware of the many questions involving apostasy, missionary activities, coercion and enticement, proselytism and its limits, the status of new or young religious movements struggling for recognition, and the social dangers that accrue from sects using manipulative tactics.

As early as 1948, when the Commission on Human Rights discussed the drafting committee's text, the issue of conversion arose. Saudi Arabia, supported by several Muslim states, submitted an amendment to delete the words "freedom to change his religion or belief." The Saudi spokesman claimed that the amendment's goal was to prevent missionaries from abusing the right based on political motivations. While Egypt's representative initially voiced reservations about the text, he ultimately voted in its favor. "By proclaiming man's freedom to change his religion or belief," he stated, "the Declaration would be encouraging, even though it might not be intentional, the machinations of certain missions, well known in the Orient."[34]

The Third Committee of the General Assembly rejected all amendments. Article 18 as a whole was adopted by 38 votes to 3, with 3 abstentions. The General Assembly adopted the declaration as a whole by 48 votes to 0, with 8 abstentions (from Saudi Arabia, South Africa, Belorussia, Czechoslovakia, Poland, Ukraine, USSR, and Yugoslavia).

The law of Islam, which is positive law in several states, inspired the Muslim objections to the explicit recognition of the right to change one's religion or belief. In Robinson's opinion, the fact that the clause was adopted by a vote of 27 to 5, with 12 abstentions, evidences the understanding that the declaration must be universal and that this clause did not represent a specific right but was the consequence of freedom of religion and thought.[35]

The controversy, however, was not over. Since 1948 the question of the recognition of the right to change one's religion or belief has dominated the debate and dealings in the area of religious human rights.[36] During the General

Assembly's discussion about the respective article of the 1981 Declaration, some forty Islamic states sought to delete the explicit reference to the right to change one's religion. Had this deletion occurred, it would have affected the validity of Article 18 of the Universal Declaration and Article 18 of the International Covenant on Civil and Political Rights. In 1981 several Islamic states, including Iran, Iraq, Jordan, Libya, Morocco, Senegal, Syria, and Tunisia, had already ratified the covenant without any reservation to Article 18.[37]

## THE KRISHNASWAMI STUDY

The first important United Nations document on change of religion in the framework of a global and comprehensive study on religious rights was Arcot Krishnaswami's *Study of Discrimination in the Matter of Religious Rights and Practices,* whose general provisions we reviewed in chapter 1.

Krishnaswami deals carefully with the issues related to change of religion. He mentions the clear distinction between freedom to maintain, or change, religion or belief, which cannot be restrained, and freedom to manifest those beliefs, already present in the writings of John Locke. Locke, whose views on toleration are not totally immune to criticism, wrote in his first *Letter Concerning Toleration* (1689):

> No man by nature is bound unto any particular church or sect, but everyone joins himself voluntarily to that society in which he believes he has found that profession and worship which is truly acceptable to God. The hope of salvation, as it was the only cause of his entrance into that communion, so it can be the only reason of his stay there. . . . A church, then, is a society of members voluntarily united to that end.[38]

For Krishnaswami, freedom to maintain or to change religion or belief falls primarily within the domain of the inner faith and conscience of an individual. However, cases of interference with this freedom exist, as followers of most religions or beliefs are members of some form of organization or community. Compelling an individual to join an organized religion or belief, or preventing an individual from leaving, must be considered an infringement of religious human rights. Even so, admits Krishnaswami, the mere existence of rules or procedures for formally joining or leaving a religion or belief is not necessarily an infringement of those rights.

Some states consider the establishment of new religious organizations dangerous because of the impact that a religion or belief normally has upon its followers. Consequently, these states may limit the freedom to change religion. Other times limitations are the result of social pressures rather than of governmental action. If a dissenting group is relatively large and tries to gain converts, the predominant group may be inclined to impose restrictions. Restrictions are more likely if the predominant religion or belief sees the new group as a splinter of the predominant group or as a schism or heresy. They may also be the result of links between a minority group and co-religionists in another country.[39]

Compulsory conversion is not merely an issue of the past. Krishnaswami mentions contemporary instances of individuals or groups being pressured to convert. Such pressures range from outright persecution to minor discriminatory measures. Frequently the public authorities simply fail to curb sufficiently pressures that are exerted by religions or beliefs enjoying a preferential position in the state,[40] although it has become increasingly rare for public authorities to exert such pressure directly. Some legal systems deny formal recognition to schismatic sectors and instead continue to consider the new group as a part of the parent group. In other instances dissenting elements are either compelled against their will to merge with the parent group or are totally denied the right to change religion or belief. Most religions clearly welcome converts formerly belonging to other faiths. The same groups reluctantly readmit the conversion of individuals who chose to leave their religion or belief. Apostasy may be prohibited by religious law or discouraged by social ostracism. In the past it was even severely punished by exile, excommunication, or death. Even now state recognition of a group's religious law as the law of the state may render a change of religion or belief legally impossible. Some states enforce the religious law of recognized communities in matters relating to personal status. In such states an individual's change of religion or belief may lead to certain incapacities or the loss of certain family rights. These same outcomes sometimes occur when a religious group refuses to grant a member the right to opt out.

Some states require an individual to register formally with religious or state authorities before granting legal effect to a change of religion. Sometimes such formalities are employed to dissuade individuals from changing religions. Problems connected with religious education and with conversion of children are particularly complicated. In some countries antenuptial agreements prevail upon the wishes of the parent or guardian. While the best interest of the child should be the paramount consideration, attention should also be paid to the expressed or presumed wishes of deceased or absent parents. The clash among parental authority, state policies, and the best interest of the child is frequently a source of difficulties, and judicial intervention is often necessary.

The methods of propagating a religion play a role as well. Determining which inducements are improper may be difficult. Some missionaries establish orphanages or schools, sometimes creating problems. Therefore, some countries have banned the running of educational institutions by missionaries. Similar objections have been voiced concerning other institutions managed by missionaries, including hospitals and social-assistance programs. Defining the scope of missionary activities is difficult, particularly when such activities take place among weak or vulnerable social sectors.

Krishnaswami emphasizes that attempts to convert individuals may conflict with their freedom to maintain their own religion or belief. This conflict may cause individuals and their respective groups to resist such attempts. Such resistance may make the coexistence of faiths difficult and cause clashes due either to the contents of the message or the methods used. Such clashes may necessitate state intervention, but the state should not exceed what is needed to restore peace.[41]

Cultural factors may dictate a society's attitude toward dissemination or propagation of a faith. Sometimes the powers that govern non-self-governing territories do not allow missionary work, even if the administering authority is of the same religion as the missionaries. This is because the activities of foreign missionaries may not be in harmony with the existing order. Krishnaswami illustrates this phenomenon by using a British government memorandum concerning Northern Nigeria, Sudan, and Somaliland.[42] The government took the line that since Northern Nigeria and the Sudan were Islamic countries and the indigenous rulers were unwilling to permit Christian preaching, it would be wrong for them to permit Christian missionary work until public opinion should change. The same approach was applied to the Somaliland Protectorate.[43] Hesitancy in such cases may have been based on the fear of the introduction of a fresh cultural impact. With the end of classic colonialism, the above situation has virtually disappeared.

In determining appropriate limitations concerning religious propagation, states must seek to preserve social stability and national security. The goal in every case should be to avoid the imposition of undue restrictions. The state has the right to limit improper inducements, such as bribes, that instigate a change of faith that is not the result of genuine conviction. When political tensions escalate between two countries, one country may deem it necessary to curtail the work of missionaries coming from the other country. Other considerations, such as morality, the general welfare, or the protection of public health, may also necessitate limitations upon faith propagation.

Sometimes the problem is not the religious message itself but the method employed that others find offensive. This may lead to special laws, such as those that prohibit activities affecting the religious feelings of the clergy or believers of a given faith. Occasionally such legislation may be so abusive that it permits censorship and regulation of publications and the media. However, blasphemy laws have become mostly, although not entirely, obsolete and are generally not applied.[44] Rather, new issues have emerged in our day, including the use of computers to disseminate religious views. This problem, not obvious at the time of Krishnaswami's work, presents an acute difficulty when the views espoused are incompatible with the legal order of a state. Regulation of computer proselytism is difficult at best.

Krishnaswami concludes that the dividing line between justifiable and more suspect restraints on religious propagation is thin. "[A]lthough the right to disseminate a faith must be safeguarded, this should be done within the framework of ensuring to everyone freedom to maintain his religion or belief." Acceptable limitations "should be such as will maintain peace and tranquility both inside and outside the country or territory, failing which no religious freedom is possible." Certain limitations upon particular forms of dissemination are permissible "in the interest of morals as conceived by society as a whole," but they should be temporary and removed as quickly as possible. The general and obvious rule is that everyone should be free to disseminate a religion or belief provided the actions "do not impair the right of any other individual to maintain his religion or belief."[45]

Consistent with this approach, Krishnaswami elaborates a series of basic rules for the attention of governments. Rule 1 states: "Everyone should be free to adhere, or not to adhere, to a religion or belief, in accordance with the dictates of his conscience." Rule 3 provides: "No one should be subjected to coercion or to improper inducements likely to impair his freedom to maintain or to change his religion or belief." Similarly, Rule 10 proclaims: "Everyone should be free to disseminate a religion or belief, in so far as his actions do not impair the right of any other individual to maintain his religion or belief." Rule 16(4), on the duties of public authorities, reads: "(a) The freedom of everyone to maintain or change his religion or belief must be ensured. . . . (c) In case of a conflict between the requirements of two or more religions or beliefs, public authorities should endeavor to find a solution assuring the greatest measure of freedom to society as a whole, while giving preference to the freedom of everyone to maintain or to change his religion or belief over any practice or observance tending to restrict this freedom."[46]

On the basis of the Krishnaswami report, the subcommission produced "Draft Principles on Freedom and Non-Discrimination in the Matter of Religious Rights and Practices." The following principles, separated into two parts, are relevant to the subject of proselytism and conversion. Part I provides: "Everyone shall be free to adhere, or not to adhere, to a religion or belief, in accordance with the dictates of his conscience. . . . 3. No one shall be subjected to material or moral coercion likely to impair his freedom to maintain or to change his religion or belief."[47] Part II provides:

8. (a) Everyone shall be free to teach or to disseminate his religion or belief, either in public or in private.

(b) No one shall be compelled to receive religious or atheistic instruction, contrary to his convictions or, in the case of children, contrary to the wishes of their parents and, when applicable, legal guardians.
9. (a) No group professing a religion or belief shall be prevented from training the personnel intending to devote themselves to the performance of its practices or observances, or from bringing teachers from abroad necessary for this purpose.[48]

The freedoms proclaimed in Part I, Krishnaswami writes, shall not be subject to any restrictions. The freedoms proclaimed in Part II can be restricted only as required by morality, health, public order, and the general welfare in a democratic society, and these restrictions should be consistent with the purposes and principles of the United Nations.[49]

Krishnaswami's study and the ensuing draft principles have added significantly to the evolution of United Nations instruments respecting change of religion and greatly influenced future texts. Their importance is further enhanced by the fact that the study was the first document prepared for the United Nations providing a comprehensive analysis of this delicate subject.

## THE 1966 COVENANTS

The International Covenants on Economic, Social, and Cultural Rights and on Civil and Political Rights, which were adopted in 1966 by Resolution 2200 A (XXI) by the United Nations, accurately reflect the general orientation and trends that inspired the 1948 Universal Declaration.

The most relevant provisions in the ICCPR, as we saw in chapter 1, are Articles 18, 20, and 27. Article 18(1) generally tracks the wording of Article 18 of the Universal Declaration but is slightly different insofar as the ICCPR does not refer explicitly to the right to *change* one's religion or belief. Rather, it uses milder compromise language, stemming from Muslim objections to the text and attempts to delete the clause. Egypt, Saudi Arabia, Yemen, and Afghanistan were among the states opposed to repetition of the 1948 wording. Western advocates argued that an explicit reference to the right was necessary to avoid uncertainties and prejudiced interpretations.[50]

The Saudi Arabian representative expressed concern that the original text of Article 18 might be understood as favoring missionary activities or the propagation of antireligious beliefs. Thus, he submitted an amendment to delete the words "to maintain or to change his religion or belief, and freedom." He later withdrew his amendment and supported one submitted by Brazil and the Philippines introducing the words "to have a religion or belief of his choice" instead of "to maintain or to change his religion or belief." Western representatives criticized this amendment for being too static and preventing more than one choice.[51] For example, the British representative proposed including the words "or to adopt" in the Brazilian-Philippine amendment. Afghanistan requested a separate vote on the British proposal; it was retained by 54 votes to 0 with 15 abstentions. The amendment as a whole was adopted by the Third Committee by 70 votes to 0 with 2 abstentions. Article 18 as a whole was approved unanimously by the Third Committee on November 18, 1960.[52] Walkate points out that six years later the General Assembly would adopt unanimously the covenant as a whole.[53] No reservations were entered regarding Article 18.

The final version of the covenant, therefore, proclaims that the right of everyone to freedom of thought, conscience, and belief "shall include freedom to have or to adopt a religion or belief of his choice." It seems quite clear that the text recognizes the right to change one's religion or belief, that is, to abandon one religion and adopt a different one. The discussion during the preparation of the Covenant supports this liberal interpretation. Nevertheless, the change in language is significant and problematic—particularly in those countries where religious law is part of the state law.

Article 18(2) confirms the approach followed in Article 18(1). It states that no one shall be subject to coercion that would impair a person's freedom to have or to adopt a religion or belief of his or her choice. *Coercion* is not defined, but it seems reasonable to interpret it not only to mean the use of force or threats but also to include more subtle forms of illegitimate influence, such as psychological and moral pressure or material enticement.

Article 18(4) deals with the liberty of parents and/or legal guardians to ensure the religious and moral education of their children in conformity with their own convictions. It should be read in conjunction with Article 13(3) of the International Covenant on Social, Cultural, and Economic Rights. Proselytism and change of religion are again intimately connected to this sensitive area. The UNESCO Convention against Discrimination in Education, the 1981 Declaration, the Convention on the Rights of the Child, and other international instruments also discuss this important interaction between religion and education.[54]

Since this interaction between religion and education is of recurring interest in both international and constitutional law, adjudication at the national and international levels has frequently been necessary. For example, in 1978 the Human Rights Committee dealt with an interesting complaint submitted by the Union of Free Thinkers in Finland on the issue of teaching the history of religion in public schools. The committee opined that such instruction, if given in a neutral and objective way that respected the convictions of parents and guardians who do not believe in any religion, does not violate Article 18 of the covenant.[55] The link between this issue and proselytism cannot be discussed in merely abstract terms. How can we ensure that religious instruction is objective and purely informative rather than an attempt to indoctrinate children who belong to other religious persuasions? Put differently, when does such religious instruction become coercive proselytism that takes advantage of the teacher's intellectual influence? This issue can only be considered specifically; it depends significantly upon other factors concurring or counter-balancing the instruction given at school.

Finally, Articles 20 and 27 of the Covenant on Civil and Political Rights are relevant to the issue of proselytism. Article 20 prohibits any advocacy of religious hatred. Article 27 reflects a restrictive approach to minority and group rights. It does not refer to proselytizing activities but does mention "the right of persons belonging to . . . minorities to profess and practice their own religion."

## THE GENERAL COMMENT

The Human Rights Committee, the body in charge of implementing the Covenant on Civil and Political Rights, issued an important General Comment in 1993 (the general provisions were analyzed in chapter 1). The General

Comment speaks to issues of proselytism and conversion and stresses that the terms *belief* and *religion* are to be broadly construed. Such an understanding leads to a rejection of "any tendency to discriminate against any religion or belief for any reason, including the fact that they are newly established or represent religious minorities that may be the subject of hostility by a predominant religious community."[56] This remark seems intended to avoid situations in which old, well-established religious groups enjoy more protection and rights than recently established or minority religious groups. Freedom of speech is also involved, and Article 18 should be read in conjunction with Article 19(1) of the covenant, which sets forth the general protection of speech.

Additionally, no one should be compelled to reveal his or her thoughts or adherence to a particular religion or belief. Paragraph 5 of the General Comment reaffirms that the Covenant on Civil and Political Rights bars any coercion that would impair the right to replace one's current religion or belief with another or with atheistic views—in other words, the right to conversion. According to the committee, coercion means the use or threat of physical force; penal sanctions; and restrictions on access to education, medical care, employment, or other rights guaranteed by the covenant. Again, the same protection is granted to holders of nonreligious beliefs.

The General Comment also discusses the relationship between education and the teaching of religion. Public school instruction regarding the history of religions and ethics is permitted if given in a "neutral" and "objective" manner. Public school instruction focusing on a particular religion or belief is inconsistent with the covenant, unless the wishes of parents and guardians are protected by nondiscriminatory exemptions or alternatives. Freedom to teach a religion or belief incorporates the liberty of parents or guardians to guarantee for their children a religious and moral education in conformity with their convictions.

The committee points out that Article 18(3) of the ICCPR, concerning limitations, should be interpreted strictly. Permissible limitations should be established by law and interpreted so as to protect the rights guaranteed under the covenant. Article 18(3) mentions limitations based on morals. The committee examines this concept, drawing from many social, philosophical, and religious traditions. The fact that a religion is recognized as a state religion (that is, considered official or traditional) or is the majority religion should not afford it special rights or privileges. Any special privileges for members of a majority religion should be considered discriminatory. Moreover, nonbelievers, members of minority religions, and adherents of religions without special state recognition should not suffer discrimination or impairment in the enjoyment of any rights under the covenant. States should report on measures taken in this area and on the rights of minorities. They should also provide information regarding practices that may be punishable, such as blasphemy, heresy, and related matters.

The 1993 General Comment summarizes the principal views of the Human Rights Committee regarding change of religion. The committee provides additional information on change of religion in its yearly reports.[57] When considering the periodic state reports, members of the committee ask relevant questions and require supplementary data from state representatives on legislation and facts regarding conversion and proselytism. For example, the committee asked Morocco to detail procedures for the recognition of religious sects and to define the meaning of terms, such as *religion of the state, revealed religions,* and *heretical sects.* When considering an Austrian report, the committee discussed the status of Jehovah's Witnesses and criminal rules concerning blasphemy. The issues of apostasy in Sudan, blasphemy in the United Kingdom, the status of non-Catholic churches in Argentina, and religious teaching in Colombia were also topics of discussion.[58]

The committee has considered very few individual complaints or communications related to religious rights, as compared to other rights. Though a few cases have made reference to proselytism and conversion, the matter has not been directly addressed. Similarly, the Committee on Economic, Social, and Cultural Rights has had no opportunity to address this subject. This is consistent with the indirect way in which this covenant refers to religious rights—mainly in connection with educational and parental rights.[59]

## THE 1981 DECLARATION

The Declaration on the Elimination of All Forms of Intolerance and Discrimination Based on Religion or Belief was promulgated by the General Assembly of the United Nations on November 25, 1981—the product of some sixteen years of negotiation, as we saw in chapter 1.[60]

Some of the major problems confronted by the General Assembly were the issues concerning change of religion, the right to proselytize, and its limits. Muslim delegations were opposed to a guarantee of these rights. The matter was ultimately settled by way of a twofold compromise. First, explicit references to the right to change one's religion were deleted from the text, both in the Preamble and in Article 1. This alteration was a departure from the wording of both the 1948 Universal Declaration and the 1966 Covenant on Civil and Political Rights. The new wording weakened the guarantee of religious freedom and jeopardized two decades of efforts. A second alteration was necessary to persuade the West to accept the change; a new Article 8 was added that states nothing in the declaration "shall be construed as restricting or derogating from any right defined in the Universal Declaration of Human Rights and the International Covenants on Human Rights."

Most experts and scholars do not consider the differences in the wording of the 1981 text as constituting a departure in meaning from previous instruments. A lingering question is whether states that did not ratify the covenants may claim that the right to change religion, although included in Article 18 of the Universal Declaration, cannot be afforded the status of customary international law insofar as those states are concerned, in light of their objections to the text.[61] However, the compromise reached in the 1981 text resulted from a collective eagerness to see the draft adopted. The compromise would have failed had it not been made clear that the right to change one's religion was preserved, though not explicitly spelled out. The Irish diplomat Declan O'Donovan, chairman of the Third Committee in 1981, did not see the retention of the words "or to adopt" as essential. He admitted, however, that its removal "was a concession by Western states that they felt obliged to make in order to advance the subject of religious belief."[62]

J. A. Walkate, who represented the Netherlands in the Third Committee, actively participated in the negotiations during the thirty-sixth session of the General Assembly (1981). He summarized the negotiations in a most illuminating account.[63] The text prepared by the Commission on Human Rights had been submitted by the Economic and Social Council (ECOSOC) on May 8, 1981, by Resolution 1981/36. The resolution recommended that the General Assembly adopt the appended declaration. The vote was 45 to 0, with 6 abstentions (Algeria and the Communist members of ECOSOC).

The Third Committee of the General Assembly discussed the draft over the course of twelve meetings. A group of Islamic states opposed the text to the extent that it concerned the question of the right to change religion. Particularly at issue were draft preambular paragraph 2, *in fine*, and part of Article I. The second paragraph of the preamble begins:

> Considering that the Universal Declaration of Human Rights and the International Covenants on Human Rights proclaim the principles of nondiscrimination and equality before the law and the right to freedom of thought, conscience, religion and belief, including the right to choose, manifest and change one's religion or belief. . . .

Article I reads:

> 1. Everyone shall have the right to freedom of thought, conscience and religion. This right shall include freedom to have or to adopt a religion or belief of his choice. . . .
> 2. No one shall be subject to coercion which would impair his freedom to have or to adopt a religion or belief of his choice.

Clearly, the phrases "to choose," "to change one's religion or belief," "to have or to adopt a religion or belief of his choice," and freedom from "coercion which would impair his freedom to have or to adopt a religion or belief of his choice" mean precisely what the Universal Declaration and the covenant proclaim. It was the confirmation and repetition of this wording that the Muslim representatives opposed. Islamic spokesmen pointed out that, according to the Qur'an, a Muslim cannot change his or her religion. For this reason, the Islamic states were ready to support the proposed text, without a vote, if the words "to adopt a religion or belief of his choice" and "to change one's religion or belief" were deleted. Alternatively, the Muslim group suggested referring the draft to the Commission on Human Rights for further work or deferring the matter to a later session.

The Western delegations tried to explain that the controversial texts were already part of the existing human rights law and that Islamic states such as Iran, Iraq, Libya, Morocco, Senegal, Syria, and Tunisia had already ratified the covenant without any reservation to the now objectionable terminology. The explanations were of no avail. Representatives of Kuwait, Egypt, Iraq, and Saudi Arabia were particularly adamant in demanding the change in wording regarding conversion.

Walkate summarizes the predicament of the Western group. They were eager to have the declaration proclaimed at the thirty-sixth session but were wary of the proposed changes. Walkate states that the Western group felt they could only accept a change if a new article were added—providing that nothing in the declaration should be construed as a derogation or restriction upon basic human rights instruments. One possibility contemplated by the Western group was to revive a Netherlands proposal in the commission's working group. This proposal asserted that there shall be no restriction upon, nor derogation from, any of the provisions of the covenant or any other international instrument relating to the elimination of intolerance and discrimination based on religion or belief "on the pretext that the present declaration does not recognize such rights or it recognized them to a lesser extent."[64] Walkate indicates that the Islamic group feared that the whole declaration, to which in general it attached importance, could be in danger. Therefore, after lengthy deliberations, they accepted the "package deal," provided no formal vote would take place in the Third Committee. Intense negotiations by the Third Committee's chairman, Declan O'Donovan, led to acceptance of this deal.

The East European states were not concerned with the issue of the right to change religion but sought to strengthen the term *belief*. O'Donovan brokered another compromise, which consisted only of adding the word "whatever" in some places, a rather modest demand. The new text, as produced by the Third Committee, incorporated these changes, eliminated the explicit references to the "right to change religion" in the Preamble and in Article 1, and added Article 8 as a general safeguard. The new text was adopted without a vote. When the modified draft came to the Plenary, the declaration was proclaimed (without a vote) on November 25, 1981.

A few Muslim delegations felt it necessary to formulate explanations for their support. Iraq (speaking on behalf of the Organization of the Islamic Conference), Syria, and Iran introduced a specific reservation as to the applicability of "any provision or wording of the Declaration which might be contrary to *Shari'a* or to any legislation or act based on Islamic law."[65]

This attitude of Muslim countries must be seen in historical perspective. In an article discussing migration as viewed by classical Islamic law, Sami A. Aldeeb Abu-Sahlieh points out that Muhammad himself dealt with the issue of conversion.[66] People who were not monotheists had to choose between conversion or war. Monotheists wishing to remain in their own religion had to accept the political authority of the Muslims and pay a tribute. Otherwise, they could expect war. Thousands of non-Muslims underwent forced conversion to Islam in Spain and elsewhere. Although the Qur'an speaks against forced conversion, such conversions of Christians and Jews took place under Muslim rule until the early decades of the twentieth century.[67] Presently, Islam is the state religion in many predominantly Muslim countries. In some, citizenship is reserved for Muslims and conversion of Muslims to another religion is forbidden.

The wording of the 1981 Declaration with regard to the right to change religion met with no other objections besides that of Muslim groups. Proselytism, with some limits, is considered a legitimate means of using freedom of expression to propagate one's faith. Similarly, conversion or opting-out of a religion is considered a legitimate human right. There is almost universal consensus on these points; the linguistic compromise in the 1981 Declaration is a typical example of international law-making accommodation of dissenting views. The result in this particular case was a weakening of the letter of Articles 18 of the Universal Declaration and of the covenant but not a departure from their spirit and meaning as interpreted by a majority of states. For some expert observers, such a weakening implies a downward thrust in the drafting process.[68]

According to Donna J. Sullivan, the parameters of the right to change one's religion or belief remain uncertain under the declaration. The phenomena of apostasy and heresy present potential conflicts between the right of individuals to believe what they choose and the right of religious groups to promulgate doctrine as a part of religious practice.

Sullivan deals with the issue under the heading of coercion. The subcommission's draft principles prohibited all coercion likely to impair a person's freedom to maintain or to change his or her religion or belief. Sullivan asserts that, if the aim of the declaration is to be achieved, coercion should be interpreted broadly. This would mean coercion would include not only physical or moral means of compulsion but also mental or psychological means, as well as a government conditioning any benefits or services upon the renunciation or acceptance of religious beliefs.

Believers should enjoy the freedom to engage in noncoercive forms of proselytizing, such as mere appeals to conscience or the display of placards or billboards, and governments should protect the right to freedom of expression. At the same time, proselytizing "may set the rights of those whose religious faith encourages or requires such activity in opposition to the rights of those targeted to be free from coercion to change their beliefs." In situations of clear conflict, "the right to engage in coercive forms of proselytizing as an expression of religious belief must yield to the right of individuals to hold a belief of their choice without impairment."[69]

Thus, bona fide proselytizing excludes coercion, intimidation, or enticement and, in Sullivan's view, is tied up with freedom of expression. Taking into account the fact that proselytizing might bring an invasion of privacy and/or the right to be left alone on matters of religion or belief, one fundamental question remains: to what extent should bona fide proselytizing be considered an unrestricted right? This is ultimately the crux of the conflict between proselytism and the right to preserve and protect one's beliefs—a conflict to which the 1981 Declaration did not provide an absolutely clear answer.

## THE WORK OF SPECIAL RAPPORTEURS

Three U.N. special rapporteurs have been reporting on the situation concerning religious rights since the promulgation of the 1981 Declaration. All of them have given substantial attention to the issue of proselytism and the restrictions imposed on proselytism by some countries. In 1987, almost three decades after the Krishnaswami study, Elizabeth Odio Benito, special rapporteur appointed by the Subcommission on Prevention of Discrimination and Protection of Minorities, submitted a study of the current dimensions of the problems of intolerance and of discrimination on grounds of religion or belief. Odio Benito does not ascribe too much weight to the differences in the wording of the main U.N. instruments dealing with changes of religion or belief. In her view a careful examination of the texts of Article 18 of the Universal Declaration of Human Rights, Article 18 of the Covenant on Civil and Political Rights, and Article 1 of the 1981 Declaration shows that, although they are slightly varied in wording, all mean precisely the same thing: every person has the right to leave one religion or belief and to adopt another, or to remain without any at all.[70] Other freedoms, such as freedom of opinion and expression and freedom of peaceful assembly and association, are intimately linked to the freedoms of thought, conscience, religion, and belief as well.

The omission of the phrase "change of religion" in Article 6 of the 1981 Declaration does not alter the right itself, Odio Benito claims. The declaration encompasses the right to change one's religion, even if it is not expressly recognized in the way it exists within the primary human rights instruments. This right "is inseparable from freedom of thought, conscience and religion." The declaration was adopted

> precisely to struggle for the elimination of each and every form of intolerance . . . something which necessarily includes a struggle against attitudes, actions or laws that prevent a human being from changing his religion or belief or having none whatsoever, for attitudes, actions or laws of this kind would be intolerant and discriminatory.[71]

Odio Benito notes that a number of states violate these freedoms. Some states officially prohibit preaching and proselytizing, teaching religion, disseminating religious materials, and other activities. In her 1987 study Odio Benito points to Eastern Europe, Albania, Afghanistan, Iran, Pakistan, and unnamed countries in the Americas, Africa, and Asia as violators of the international norms related to religious freedoms—especially by taking action against foreign missionaries. Repressive practices include imprisonment, torture, and even death sentences. Some countries prohibit conversion either by law or by their constitution; governments have arrested persons simply because they adopted a different religion.[72]

Twenty-six governments made information available for Odio Benito's study. Using this information, Odio Benito studied laws prohibiting coercion impairing the freedom to choose a religion or belief. Comparing this information with the text of Article 1(2) of the 1981 Declaration, the rapporteur concluded that only four states (Cyprus, Israel, Qatar, and Spain) prohibit coercion to leave one's religion or belief or to adopt a new one. Other constitutional or legal provisions prohibit forms of coercion likely to impair the freedom to change religion. The special rapporteur alludes to practices of specific countries: coercion to participate in, or not to participate in, ceremonies of a religion or belief not one's own (Barbados, Germany, Jamaica, Mauritius, Morocco, Pakistan, Spain, Switzerland, and Turkey); coercion to reveal one's religion or belief (Cyprus, Ecuador, Germany, Peru, Portugal, Spain, Turkey, and Ukraine); coercion to receive religious education in a religion other than one's own (Barbados, Israel, Italy, Jamaica, Pakistan, Switzerland, and Trinidad and Tobago); coercion to contribute to a fund used for the purposes of a religion other than one's own (Cyprus, Denmark, and Pakistan); and coercion to practice a particular religion or belief (Mauritius and Morocco).

Odio Benito concludes that the right to change religion is not fully protected or respected. Only a few states have constitutional provisions providing full protection.[73] The rights of children, however, do receive special attention. A child's right not to be compelled to receive religious teaching against the wishes of the child's parents or legal guardians is mentioned by twenty governments and has yielded several judicial decisions.[74]

The Commission on Human Rights appointed Angelo Vidal d'Almeida Ribeiro as special rapporteur in 1986. The author of seven reports on the implementation of the 1981 Declaration,[75] Ribeiro does not deal with the terminology question. Rather, he discharges his monitoring duties by highlighting difficulties many countries have faced in applying Article 1 of the 1981 Declaration. Among other cases, Ribeiro addresses the prohibition of missionary activities in China; the illegal propaganda for Jehovah's Witnesses, considered an unlawful association in Cuba; the forced conversion of Coptic Christians into Islam in Egypt; the persecution of Jehovah's Witnesses on grounds of proselytism in Greece; the intimidation of Christian missionaries in India; the persecution of the Bahá'í religion in Iran; forced conversions and persecution of converts in Pakistan, Saudi Arabia, and Sudan; and prohibition of proselytism in Vietnam. The special rapporteur concludes that intolerance and discrimination based on religion or belief concern "the right to have the religion or belief of one's choice, the right to . . . change one's religion or belief, . . . the right to teach a religion or belief in places suitable for those purposes, . . . the rights of parents to bring up children in accordance with the religion or belief of their choice. . . . "[76] In contrast with the situation prevailing in the

West, in most countries where Islam is the prevalent or official religion and where the *shari'a* is in force, "proselytism and apostasy were particularly sensitive issues."[77]

Following the resignation of Angelo Vidal d'Almeida Ribeiro, the chairman of the Commission on Human Rights appointed Abdelfattah Amor as special rapporteur. Amor also deals with the issues of conversion and proselytism in his reports since 1994.[78] He emphasizes that the right to change one's religion is recognized within the framework of internationally established standards in the field of human rights, including the 1981 Declaration. The right is also recognized by the interpretation of the Human Rights Committee, as expressed in General Comment 22 of 1993, summarized earlier. The rapporteur also stresses that Article 18(2) of the ICCPR bars coercion that would impair the right to have or adopt a religion or belief. Thus, Article 18(2) bans the threat of physical force or penal sanctions as a means to compel believers or nonbelievers to adhere to religious beliefs, to recant their religion or belief, or to convert.[79] He specifically emphasizes that a Muslim's conversion to another religion should in no way give rise to pressures, bans, or restrictions on the Protestant community, on the converts, or on ministers of religion.[80]

During a visit to the Islamic Republic of Iran in December 1995 government representatives acknowledged to Amor that Article 18 of the Universal Declaration expressly recognized conversion, that the Islamic countries had expressed reservations about it, and that Article 18 of the covenant did not refer to conversion.[81] Amor notes that the proportion of Muslim converts into Protestant communities is increasing but in a clandestine way. The authorities in Iran prohibit all forms of proselytism and conversion of a Muslim to another religion, and this explains the limitations placed on the religious activities of the Protestant churches.[82]

Amor notes that prohibitions against proselytizing are among the main violations of Article 1 of the 1981 Declaration. Forced conversions are another major violation. These have frequently occurred in countries such as Indonesia, Myanmar, Sudan, the Maldives, Malaysia, Egypt, Morocco, Nepal, and Greece. In Sudan a new law restricting missionary societies was repealed after a meeting between the pope and the president.[83] In an addendum concerning a visit to Pakistan, the special rapporteur states that indications exist that the subordinate Pakistani judiciary tends to hold that conversion from Islam to another faith is an offense, even though Pakistani authorities assert that conversion and proselytism are not persecuted.[84]

In his detailed report for 1994 the rapporteur records some relevant findings: non-Muslims are allegedly forbidden to proselytize in Afghanistan; in Bhutan, the local Hindu population resents the continuous attempts to convert them to Christianity and has taken steps to ban missionary activities; in Egypt, the government invoked articles of the Penal Code to punish the conversion of Muslims and expelled foreigners for proselytizing; in India, the laws of some provinces discourage proselytism; in Malaysia, the state of Johor adopted a law in 1991 that controls and restricts the propagation of non-Islamic religions; and in Mexico, reprisals have been adopted against a few hundred people for abandoning the Chamula religion to adopt Christianity.[85]

The report submitted by Rapporteur Amor on December 30, 1996, refers especially to some urgent appeals sent to Iran, Egypt, and the United Arab Emirates concerning conversion or apostasy issues.[86] The rapporteur analyzes the different categories of religious freedom violations and points out that the freedom to change one's religion is being violated in several countries. Violations of the freedom to manifest one's religion or belief often involve a ban on proselytizing, including prison sentences. In Armenia, Bhutan, Brunei Darussalam, and the Maldives, the ban on proselytizing effectively applies only to certain religious communities. The Lao People's Democratic Republic, Morocco, Mexico, and Greece are singled out because of their limitations on proselytizing. Amor reemphasizes the right to change religion as a legally essential aspect of religious freedom. Dealing with the distinction between a religion and a sect, he concludes that "it is not the business of the State or any other group or community to act as the guardian of people's consciences and encourage, impose or censure any religious belief or conviction."[87]

In his report submitted on January 22, 1998, Special Rapporteur Amor concentrates his analysis on the sphere of tolerance, in the light of replies to a questionnaire received from seventy-seven states. He deals with the issue of religious instruction and surveys the different categories of violations of religious rights, including the freedom to change one's religion and the question of proselytism. The special rapporteur suggests changing his official title to Special Rapporteur on Freedom of Religion and Belief, so as to encompass freedom of belief (agnosticism, freethinking, atheism, and rationalism) and evade the negative connotations of intolerance and discrimination. He also recommends that he be provided with the resources to undertake a study on proselytism, freedom of religion, and poverty.[88]

Amor refers to the issue of sects and new religious movements, complicated by the fact that human rights instruments do not define religion and do not mention the new phenomena.[89]

## OTHER GLOBAL INSTRUMENTS

A few other international global instruments deal with proselytism and change of religion indirectly, and these may be useful to mention.

### Minorities

The issue of minorities has been dealt with in general in chapter 3. By its nature the 1992 United Nations Declaration on the Rights of Persons belonging to National or Ethnic, Religious, and Linguistic Minorities must be particularly mentioned. Religious and ethno-religious groups may be seriously affected by the attitude of the majority in the state and by national legislation concerning religious interaction. Inspired by Article 27 of the International Covenant on Civil and Political Rights, the 1992 declaration reflects the reluctance of the organized international community to recognize the role of group rights. Nevertheless, it does acknowledge some rights and needs of minorities—including the protection of their existence and identity. This protection extends to religious minorities. The declaration even encourages conditions for the promotion of group religious identity.

Article 2(5) of the declaration is of special relevance. It recognizes the right of persons belonging to, inter alia, religious minorities

> to establish and maintain, without any discrimination, free and peaceful contacts with other members of their group and with other persons belonging to other minorities, as well as contacts across frontiers with citizens of other states to whom they are related by national or ethnic, religious or linguistic ties.

It may be an overstatement to interpret this provision as authorizing contacts intended to proselytize or teach one's religion to persons belonging to other minorities. However, Article 8(2) does state that the exercise of the rights proclaimed in the declaration shall not prejudice the enjoyment of universally recognized human rights and fundamental freedoms. Beyond that, however, the declaration contains no reference to proselytism and conversion.

### Migrant Workers

The United Nations adopted the International Convention on the Protection of All Migrant Workers and Members of Their Families in 1990.[90] A comprehensive and detailed text, the convention follows the wording of the ICCPR and deals specifically with the right to change one's religion.

Article 12 of the convention reads:

> 1. Migrant workers and members of their families shall have the right to freedom of thought, conscience and religion. This right shall include freedom to have or to adopt a religion or belief of their choice and freedom either individually or in community with others and in public or private to manifest their religion or belief in worship, observance, practice and teaching.
> 2. Migrant workers and members of their families shall not be subject to coercion that would impair their freedom to have or to adopt a religion or belief of their choice.

Article 12 also addresses limitations on the freedom of religion, stating in paragraph 3 that the freedom

> may be subject only to such limitations as are prescribed by law and are necessary to protect public safety, order, health or morals, or the

fundamental rights and freedoms of others, and the rights of parents to ensure the religious and moral education of their children in conformity with their own convictions.

Also relevant is Article 13(2), which proclaims the right to impart information and ideas, regardless of frontiers.

### Indigenous Populations

The United Nations' designation of 1993 as the International Year for the World's Indigenous People prompted the U.N. working group on indigenous populations to initiate a study on the hundreds of treaties, agreements, and other arrangements between governments and indigenous groups. Indigenous groups are closely related to some of the issues discussed here. The problems concerning cultural relativism and the preservation of traditional religions are obviously also implicated.

In a document prepared by the working group, the rights of indigenous populations "to manifest, teach, practice and observe their own religious traditions and ceremonies, and to maintain, protect, and have access to (sacred) sites for these purposes," and their right "to preserve their cultural identity and traditions" are recognized.[91]

Also important in this respect is the 1989 International Labor Organization Convention concerning Indigenous and Tribal Peoples in Independent Countries, which amended the 1957 Indigenous and Tribal Populations Convention.[92] The 1989 convention does not contain specific provisions concerning proselytism or conversion, but it does address these issues indirectly. The preamble refers to the aspirations of the indigenous peoples to exercise control over their "ways of life" and to "maintain and develop their identities, languages and religions." Article 5 ensures recognition of the spiritual values and practices of the indigenous peoples, while Article 7 proclaims that the peoples concerned have the right to decide "their own priorities for the process of development as it affects their lives, beliefs, institutions and spiritual well-being. . . . " Article 8 provides that due regard shall be had for the customs or customary law of the peoples concerned, "except where these are incompatible with internationally recognized human rights."

### Rights of the Child

When the 1981 Declaration was discussed, one of the major difficulties related to the article on rights of children. Religious issues are closely connected with educational rights, and the issue of change of religion is no exception. Differences of view arose about several topics: parental rights; conflicts between parents regarding the religion of the child; the age a child must reach before he or she is capable of making autonomous decisions concerning religion or belief; and how to balance the roles of the state, the parents, and the generally accepted principle of the best interest of the child.

The main international text on the subject is the 1989 Convention on the Rights of the Child. The convention was unanimously adopted and followed in the steps of the 1959 United Nations Declaration on the Rights of the Child.[93] Article 14 of the convention deals with religion; it proclaims that states shall respect the right of the child to freedom of thought, conscience, and religion, as well as the rights and duties of the parents or legal guardians to "provide direction" to the child in the exercise of his or her rights. Attempts to use the wording of the International Covenant on Civil and Political Rights in Article 14 engendered opposition. Muslim representatives opposed such attempts, invoking the Qur'an and various pieces of national legislation. They asserted that a child is not able to choose a religion or belief or to change one. The Maldives even attached a reservation stipulating that "all Maldivians should be Muslims." Iran stated that it would enter reservations to any provision that contradicted traditional Islamic rules. Other Islamic states submitted similar reservations. Western states generally supported the classic line of human rights law, though some Catholic states also expressed reservations. The United States ultimately failed in its attempts to include a guarantee of the freedom to change religion.

Many see Article 14 as a step back when compared to the standards contained in the 1948 Universal Declaration, the 1966 Covenant, and the 1981 Declaration on the Elimination of All Forms of Intolerance and of Discrimination Based on Religion or Belief. In the words of Bahiyyih G. Tahzib, Article 14 is "less broad in its scope of protection."[94] However, the same author acknowledges that the convention contains a saving clause: Article 43 preserves the application of international law provisions more favorable to the rights of the child.

Difficulties also arose in connection with Article 20, which concerns adoption. Further, no solution was provided for problems caused by clashes between the parents as to the religion of the child. The major issue of conflict between the state and the parents in deciding what kind of education the child will receive in matters of religion has arisen in several judicial decisions.[95]

### Discrimination in Education

The Convention against Discrimination in Education was adopted in 1960 by the General Conference of UNESCO.[96] It does not refer specifically to change of religion. Even so, the interaction between religion and education is well known. Frequently, educational policies of some states cause resentment among religious groups that believe such policies involve attempts to induce pupils to change their religious convictions. More than once opponents have claimed that proselytism is an indirect intention of some religious education, particularly when such education is opposed to the desires of parents or legal guardians. This issue was mentioned above in connection with the article addressing the rights of the child in the 1981 Declaration.

Article 5,1(b) of the UNESCO convention reaffirms the right of parents or legal guardians to ensure "the religious and moral education of the children in conformity with their own convictions, and no person or group of persons should be compelled to receive religious instruction inconsistent with his or their conviction." Judicial or quasi-judicial decisions at the European level have dealt with religious instruction allegedly involving indoctrination or proselytism.

### Draft Convention on Religious Intolerance and Discrimination

The treatment of change of religion in the draft Convention on the Elimination of All Forms of Intolerance and of Discrimination Based on Religion or Belief merits attention in this section on global international instruments. The draft convention was already penned by 1965. We have already discussed in chapter 1 the rather dim prospects of the renewal of the consideration of such a convention.

According to the draft convention, states must undertake to ensure the right to freedoms of thought, conscience, religion, and belief. Article III 1(a) of the draft provides that this right shall include

> freedom to adhere or not to adhere to any religion or belief and to change his religion or belief in accordance with the dictates of his conscience without being subjected either to any of the limitations referred to in Article XII or to any coercion likely to impair his freedom of choice or decision in the matter, providing that this paragraph should not be interpreted as extending to manifestations of religion or belief.

The limitations listed in draft Article XII are the usual ones. Article III 1(b) ensures to everyone "the freedom to teach, to disseminate and to learn his religion or belief and its sacred languages or traditions, to write, print and publish religious books and texts. . . . " The differences in the language of the draft as compared to the already adopted instruments are obviously due to the time when the draft was prepared.[97]

## REGIONAL INSTRUMENTS

The provisions on the issue of proselytism incorporated into regional or sectorial human rights instruments reflect the approach of the respective groups of states involved.

### European Convention

Article 9(1) of the European Convention for the Protection of Human Rights and Fundamental Freedoms (1950), ratified by all member states of the Council of Europe, provides that "[e]veryone has the right to freedom of thought, conscience and religion; this right includes freedom to change his religion or belief. . . . " The convention follows the pattern of the Universal Declaration, thus differing from the wording of the International Covenant on Civil and Political Rights and the 1981 Declaration. The 1990 Copenhagen Meeting of the Conference on the Human Dimension of the Conference on Security and Cooperation in Europe (CSCE) follows a similar approach, carrying an almost identical wording in its Article 9(4). The Vienna Concluding Document of 1989 does not contain specific references to change of religion, though Article 16 does refer to religious education, training of personnel, and other rights related to the issue under consideration.

## AMERICAN CONVENTION ON HUMAN RIGHTS

The American Convention on Human Rights, adopted in 1969, deals with freedom of conscience and religion (Article 12) separately from freedom of thought and expression (Article 13). Article 12(1) says that "everyone has the right to freedom of conscience and religion: This right includes freedom to maintain or to change one's religion or beliefs. . . . " Article 12(2) adds that "[n]o one shall be subject to restrictions that might impair the freedom to maintain or to change his religion or beliefs." Article 13(1) includes the freedom to "impart information and ideas of all kinds . . . through [any] medium of one's choice as part of the right to freedom of thought and expression." The Inter-American Court of Human Rights gave this article a broad interpretation, stressing that the expression and dissemination of ideas are indivisible concepts.[98]

## CAIRO DECLARATION ON HUMAN RIGHTS

For Islamic states, members of the Islamic Conference, the Cairo Declaration on Human Rights (1990) is considered an authoritative document reflecting the Islamic view on international human rights. On the issue of proselytism, Article 10 of the declaration prohibits "any form of compulsion on man or to exploit his poverty or ignorance in order to convert him to another religion or to atheism." Article 22 allows freedom of expression in a manner as would not be contrary to the principles of the *shari'a*.

## OSCE HUMAN DIMENSION SEMINAR

The Organization for Security and Cooperation in Europe (OSCE) has devoted considerable attention to the issues of proselytism and change of religion, partly because of situations prevailing in Eastern Europe. The OSCE Office for Democratic Institutions and Human Rights convened a Human Dimension Seminar on constitutional, legal, and administrative aspects of the freedom of religion on April 16-19, 1996. The seminar covered such themes as state, church, religious communities, and organization; law, church, and religious communities; and state and individual believer. Representatives of forty-seven participating states and one nonparticipating state, as well as of several international organizations, attended the seminar, which was held in Warsaw. Fifty-five nongovernmental organizations were also represented.

The issues of change of religion and proselytism came up repeatedly in three discussion groups. This likely reflected the "deep concern" caused by the "intolerance exhibited by some religious groups in some OSCE states," including the prohibition of proselytism in some countries.[99] The participants recommended that the office conduct a comprehensive survey of the relevant constitutional, legal, and administrative provisions relevant to freedom of religion in OSCE states and also organize a future seminar on the topic of tolerance and proselytism.

The consolidated summary of the seminar stresses that the participants reached broad agreement on the fact that freedom of conscience and belief is an absolute right under the OSCE commitments. Further, they agreed that freedom of conscience and belief incorporates the right to believe and to change one's faith. It was acknowledged that "a tension exists between traditional religions in their perceived role in maintaining historical values and the rights of new indigenous religious groups." Participants stressed the need to achieve a balance between individual rights and cultural and historical interests.

Freedom of religion in education also received attention at the seminar. In many of the participating OSCE countries the tenets of the majority religion or religions are taught in the public schools. Recognition of this fact led to a discussion regarding proselytism and the wearing of religious symbols in public schools.[100] One of the groups noted that most religions engage in persuasion at some level, including promises of spiritual or material benefits—an uncharted area of law that remains unclear in many of the human rights instruments.[101]

## FRAMEWORK CONVENTION ON MINORITIES

The Council of Europe Committee of Ministers adopted the Framework Convention on November 10, 1994. The Framework Convention for the Protection of National Minorities does not specifically mention the issues of change of religion and proselytism, but several of its articles are clearly relevant. To be seen accurately, the Framework Convention must be viewed in the context of connected instruments, such as the European Convention on Human Rights and the OSCE documents.

The preamble of the Framework Convention refers to the need to respect the religious identity of each person belonging to a national minority.[102] A pluralist and genuinely democratic society "should create appropriate conditions enabling [each person] to express, preserve and develop this identity." Under Article 5(1) religion is seen as an essential element of the identity of national minorities. Article 6(1) states that societies should encourage a "spirit of tolerance and intercultural dialogue, irrespective of religious identity or other factors." Under Article 7, the freedoms of peaceful assembly, association, expression, thought, conscience, and religion should be respected. Under Article

8, every member of a minority has the right to manifest his or her religion or belief and to establish religious institutions, organizations, and associations.

Article 12 dictates that states shall foster knowledge of, inter alia, the religion of the minorities as well as of the majority. Under Article 13(1), persons belonging to a national minority have the right to set up and to manage their own private educational establishments. Article 17, which draws upon provisions of the 1990 Document of the Copenhagen Meeting of the CSCE Conference on the Human Dimension, requires free and peaceful contacts across frontiers with persons staying in other states with whom they share, inter alia, a religious identity.

## CASE LAW

International case law on religious matters is scarce. The European Court of Human Rights has dealt with religion and education in a few cases. In *Hoffman v. Austria* the court reviewed an Austrian Supreme Court case. The Austrian court had held that the father should receive parental rights over his children because the applicant-mother (his ex-wife) was raising the children according to the principles of Jehovah's Witnesses. Overturning lower rulings, the highest Austrian tribunal held that its decision was required by Austrian law, which prohibited changing a child's religion without the consent of both parents. The European Court found the Austrian decision to be in violation of the 1950 European Convention. Specifically, it violated Article 14, because it involved discrimination on the basis of religion in the exercise of Article 8. The European Court decided that the interests of the child are paramount. Using this benchmark, the court reasoned that the applicant's views on blood transfusions posed a risk to the children, and the court thus awarded custody to the father.[103]

In another relevant decision, *Otto Preminger Institute v. Austria*, the European Court stressed the need for toleration when others propagate doctrines hostile to one's own faith.[104] The court took into consideration the religious feelings of the affected population and rejected an Austrian regional court's seizure of a film. Other cases, such as *Angelini v. Sweden, Hartikainen v. Finland*, and *Kjeldsen et al. v. Denmark*, have already been mentioned earlier in this chapter.

### THE KOKKINAKIS CASE

The *Kokkinakis* case is the first decision of an international tribunal on the issue of proselytism.[105] The division of the nine-judge chamber and the criticism by legal commentators reflect and underscore the controversial nature of the case.[106] The European Commission on Human Rights concluded unanimously that *Kokkinakis* involved a violation of Article 9 of the European Convention. On May 25, 1993, the European Court on Human Rights followed this opinion. The court decided by a 6 to 3 vote that Article 9 had been violated; it decided by 8 votes to 1 that Article 7 of the Convention had not been breached; and it unanimously found it unnecessary to examine the case under Article 10 or under Article 14 taken together with Article 9. The court required Greece, the respondent state, to pay the applicant, Mr. Kokkinakis, two monetary judgments: one amount to compensate his nonpecuniary damage, and a second, larger amount for costs and expenses.

Minos Kokkinakis, an elderly Greek businessman, was born in 1919 into an Orthodox family in Crete. He became a Jehovah's Witness in 1936. Since then, authorities had arrested him more than sixty times for proselytism. He has been interned and imprisoned on several occasions and was the first member of the Jehovah's Witnesses to be convicted under Greece's respective constitutional and legal provisions against proselytism. Greek courts now frequently apply these provisions.

In 1986 Mr. Kokkinakis and his wife visited the home of a Mrs. Kyriakaki, in Sitia, Crete, and initiated a discussion with her. Mr. Kyriakaki, the cantor of a local Orthodox church, informed the police, who subsequently arrested the couple. Mr. and Mrs. Kokkinakis were later prosecuted under Law 1363/1938, which makes proselytism an offense, and were tried at the Lasithi Criminal Court. On March 20, 1986, the court found both Mr. and Mrs. Kokkinakis guilty of proselytism and sentenced each to four months in prison, commutable into a pecuniary penalty. The court also ordered the confiscation and destruction of the booklets they had tried to sell.

Mr. and Mrs. Kokkinakis appealed to the Crete Court of Appeal, which quashed Mrs. Kokkinakis's conviction. The court upheld her husband's conviction but reduced it to three months in prison, also commutable. Mr. Kokkinakis appealed on points of law, claiming that the 1938 law contravened the Greek Constitution. On April 22, 1988, the Court of Cassation rejected the plea of unconstitutionality, as it had always done in the past.

On August 22, 1988, Mr. Kokkinakis applied to the European Commission on Human Rights. The commission declared the application partially admissible and ultimately decided that there had been a violation of Article 9. When the case came to the European Court, the court analyzed the general principles involved as enshrined in Article 9. Article 9 sees freedom of thought, conscience, and religion as one of the foundations of a democratic society and one of the most vital elements constituting the identity of believers and their conception of life. It is also "a precious asset for atheists, agnostics, skeptics and the unconcerned." It also includes, in principle, the right to try to convince one's neighbor—through teaching, for example.

The European Court found that the sentences of the Greek courts amounted to an interference with the right and freedom to manifest one's religion or belief. Such an interference was contrary to Article 9, unless it was: (1) "prescribed by law"; (2) directed at one or more of the legitimate aims in Article 9(2); and (3) "necessary in a democratic society" for achieving those aims. The court analyzed each side's argument, noting that the wording of many of the statutes is rather vague—including criminal law provisions on proselytism. The court also declared that the constitutionality of a law should be interpreted by its national authorities.

Considering the circumstances of the case and the terms of the judicial decisions, the court held that the impugned measure was in pursuit of a legitimate aim under Article 9(2)—the protection of the rights and freedoms of others. Mr. Kokkinakis contended that, in a democratic society, it is not necessary to limit a person's right to speak to a neighbor about religion, that such a conversation cannot be made a criminal offense, and that he had been convicted not for something he had done but rather for what he was. In examining these arguments the court referred to the government's allegations. These allegations included Mr. Kokkinakis's insistence on entering the Kyriakaki home under false pretenses and his skillful analysis of the religious texts calculated to delude the complainant, who did not possess an adequate grounding in doctrine.

The court recognized that individual states retain a margin of appreciation. However, the court held that this margin is subject to European supervision; this holds true for both legislation and the decisions applying the legislation, and includes the decisions of an independent court. The court must look at the impugned judicial decisions against the background of the case as a whole. Here, the European Court made a controversial distinction

> between bearing Christian witness and improper proselytism. The former corresponds to true evangelism. . . . The latter represents a corruption or deformation of it. It may . . . take the form of activities offering material or social advantages with a view to gaining new members of a Church or exerting improper pressure on people in distress or in need; it may even entail the use of violence or brainwashing. . . . [107]

The court's distinction, based on a 1956 document of the World Council of Churches, has received criticism.[108]

The court noted that the Greek tribunals did not sufficiently specify in what way the accused had utilized "improper means," nor did they show that the applicant's conviction was justified by a "pressing social need." "The contested measure therefore does not appear to have been proportionate to the legitimate aim pursued or, consequently, necessary in a democratic society . . . for the protection of the rights and freedoms of others."

Judge Pettiti issued a partly concurring opinion.[109] In his view the current Greek criminal legislation on proselytism was in itself contrary to Article 9 of the European Convention. *Kokkinakis* was the first real case concerning freedom of religion to come before the European Court. Freedom of religion and conscience entails "accepting proselytism even where it is 'not respectable.' . . . The only limits on the exercise of this right are those dictated by respect for the rights of others where there is an attempt to coerce the person into consenting or to use manipulative techniques."[110] States may legislate against "brainwashing, breaches of labor law, endangering of public health and incitement to immorality . . . found in the practices of certain pseudo-religious groups," in order to avoid abuses and deviation leading to attempts at brainwashing. Such activities may be alleviated by ordinary civil and criminal law. However, states may *not* regulate legitimate proselytism under the guise of eliminating the above activities. Noncriminal proselytism remains the mere expression of freedom of religion.[111]

Judge Pettiti dissented from the majority's view that the applicant's conviction was not justified under the circumstances. In his opinion the majority's wording leaves too much room for a repressive interpretation by the Greek courts in the future. He opined that permissible limits of proselytism can be defined. Examples include cases of coercion, abuse of one's rights in a way that infringes the rights of others, and manipulation by methods that lead to a violation of conscience.[112]

Judge Valtikos dissented radically from the court's decision. He accepted the definition of proselytism provided by Greek criminal law, which defines proselytism as

> any direct or indirect attempt to intrude on the religious beliefs of a person of a different religious persuasion, with the aim of undermining those beliefs, either by any kind of inducement or promise of an inducement or moral support or material assistance, or by fraudulent means or by taking advantage of his inexperience, trust, need, low intellect or naivety.

He then added his own definition: "the rape of the belief of others."[113]

Judges Foighel and Loizou also dissented, finding no violation of Article 9(1). They stated that those engaged in teaching their religion have a duty to respect the religion of others. Religious tolerance implies respect for the religious beliefs of others. "The persistent efforts of some fanatics to convert others to their own beliefs by using unacceptable psychological techniques on people, which amount in effect to coercion, do not come within the meaning of the term teach."[114]

Judge Martens dissented in part. He, too, found a breach of Article 9, but for reasons different from those relied upon by the court. Article 7(1) of the convention had also been violated, in his view. Martens did not believe that Article 9 allows member states to make it a *criminal offense* to attempt to induce a person to change his or her religion. The freedoms of thought, conscience, and religion enshrined in Article 9(1) are absolute and involve the human rights principles of respecting human dignity and human freedom. It is not within the province of the state to interfere in the conflict between proselytizer and proselytized, except in some very special situations in which the state has a particular duty of care. This holds true even when one particular religion enjoys a dominant position in a state. Martens added that the "rising tide" of religious intolerance makes it imperative to keep the state's powers in this field within "the strictest possible boundaries." Unfortunately, the court attempted to settle those boundaries by means of the elusive notion of improper proselytism, which the court left undefined. Except when an ordinary crime is involved, civil law, not criminal law, should prescribe the legal remedies for proselytism.[115]

The *Kokkinakis* decision is of great importance because it was the first full pronouncement on proselytism by an international court. Since Article 9 of the European Convention follows the wording of Articles 18 of the Universal Declaration and of the International Covenant on Civil and Political Rights, the case acquires a universal dimension.

Prior to *Kokkinakis* the European Court had made passing reference to the issue of misplaced proselytism but had not addressed the topic directly.[116] The European Commission on Human Rights dealt with a number of cases involving Article 9, but this time the issue of proselytism as a whole came before the court. Article 9 was dealt with (but not applied) in only one of the cases considered admissible by the commission prior to *Kokkinakis*.[117]

The court's decision engendered much criticism. However, this was foreseeable, given the varying points of view in the opinion. T. Jeremy Gunn observes that the court was moving toward a predetermined result from the very beginning, and that the court did not examine carefully the arguments before it. The court "made no effort to understand or interpret the scope of the fundamental right to manifest a belief," and was "satisfied that several earlier decisions from Greek courts had sufficiently defined the offense of proselytism."[118] Gunn criticizes the court for ignoring the vagueness problem, for finding that the Greek government had a legitimate aim when restricting manifestations of belief, and for focusing exclusively on Mr. Kokkinakis's specific conviction rather than considering the anti-proselytism statute as a whole. The court "refused to criticize the law that had been repeatedly used to incarcerate minority believers." The decision, therefore, exemplifies the European Court's failure "to take rights of conscience seriously" and to require governments to impose less restrictive burdens on manifestations of freedom of religion and conscience. It also shows a bias against nontraditional, nonmainstream religions. Gunn emphasizes the court's bias against non-Christian religions. He also describes Judge Valtikos's dissenting opinion as vituperative—"an opinion that would be unimaginable by a judge in the United States in the 1990s."[119]

Rigaux also attacked the dissenting judge's language, arguing that it was out of place in a decision that should respect the rule of religious pluralism and the equality between different forms of beliefs.[120] In his view the court had a duty to verify the constitutionality of the particular legislation and to determine when the incrimination of proselytism violates freedom of expression in religious matters.

Garay reviewed the extent to which European national constitutions and legislation generally protect the freedom of religious expression; Greece is an exception. He points out that religious minorities do not generally suffer in Europe due to a refusal to recognize their spiritual identity; they suffer because society is organized in a way that reflects the dominating religious cultures. In this way the neutrality of the state becomes a myth. Garay referred to the dangers involved in radical forms of proselytism that may, in some cases, become a threat to human rights. He also elaborated on possible abuses that may emanate from monopolistic situations in public education and from the intensive, exclusive use of the primary means of communication by the majority religion for religious purposes.[121]

In conclusion, in spite of the weaknesses pointed out, *Kokkinakis* is important because of its scope and the opportunity it afforded the court to deal with the issue of proselytism. The diverse views of the members of the court reflect the difficulties involved.

## THE LARISSIS CASE

The *Case of Larissis and Others v. Greece* provided the European Court of Human Rights with an opportunity to consider the legitimacy of proselytizing persons under military duty, namely, what has been described as a captive audience.[122] This is an important aspect that did not come up in the *Kokkinakis* case. In the judgment, delivered at Strasbourg on February 24, 1998, the court held that there had been no violation of Article 7 of the European Convention, that there had been no violation of Article 9, in respect of measures taken against the applicants for proselytizing airmen, and that there had been a violation of Article 9 in respect of measures taken against them for proselytizing civilians. The applicants were awarded nonpecuniary damages and legal costs and expenses.

The three applicants were Greek citizens. At all material times they were officers in the Greek Air Force and followers of the Pentecostal Church. They were accused of approaching, during the years 1986 to 1989, several airmen serving under them, all of them Orthodox Christians, trying to convey to them the teachings of the Pentecostal Church. Two of the three applicants were also accused of attempting to convert a number of civilians. They were charged with offenses of proselytism under section 4 of Law No. 1363/1938.[123] In 1992 the applicants stood trial before the Permanent Air Force Court of Athens. The claim that section 4 was unconstitutional was dismissed, and the applicants were convicted of proselytism against airmen and civilians. They were sentenced to various terms of imprisonment, not to be enforced provided that they did not commit new offenses in the following three years. The applicants appealed to the Court-Martial Appeal Court, which upheld the judgment but reduced the sentences. An appeal to the Court of Cassation on points of law was dismissed in 1993. The court did not find any contravention of the Greek Constitution or of Article 9 of the European Convention on Human Rights.

In 1994 the applicants started proceedings before the European Commission. They were declared admissible in November 1995, there was no friendly settlement, and the commission adopted, on September 12, 1996, a report establishing the facts and expressing its opinion. The commission declared that Article 9 of the convention had been violated insofar as two of the applicants were convicted for the proselytism of civilians. There had been no violation of Article 9 insofar as the applicants were convicted for the proselytism of airmen. The commission also decided, by 28 votes to 1, that there had been no violation of Article 7, and, unanimously, that no separate issue arose under Article 10 or under Article 14 taken in conjunction with Article 9.

The court took up the case on October 28, 1996. The court referred to the *Kokkinakis* case and did not see any difference with regard to its interpretation of the Greek law in the 1993 case. There was therefore no violation of Article 7.[124] The measures in question were prescribed by law and had the legitimate aim of protecting the rights and freedoms of others. The court emphasized that religious freedom implied freedom to manifest one's religion, including the right to try to convince one's neighbor. Article 9 did not, however, protect improper proselytism, such as the offering of material or social advantage or the application of improper pressure with a view to gaining new members for a church. Since different factors came into the balance in relation to the proselytizing of the airmen and that of the civilians, the two matters had to be assessed separately.

States might, in certain circumstances, be justified in taking special measures to protect subordinate members of the armed forces from harassment or abuse of power. Subordinates could find it difficult to rebuff the approaches of an individual of superior rank or to withdraw from a conversion initiated by him. The court found that the three airmen with whom the applicants had discussed religion appeared to have felt themselves constrained and subject to a certain degree of pressure owing to the applicants' status as officers. The measures taken against the applicants were not particularly severe and were not disproportionate. There had not been therefore a violation of Article 9 in relation to the proselytizing of the airmen.

The case with the civilians came out differently. They were not under constraints of the same kind as the airmen, and they did not require special protection. The court considered that the applicants did not act improperly toward the civilians and that the measures taken against them in this respect were unjustified and amounted to a violation of Article 9.[125]

The court decided that no separate issues arose under Article 10 or under Article 14 and 9 taken together.[126] The court awarded, by way of compensation for nonpecuniary damage, GRD 500,000 (US$1,556) to each of the two applicants in respect of whom it had found a violation of Article 9, as well as legal costs and expenses.

## CONCLUSIONS

This present chapter deals with proselytism and its limits, and the right to change one's religion within the framework of modern international human rights law as developed in the United Nations era. The following conclusions may be deduced.

First, the right to proselytize and try to convince people to adopt a specific religion, on the one hand, and the right of a person to abandon and/or change his or her religion, on the other, are closely connected. These are not absolute rights, and some societies have placed restrictions on both of them. Proselytism is related to the freedoms of expression, association, scientific research and work, and teaching; change of religion is related to the right to opt-out of organized religious frameworks, congregations, or churches—a matter that is regulated in some societies. Where religious frameworks are regulated by law, the right to join an organized religion may also require some formalities. Complicated situations exist in countries where family law is under the influence of religion.

Second, to the extent that the freedoms of thought, conscience, and religion belong to the strict internal forum, they cannot be interfered with except by applying techniques that only totalitarian states have the power to impose. It is the right to manifest religious views, expressed through proselytizing activities or through formal steps to change one's religious framework, that may require regulation and protection.

Third, in a democratic society people should be free to disseminate their religious views. They should not be silenced simply because some people prefer not to hear those views. There is, however, a right to privacy, and uninvited speech should not necessarily prevail over this right.

Fourth, this is particularly true when proselytism is conducted in places where people are present by force of law and constitute a captive audience: classrooms, military installations, prisons, hospitals, and the like. Exposing people in captive audiences to undesired or uninvited proselytism may be considered a violation of their rights and a form of coercion. The *Larissis* case is relevant in this respect.

Fifth, proselytism involving material enticement—money, gifts, or privileges—should be considered a form of coercion and, thus, may be limited by law. Such material enticements exceed the area of freedom of speech and expression. However, the borderline cases are not easy to judge.

Sixth, one of the limits of the right to proselytism is the protection of communal or collective identities. Minority rights are relevant to this concept. The international community has been reluctant to abandon the individualistic approach followed since the establishment of the United Nations. A change in this approach seems necessary since group rights deserve to be protected.

Seventh, religious rights and education are closely connected. Religious education is therefore a difficult area requiring careful treatment. State education may include religious teachings, but within certain limits. When the teaching becomes proselytism and affects children whose parents or legal guardians are against exposing them to such teachings, precautionary provisions are necessary. International judicial activity has taken place in this area, although almost exclusively in Europe.

Eighth, a downward or deteriorating trend in the recognition of both rights—to proselytize and to change one's religion—has characterized international instruments. The 1948 Universal Declaration is far-reaching in both respects; the 1966 Covenants had to use milder language; the 1981 Declaration was in danger of not being adopted if a compromise had not been reached. This could mean that there has been a change in the attitude of the international community in this respect. Alternatively, it could simply evidence a growing split of opinion that can no longer be readily resolved.

Ninth, Western international lawyers argue that the international attitude has not changed. U.N. special rapporteurs consider the change of wording to be more or less cosmetic or superficial; they claim that no interpretation limiting the scope of these rights is acceptable, as proclaimed in the Universal Declaration and in the ICCPR. Article 8 of the 1981 Declaration was intended to safeguard those rights. Representatives of some religious communities take a different view, claiming that their communities cannot be expected to depart from deeply rooted traditions. In view of the intensity of their objections, it seems difficult to assert that these opponents should be expected to consider the rights to change religion and to proselytize as reflecting binding customary law for them. The issue of universalism versus particularism is relevant in this respect. For example, the particular situation of indigenous populations must be contemplated.

Tenth, the Human Rights Committee's General Comment on Article 18 follows the classic universalist approach. Jurisprudence is scarce in this respect. The delays and difficulties in the quest for a mandatory treaty on religious rights are, however, an indication of the ideological controversy. In recent years religious fundamentalism and the confusion between politics and human rights, particularly in the religious sphere, have further complicated the issue.

Proselytism and the right to change one's religion are, of course, not absolute rights. However, they do need to be protected and, to that effect, legal formulation seems to be rather pressing.

# Summary and Conclusions

————————◆————————

In this book I have tried to provide a concise picture of how modern human rights law protects freedom of religion and belief while highlighting the shortcomings of the system. When writing about *human rights law*, I have been mostly referring to the positive international law that has been developed mainly after the establishment of the United Nations. When writing about *freedom of religion and belief*, I have been referring to the enjoyment of individual and collective rights related to religion and belief as well as to the rights of the collective entity, such as a religious group or community.

Human rights is a concept that has evolved, gradually, long before the twentieth century, and its roots can be traced to ancient religious teachings. Those teachings have been variously expressed in natural law, the ideas of pluralism and toleration, the preoccupation with the rights of minority groups, and the general principles of international and constitutional law. Nevertheless, it is only since 1948 that it is appropriate to refer to human rights law as a coherent system of principles and rules, some of them *jus cogens*, or peremptory norms, that may have reached an autonomous status within international, constitutional, criminal, family, and humanitarian law.

That modern human rights are organized as a system implies that all human rights are universal, indivisible, and interdependent. Nevertheless, the wide spectrum of global and regional instruments intended to guarantee and protect human rights have fundamental dissimilarities. Although human rights related to religion and belief are acknowledged, they have been neglected by the international community. This may be a consequence of the profound sentiments and emotions that religious beliefs provoke among followers and adversaries.

Human rights law, including laws generated by the United Nations and regional instruments, does not define the term *religion*. Nor does domestic law provide a suitable definition, despite judicial efforts. The desire to avoid ideological or philosophical controversy has prevailed, and agreements between states that are influenced by different religious creeds are more easily attained by avoiding specific references to religion. Despite potentially conflicting views as to what *religion* means, human rights texts have been able to express a basic agreement: in United Nations law and in modern human rights law more generally, the term *religion* or *belief* means theistic convictions involving a transcendental view of the universe and a normative code of behavior, as well as atheistic, agnostic, rationalistic, and other views in which both elements are absent.

Whether this notion of religion includes sects, cults, or new religious movements is debatable. Human rights instruments, in general, do not use this terminology. The word *sect*, despite its original neutral meaning, has a pejorative connotation today that cannot be dissociated from tragic events involving some groups with questionable religious aspirations. Groups or sects with legitimate religious aims must therefore be wary of gratuitous violations of freedom of religion. Several governments have taken steps to clarify the issue, and the United Nations special rapporteur on freedom of religion, who has reviewed the problem in several countries, has recommended further study.

Another delicate problem is the attempt to establish a balance between the universality of human rights and idiosyncrasies of particular religions. The aim of such balancing should be to reach a minimum standard acceptable to all cultures and religions.

When attempting such balancing, it is important to keep in mind that religion is the result of deeply rooted cultural, anthropological, social, and historical factors. These factors are so deeply rooted that they can determine group membership irrespective of individual preferences or will. Religion is based on faith, and faith is, of course, an individual phenomenon. But religious rights are also collective rights and encompass the rights of an entire group or community. Therefore, it is imperative to establish a catalog of rights to protect religion at the three levels indicated in this book, namely, the individual level, the joint or collective level, and the level of the group as such. International law, as expressed in instruments of the United Nations, has tried to provide such a catalog.

Chapter 1 discussed the evolution of the United Nations approach to the protection of religion and belief. It was in the period following World War II that specific steps regarding religious rights were taken. This was done on a gradual basis, with an evident emphasis on individual rights and the rule of nondiscrimination.

The 1981 Declaration contains the most detailed catalogue of both individual and group religious rights, and they have been analyzed at length in this book. The draft convention was also reviewed. At this stage it appears that further work on the convention has been suspended, and there is little hope that it will be renewed. The fact that the special rapporteurs on the 1981 Declaration have been able to develop their own monitoring system makes the need for a convention less urgent. Moreover, member-states of the United Nations are expected to cooperate with the special rapporteurs, thus creating greater compliance than a treaty that is only followed by ratifying states.

With the exception of the minorities system under the League of Nations, international law did not concern itself with religious groups until recently, even though discrimination is generally based on group membership. This can be explained in part by the fact that religious issues are sometimes complicated by the difficulty of separating ethnicity and cultural background from religious affiliation.

Religious groups are collective entities and not mere aggregations of individuals. Sometimes they may not be part of well-established, historical religions, and this can make a particular religion hard to define. In addition, some religions lack the permanency that could more readily help to identify them. Individuals can, in principle, voluntarily change their religion or adopt certain procedures or beliefs of a major religion in order to form a minor one. But unless individual decisions lead to mass movement, the most common religious groups will continue their existence.

I have mentioned the League of Nations system for the protection of minorities. For the purposes of this book, this protection was significant because it extended to religious minorities and it established an important precedent for the United Nations' work on religious rights. The League of Nations system failed because of political circumstances, but it still contained elements that could help ensure basic rights of religious minorities. These rights not only included freedom from discrimination but also addressed issues of equality, free exercise of religion, use of minority languages, establishment of institutions of charitable, religious, or educational nature, and other rights likely to provide a reasonable *modus vivendi* for minority groups within a pluralistic society.

Under the United Nations the prewar mechanisms addressing the rights of minorities ceased to exist, and a completely different approach prevailed. The United Nations Charter does not refer to minorities. Instead, it reflects the view that the protection of individual rights is primary. Minority rights, collective rights, and group rights are treated as suspect. This attitude continues to manifest itself today in new international instruments, despite the fact that recent events show the need to go beyond a system based on purely individual rights. The Convention on Genocide, with its emphasis on rights of minorities, is an exception and was therefore examined in a chapter addressing the protection of religious groups from persecution.

Nevertheless, the present system of protecting human rights related to religion has developed concurrently with the existence of the United Nations. This was the result of the adoption of instruments developed at the initiative or under the aegis of the United Nations. Similar initiatives and programs of regional organizations, mainly in Europe, have also been important. Yet the current system, which is still evolving, has provided limited protection of religious freedoms. Protective provisions do exist, and they have exercised a considerable influence on domestic legislation. But there is no mandatory global treaty regarding religious human rights.

Article 18 of the International Covenant on Civil and Political Rights, based on Article 18 of the Universal Declaration on Human Rights, and other provisions related to religious rights in the covenants and in other treaties, are, of course, mandatory for the states that have ratified them. Many of these are seen today as reflecting customary international law. Some, such as the prohibition of discrimination on grounds of religion or the outlawing of genocide against religious groups, belong to the restricted category of *jus cogens*. Freedom of religion is one of the fundamental rights that cannot be derogated in states of emergency. The 1981 Declaration on the Elimination of All Forms of Intolerance and Discrimination Based on Religion or Belief produced a coherent picture of human rights principles in the broad sphere of religion and belief. The Human Rights Committee issued a General Comment that constitutes an authoritative source for the implementation of the covenant clauses. But many claim that this is not enough, particularly at a time when international and intranational tensions are strongly connected with religious problems and conflicts.

It is against this background that a discussion on the need for a treaty on religious rights is taking place. The main argument in favor of preparing such a binding instrument is the desire to give religious rights an affirmative protection that is granted to other basic rights. Arguments against it include the risk of trying to find a mutually satisfying compromise among many states and the possible reluctance of some states to ratify a mandatory instrument that might clash with long-established systems of law, especially as those systems relate to religious and interpersonal issues. These arguments have been more fully explored in chapter 1.

Chapter 2 provided an overview of regional protections of religious human rights in Europe, America, Africa, and Islam. The most elaborated system is that of Europe and encompasses the European Convention for the Protection of Human Rights and Fundamental Freedoms and the Organization (formerly Conference) on Security and Cooperation in Europe. The principles of the European system are fundamentally similar to the United Nations system, although the European system is more effective at implementation. In fact, the monitoring mechanisms and the institutional framework for the protection of human rights developed by the Council of Europe, the OSCE, and the European Union have produced important case law precedent with regard to religious rights. Specifically, this case law has addressed a number of issues including the manifestation of religious rights, religious education, freedom of expression, conscientious objection, medical issues, parental rights, employment, blasphemy, and proselytism.

In America, by comparison, the 1960 Convention on Human Rights followed the model of the universal texts vis-à-vis religious rights. A preexisting Commission on Human Rights has been in charge of monitoring, and there is an Inter-American Court on Human Rights in place to settle disputes. But few cases concerning religion have come to the attention of the monitoring institutions because of both institutional and political exigencies and a focus on other basic human freedoms.

While the African Charter on Human and Peoples' Rights guarantees freedom of conscience and free practice of religion, the African Commission on Human Rights has failed to determine clearly what constitutes violation of freedom of conscience. Islam is a world religion and not a regional system, but it nevertheless has had a major influence on religious rights. In fact, the 1990 Cairo Declaration on Human Rights reflects the Islamic approach. This is noteworthy because Islamic law contains rules that may contradict modern human rights formulations.

Chapter 3 addressed the ways of protecting religious groups from persecution and incitement. This issue cannot be analyzed in isolation and must be considered in connection with other measures intended to prevent attacks against groups, regardless of whether they are religious in orientation. The prohibition of discrimination is well grounded in international law; it now becomes necessary to extend that prohibition to religious persecution. Along with analyzing specific provisions of the instruments on religion, this chapter addressed (1) the relevance of the Convention on Racial Discrimination, particularly Article 4; (2) group libel or defamation; and (3) international criminal law, specifically the outlawing of genocide and "ethnic cleansing." The phrase *ethnic cleansing* must be interpreted to include religion, because "ethnic cleansing" is often motivated by religious hatred.

The Convention on Racial Discrimination was originally intended to be part of two parallel sets of instruments: a declaration and convention on racial discrimination, and a declaration and convention on religious discrimination and intolerance. Article 4, the result of controversial compromise, is relevant when interpreting the provisions of the Declaration on Religion. The first General Recommendation that was adopted by the Committee on the Elimination of Racial Discrimination (CERD) overrode objections by asserting that the implementation by states parties of the provisions envisaged in Article 4 is obligatory, and, if domestic legislation is not sufficient, it should be supplemented by adequate additional measures. In other words, CERD determined that the application of Article 4 is mandatory, not discretionary.

A formula (known as "with due regard") was introduced to help states support the rules of free expression and freedom of association. This formula, however, was not accepted without reluctance. For example, the use of the term *hatred* was troubling to some states because the term does not describe a clearly established legal interest. Rules outlawing racist organizations and propaganda were also seen as vague. Until universal definitions are achieved, however, Article 4 and other provisions of the convention will serve as essential ways to extend protection to religion and religious groups.

Along with the Convention on Racial Discrimination, other instruments have addressed the issue of protecting religious groups from persecution. The controversial International Religious Freedom Act, signed by the president of the United States in October 1998, is one such example. Even though this does not technically qualify as international law, it does have obvious international implications.

*Group libel* or defamation is one concept that might help religious groups to achieve protection from prosecution. But lawyers are divided in this respect.

Strict civil libertarians view the acceptance of group libel as a risk to freedom of expression. Some insist that the victims of libel should always be identifiable persons. Furthermore, the mechanics of group representation creates legal uncertainty. There are new proposals for legislation in this area, and several countries have already adopted legislation making it possible for affected groups to make a claim. Additionally, several of the main international instruments also contain some sort of group libel provision.

The final part of chapter 3 addressed international criminal law, which is a particularly salient area given the recent tragic events in former Yugoslavia and Rwanda. The crimes committed in these and other places have provoked the Security Council to establish ad hoc tribunals that deal with such crimes. Additionally, in June 1998 a world conference that took place in Rome decided to establish a general international criminal court, and this has been seen as an important step toward the codification and implementation of penal law at the international level. The birth of this court was not without objection, but it was eventually adopted by a large majority.

The main legal text in this area, and the first human rights treaty adopted by the United Nations, is the 1948 Convention on the Prevention and Punishment of the Crime of Genocide. Genocide is a crime, in the words of the International Court of Justice, that involves "a denial of the right of existence of entire human rights groups, a denial which shocks the conscience of mankind and results in great losses to humanity. . . . " The prohibition of genocide, whether committed in time of peace or war, is seen today as part of *jus cogens*, but the convention has exerted little influence in preventing genocidal situations. The convention does not provide measures of implementation, and it therefore requires updating. Despite this shortcoming, the convention remains a significant part of evolution of international criminal law over the past five decades.

The phrase *ethnic cleansing* has been used frequently to refer to the tragic events in former Yugoslavia. In general, the phrase has described a form of genocide, or a war crime, or a crime against humanity, or a hate crime. The phrase also refers to the motivation behind the offense. In all cases the religious affiliation of the victims was significant, and religious sites and monuments were targeted as an extension of the policy. As defined by a U.N. special rapporteur on religious rights, "ethnic cleansing" is aimed at eradicating the religious and cultural base of ethnic communities living in a given area in order to encourage their departure and prevent their eventual return.

The United Nations has reacted to such policies. For example, the General Assembly has adopted several resolutions, and the Security Council has established special tribunals to address the situations in former Yugoslavia and Rwanda. These responses, developed in connection with chapter VII of the United Nations Charter, were important factors in the recent decision on the permanent international criminal court. The General Assembly has equated "ethnic cleansing" with racist hatred, and views "ethnic cleansing" as a violation of both humanitarian and human rights law.

The Human Rights Committee and the Committee on the Elimination of Racial Discrimination as well as other U.N. bodies define *ethnic* as a distinct group of ethnic, racial, religious, or cultural characteristics. Other documents view "ethnic cleansing" as a corollary to "the principle that persons of different religions . . . could not live side by side."

In conclusion, many international texts and instruments should be considered when describing the steps taken by the international community to protect religious groups. These include specific anti-discrimination treaties and rules of criminal law intended to guarantee the rights of religiously based groups.

Chapter 4 addressed the issue of proselytism and change of religion. The controversy on the right to proselytize has become a major obstacle to the adoption of a mandatory treaty addressing religious rights. The freedom to teach one's religion and convince others to join a particular creed, and the right of a person to abandon or change his or her religion, involve the freedom of expression and association as well as the relationship between organized religion and its members. Family law is also affected in countries where religion predominates. While individual freedom of thought, conscience, and religion is generally irreproachable, it sometimes requires protection and regulation when threatened by aggressive proselytism.

In a democratic society everyone should be free to disseminate religious views, whether or not they are shared by the majority. But there is also a right to privacy. Uninvited speech should not necessarily prevail over this right to privacy, particularly when proselytism is conducted in places where people are constructively captive. Such places include military installations, schools, prisons, and hospitals. Proselytism conducted in those places can be coercive, especially when done against the will of the recipient. There is also a coercive effect when proselytism involves material inducement (money, gifts, or privileges). Such material inducement exceeds freedom of speech. The dividing line, however, is not absolutely clear. In the *Larissis* case the European Court of Human Rights decided that proselytism conducted among members of the armed forces is improper, while it may be legitimate when the targets are civilians. This decision followed the *Kokkinakis* case, where the issue of proselytism was first considered by an international court.

Communities and collective identities warrant protection, especially when minority rights are concerned. Issues involving religious education also require careful treatment. State education may include religious teachings, but those limits should be defined. European case law has tried to define the limits, but they are elusive because religious rights and education are often closely intertwined.

The legislative history of the international instruments dealing with religious rights—especially the 1948 Universal Declaration, the 1966 Covenants, and the 1981 Declaration—shows the extent to which proselytism and change of religion were major obstacles to agreement. A comparison of the wording of these three documents shows an erosion in the recognition of these rights. While Western jurists and U.N. rapporteurs consider the changes to be only slight, spokesmen for some religious communities take a different view, claiming that religiously based communities cannot be expected to give up deeply rooted traditions. For them, the right to change religion or proselytize should not be overridden by secular law. They further assert that cultural relativism should not be beholden to universalism. The particular situation of indigenous populations was contemplated in some texts. For example, when Muslim states objected to the original wording of the Universal Declaration, softer language was used in subsequent texts.

The classic universalistic approach was followed by the Human Rights Committee's important General Comment of 1993. The insistence on this approach was partly responsible for a lack of progress toward a treaty on religious rights. The controversy between universalism and cultural relativism cannot be dissociated from the recent advances in religious fundamentalism and the murkiness between human rights and political issues.

In conclusion, proselytism and change of religion are recognized rights, although not absolute rights. They belong, with some limitations, to a current minimum common standard that is incorporated into human rights law. A clash between rights might occur when the right to teach one's religious ideas endangers privacy or affects captive audiences. Limits to the right to proselytize may also be imposed in order to avoid offending the religious sensibilities of others. Change of religion is sometimes subjected to formal restrictions when applied to religious communities that are regulated by law.

The recent events in Russia and other areas of the former Soviet bloc show the impact of proselytism on certain societies. International case law, particularly in Europe, underscores the connection between this subject and other human rights areas. When developing a catalogue of human rights related to religion and beliefs, one cannot overlook the importance of proselytism.

Since the establishment of the United Nations, the international community has made considerable progress toward the consolidation of a legal order likely to ensure respect for and observance of religious rights. The result is not a perfect protective system and falls short of the progress made in the area of racial discrimination. Moreover, it appears at present that the development of religious rights has been beset by stagnation. In the past few years the United Nations General Assembly has played a limited role, merely calling upon states to ensure domestic guarantees of freedom of religion and belief and to express concern at attacks upon religious places and sites. This stagnation is particularly distressing when viewed in the context of the role that religion is playing in international life, especially as it becomes a predominant factor in the increase in tension and violence.

This book is being published at a time when the interaction between religious rights and the international world order is particularly tense. Alarmingly, little is being done to improve the legal system envisaged to ensure such rights, although such a system does exist. The time may be ripe to renew the debate on the need for a mandatory treaty. Even if it does not go beyond the provisions of the 1981 Declaration, a new treaty adopted and ratified by a significant number of states may be meaningful as the expression of the will of the international community.

In any case, human rights related to religion and belief should not remain a neglected chapter in the universal quest for a more secure international order.

# Appendix

# SELECTED INTERNATIONAL HUMAN RIGHTS INSTRUMENTS ON RELIGIOUS HUMAN RIGHTS

———————◆———————

## 1. UNIVERSAL DECLARATION OF HUMAN RIGHTS (1948)[1]

*Article 18.* Everyone has the right to freedom of thought, conscience and religion; this right includes freedom to change his religion or belief, and freedom, either alone or in community with others and in public or in private, to manifest his religion or belief in teaching, practice, worship and observance.

## 2. CONVENTION ON THE PREVENTION AND PUNISHMENT OF THE CRIME OF GENOCIDE (1948)[2]

*Article II.* In the present Convention, genocide means any of the following acts committed with intent to destroy, in whole or in part, a national, ethnical, racial or religious group, as such:
   a. Killing members of the group;
   b. Causing serious bodily or mental harm to members of the group;
   c. Deliberately inflicting on the group conditions of life calculated to bring about its physical destruction in whole or in part;
   d. Imposing measures intended to prevent births within the group;
   e. Forcibly transferring children of the group to another group.

## 3. EUROPEAN CONVENTION FOR THE PROTECTION OF HUMAN RIGHTS AND FUNDAMENTAL FREEDOMS (1950)[3]

*Article 9.*
1. Everyone has the right to freedom of thought, conscience and religion; this right includes freedom to change his religion or belief and freedom, either

alone or in community with others and in public or in private, to manifest his religion or belief, in worship, teaching, practice and observance.

2. Freedom to manifest one's religion or beliefs shall be subject only to such limitations as are prescribed by law and are necessary in a democratic society in the interests of public safety, for the protection of public order, health or morals, or for the protection of the rights and freedoms of others.

## 4. INTERNATIONAL CONVENTION ON THE ELIMINATION OF ALL FORMS OF RACIAL DISCRIMINATION (1965)[4]

*Article 4*. States Parties condemn all propaganda and all organizations which are based on ideas or theories of superiority of one race or group of persons of one colour or ethnic origin, or which attempt to justify or promote racial hatred and discrimination in any form, and undertake to adopt immediate and positive measures designed to eradicate all incitement to, or acts of, such discrimination and, to this end, with due regard to the principles embodied in the Universal Declaration of Human Rights and the rights expressly set forth in article 5 of this Convention, *inter alia*:

a. Shall declare an offence punishable by law all dissemination of ideas based on racial superiority or hatred, incitement to racial discrimination, as well as all acts of violence or incitement to such acts against any race or group of persons of another colour or ethnic origin, and also the provision of any assistance to racist activities, including the financing thereof;

b. Shall declare illegal and prohibit organizations, and also organized and all other propaganda activities, which promote and incite racial discrimination, and shall recognize participation in such organizations or activities as an offence punishable by law;

c. Shall not permit public authorities or public institutions, national or local, to promote or incite racial discrimination.

*Article 5*. In compliance with the fundamental obligations laid down in article 2 of this Convention, States Parties undertake to prohibit and to eliminate racial discrimination in all its forms and to guarantee the right of everyone, without distinction as to race, colour, or national or ethnic origin, to equality before the law, notably in the enjoyment of the following rights: . . .

(d) (vii) the right to freedom of thought, conscience and religion.

## 5. INTERNATIONAL COVENANT ON CIVIL AND POLITICAL RIGHTS (1966)[5]

*Article 18*.

1. Everyone shall have the right to freedom of thought, conscience and religion. This right shall include freedom to have or to adopt a religion or

belief of his choice, and freedom, either individually or in community with others and in public or private, to manifest his religion or belief in worship, observance, practice and teaching.

2. No one shall be subject to coercion which would impair his freedom to have or to adopt a religion or belief of his choice.

3. Freedom to manifest one's religion or beliefs may be subject only to such limitations as are prescribed by law and are necessary to protect public safety, order, health, or morals or the fundamental rights and freedoms of others.

4. The State Parties to the present Covenant undertake to have respect for the liberty of parents and, when applicable, legal guardians to ensure the religious and moral education of their children in conformity with their own convictions.

*Article 20.*

2. Any advocacy of national, racial or religious hatred that constitutes incitement to discrimination, hostility or violence shall be prohibited by law.

## 6. DRAFT CONVENTION ON THE ELIMINATION OF ALL FORMS OF RELIGIOUS INTOLERANCE (1965-1967)[6]

*Preamble*
*The States Parties to the Present Convention*

*Considering* that one of the basic principles of the Charter of the United Nations is that of the dignity and equality inherent in all human beings, and that all States Members have pledged themselves to take joint and separate action in co-operation with the Organization to promote and encourage universal respect for and observance of human rights and fundamental freedoms for all, without distinction as to race, sex, language or religion,

*Considering* that the Universal Declaration of Human Rights proclaims the principle of non-discrimination and the right to freedom of thought, conscience, religion and belief,

*Considering* that the disregard and infringement of human rights and fundamental freedoms, and in particular of the right to freedom of thought, conscience, religion and belief, have brought great suffering to mankind,

*Considering* that religion or belief, for anyone who professes either, is a fundamental element in his conception of life, and that freedom to practice religion as well as to manifest a belief should be fully respected and guaranteed,

*Considering* it essential that Governments, organizations and private persons should strive to promote through education, as well as by other means, understanding, tolerance and respect in matters relating to freedom of religion and belief,

*Noting with satisfaction* the coming into force of conventions concerning discrimination, inter alia, on the ground of religion, such as the International Labour Organization Convention on Discrimination in Respect to Employment and Occupation, adopted in 1958, the United Nations Educational, Scientific and Cultural Organization Convention against Discrimination in Education, adopted in 1960, and the United Nations Convention on the Prevention and punishment of the Crime of Genocide, adopted in 1948,

*Concerned* by manifestations of intolerance in such matters still in evidence in some areas of the world,

*Resolved* to adopt all necessary measures for eliminating speedily such intolerance in all its forms and manifestations and to prevent and combat discrimination on the ground of religion or belief,

*Have agreed as follows*:

## Article I

For the purpose of this Convention:

(a) The expression religion or belief shall include theistic, non-theistic and atheistic beliefs;

(b) The expression "discrimination on the ground of religion or belief" shall mean any distinction, exclusion, restriction or preference based on religion or belief which has the purpose or effect of nullifying or impairing the recognition, enjoyment or exercise, on an equal footing, of human rights and fundamental freedoms in the political, economic, social, cultural or any other field of public life;

(c) The expression religious intolerance shall mean intolerance in matters of religion or belief;

(d) Neither the establishment of a religion nor the recognition of a religion or belief by a State nor the separation of Church from State shall by itself be considered religious intolerance or discrimination on the ground of religion or belief; provided that this paragraph shall not be construed as permitting violation of specific provisions of this Convention.

## Article II

State Parties recognize that the religion or belief of an individual is a matter for his own conscience and must be respected accordingly. They condemn all forms of religious intolerance and all discrimination on the ground of religion or belief and undertake to promote and implement policies which are designed to protect freedom of thought, conscience, religion or belief, to secure religious tolerance and to eliminate all discrimination on the ground of religion or belief.

## Article III

1. State Parties undertake to ensure to everyone within their jurisdiction the right to freedom of thought, conscience, religion or belief. This right shall include:

(a) Freedom to adhere or not to adhere to any religion or belief and to change his religion or belief in accordance with the dictates of his conscience without being subjected either to any of the limitations referred to in Article XII or to any coercion likely to impair his freedom of choice or decision in the matter, provided that this sub-paragraph shall not be interpreted as extending to manifestations of religion or belief;

(b) Freedom to manifest his religion or belief either alone or in community with others, and in public or private, without being subjected to any discrimination on the ground of religion or belief;

(c) Freedom to express opinions on questions concerning a religion or belief.

2. State parties shall in particular ensure to everyone within their jurisdiction:

(a) Freedom to worship, to hold assemblies related to religion or belief and to establish and maintain places of worship or assembly for these purposes;

(b) Freedom to teach, to disseminate and to learn his religion or belief and its sacred languages or traditions, to write, print and publish religious books and texts, and to train personnel intending to devote themselves to its practices or observances;

(c) Freedom to practice his religion or belief by establishing and maintaining charitable and educational institutions and by expressing in public life the implications of religion or belief;

(d) Freedom to observe the rituals, dietary and other practices of his religion or belief and to produce or if necessary import the objects, foods and other articles and facilities customarily used in its observances and practices;

(e) Freedom to make pilgrimages and other journeys in connection with his religion or belief whether inside or outside his country;

(f) Equal legal protection for the places of worship or assembly, the rites, ceremonies and activities, and the places of disposal of the dead associated with his religion or belief;

(g) Freedom to organize and maintain local, regional, national and international associations in connection with his religion or belief, to participate in their activities, and to communicate with his co-religionists and believers;

(h) Freedom from compulsion to take an oath of a religious nature.

### Article IV

1. The State Parties undertake to respect the right of parents and, where applicable, legal guardians, to bring up in the religion or belief of their choice their children or wards who are as yet incapable of exercising the freedom of choice guaranteed under Article III, paragraph 1(a).

2. The exercise of this right carries with it the duty of parents and legal guardians to inculcate in their children or wards tolerance for the religion or belief of others, and to protect them from any precepts or practices based on religious intolerance or discrimination on the ground of religion or belief.

3. In the case of a child who has been deprived of his parents, their expressed or presumed wishes shall be duly taken into account.

4. In applying the provisions of this article, the best interests of the child shall be the guiding principle for those who are responsible for his upbringing and education.

### Article V

State Parties shall ensure to everyone freedom to enjoy and to exercise political, civic, economic, social and cultural rights without discrimination on the ground of religion or belief.

### Article VI

State Parties undertake to adopt immediate and effective measures, particularly in the fields of teaching, education, culture and information, with a view to combating prejudices as, for example, antisemitism and other manifestations which lead to religious intolerance and to discrimination on the ground of religion or belief, and to promoting and encouraging, in the interest of universal peace, understanding, tolerance, co-operation and friendship among nations, groups and individuals, irrespective of differences in religion or belief, in accordance with the purposes and principles of the Charter of the United Nations, the Universal Declaration of Human Rights and this Convention.

### Article VII

1. In compliance with the fundamental obligations laid down in Article II, States Parties shall take effective measures to prevent and eliminate discrimination on the ground of religion or belief, including the enactment or abrogation of laws or regulations where necessary to prohibit such discrimination by any person, group or organization.

2. States Parties undertake not to pursue any policy or enact or retain laws or regulations restricting or impeding freedom of conscience, religion or belief or the free and open exercise thereof, nor discriminate against any person, group or organization on account of membership or non-membership in, practice or non-practice of, or adherence or non-adherence to any religion or belief.

### Article VIII

States Parties undertake to ensure to everyone equality before the law without any discrimination in the exercise of the right to freedom of thought, conscience, religion or belief, and to equal protection of the law against any discrimination on the ground of religion or belief.

### Article IX

States Parties shall ensure equal protection of the law against promotion of or incitement to religious intolerance or discrimination on the ground of religion or belief. Any act of violence against the adherents of any religion or belief or against the means used for its practice, any incitement to such acts or incitement to hatred likely to result in acts of violence against any religion or belief or its adherents, shall be considered as offences punishable by law. Membership in an organization based on religion or belief does not remove the responsibility for the above-mentioned acts.

## Article X

States Parties shall ensure to everyone within their jurisdiction effective protection and remedies, through the competent national tribunals and other State institutions, against any acts, including acts of discrimination on the ground of religion or belief, which violate his human rights and fundamental freedoms contrary to this Convention, as well as the right to seek from such tribunals just and adequate reparation or satisfaction for any damage suffered as a result of such acts.

## Article XI

Nothing in this Convention shall be interpreted as giving to any person, group, organization or institution the right to engage in activities aimed at prejudicing national security, friendly relations between nations or the purposes and principles of the United Nations.

## Article XII

Nothing in this Convention shall be construed to preclude a State Party from prescribing by law such limitations as are necessary to protect public safety, order, health or morals, or the individual rights and freedoms of others, or the general welfare in a democratic society.

## 7. AMERICAN CONVENTION ON HUMAN RIGHTS (1969)[7]

*Article 12.*

1. Everyone has the right to freedom of conscience and of religion. This right includes freedom to maintain or to change one's religion or beliefs, and freedom to profess or disseminate one's religion or beliefs, either individually or together with others, in public or in private.

2. No one shall be subject to restrictions that might impair his freedom to maintain or to change his religion or beliefs.

3. Freedom to manifest one's religion and beliefs may be subject only to the limitations prescribed by law that are necessary to protect public safety, order, health, or morals, or the rights or freedoms of others.

4. Parents or guardians, as the case may be, have the right to provide for the religious and moral education of their children or wards that is in accord with their own convictions.

## 8. AFRICAN CHARTER ON HUMAN AND PEOPLES' RIGHTS (1969)[8]

*Article 8.* Freedom of conscience, the profession and free practice of religion shall be guaranteed. No one may, subject to law and order, be submitted to measures restricting the exercise of these freedoms.

## 9. UNITED NATIONS DECLARATION ON THE ELIMINATION OF ALL FORMS OF INTOLERANCE AND DISCRIMINATION BASED ON RELIGION OR BELIEF (1981)[9]

*Preamble*

*Considering* that one of the basic principles of the Charter of the United Nations is that of the dignity and equality inherent in all human beings, and that all Member States have pledged themselves to take joint and separate action in co-operation with the Organization to promote and encourage universal respect for and observance of human rights and fundamental freedoms for all, without distinction as to race, sex, language or religion,

*Considering* that the Universal Declaration of Human Rights and the International Covenants on Human Rights proclaim the principles of non-discrimination and equality before the law and the right to freedom of thought, conscience, religion and belief,

*Considering* that the disregard and infringement of human rights and fundamental freedoms, in particular of the right to freedom of thought, conscience, religion or whatever belief, have brought, directly or indirectly, wars and great suffering to mankind, especially where they serve as a means of foreign interference in the internal affairs of other States and amount to kindling hatred between peoples and nations,

*Considering* that religion or belief, for anyone who professes either, is one of the fundamental elements in his conception of life and that freedom of religion or belief should be fully respected and guaranteed,

*Considering* that it is essential to promote understanding, tolerance and respect in matters relating to freedom of religion and belief and to ensure that the use of religion or belief for ends inconsistent with the Charter of the United Nations, other relevant instruments of the United Nations and the purposes and principles of the present Declaration is inadmissible,

*Convinced* that freedom of religion and belief should also contribute to the attainment of the goals of world peace, social justice and friendship among peoples and to the elimination of ideologies or practices of colonialism and racial discrimination,

*Noting with satisfaction* the adoption of several, and the coming into force of some, conventions, under the aegis of the United Nations and of the specialized agencies, for the elimination of various forms of discrimination,

*Concerned* by manifestations of intolerance and by the existence of discrimination in matters of religion or belief still in evidence in some areas of the world,

*Resolved* to adopt all necessary measures for the speedy elimination of such intolerance in all its forms and manifestations and to prevent and combat discrimination on the grounds of religion or belief.

*Proclaims* this Declaration on the Elimination of All Forms of Intolerance and of Discrimination Based on Religion or Belief:

## Article 1

1. Everyone shall have the right to freedom of thought, conscience and religion. This right shall include freedom to have a religion or whatever belief of his choice, and freedom, either individually or in community with others and in public or private, to manifest his religion or belief in worship, observance, practice and teaching.

2. No one shall be subject to coercion which would impair his freedom to have a religion or belief of his choice.

3. Freedom to manifest one's religion or belief may be subject only to such limitations as are prescribed by law and are necessary to protect public safety, order, health or morals or the fundamental rights and freedoms of others.

## Article 2

1. No one shall be subject to discrimination by any State, institution, group of persons or person on the grounds of religion or other beliefs.

2. For the purposes of the present Declaration, the expression "intolerance and discrimination based on religion or belief" means any distinction, exclusion, restriction or preference based on religion or belief and having as its purpose or as its effect nullification or impairment of the recognition, enjoyment or exercise of human rights and fundamental freedoms on an equal basis.

## Article 3

Discrimination between human beings on the grounds of religion or belief constitutes an affront to human dignity and a disavowal of the principles of the Charter of the United Nations, and shall be condemned as a violation of the human rights and fundamental freedoms proclaimed in the Universal Declaration of Human Rights and enunciated in detail in the International Covenants on Human Rights, and as an obstacle to friendly and peaceful relations between nations.

## Article 4

1. All States shall take effective measures to prevent and eliminate discrimination on the grounds of religion or belief in the recognition, exercise and enjoyment of human rights and fundamental freedoms in all fields of civil, economic, political, social and cultural life.

2. All States shall make all efforts to enact or rescind legislation where necessary to prohibit any such discrimination, and to take all appropriate measures to combat intolerance on the grounds of religion or other beliefs in this matter.

## Article 5

1. The parents or, as the case may be, the legal guardians of the child have the right to organize the life within the family in accordance with their religion or belief and bearing in mind the moral education in which they believe the child should be brought up.

2. Every child shall enjoy the right to have access to education in the matter of religion or belief in accordance with the wishes of his parents or, as the case may be, legal guardians, and shall not be compelled to receive teaching on religion or belief against the wishes of his parents or legal guardians, the best interests of the child being the guiding principle.

3. The child shall be protected from any form of discrimination on the ground of religion or belief. He shall be brought up in a spirit of understanding, tolerance, friendship among peoples, peace and universal brotherhood, respect for freedom of religion or belief of others, and in full conscience that his energy and talents should be devoted to the service of his fellow men.

4. In the case of a child who is not under the care either of his parents or of legal guardians, due account shall be taken of their expressed wishes or of any other proof of their wishes in the matter of religion or belief, the best interest of the child being the guiding principle.

5. Practices of a religion or belief in which a child is brought up must not be injurious to his physical or mental health or to his full development, taking into account article 1, paragraph 3, of the present Declaration.

### Article 6

In accordance with article 1 of the present Declaration, and subject to the provision of article 1, paragraph 3, the right to freedom of thought, conscience, religion or belief shall include, *inter alia*, the following freedoms:

(a) To worship or assemble in connexion with a religion or belief, and to establish and maintain places for these purposes;

(b) To establish and maintain appropriate charitable or humanitarian institutions;

(c) To make, acquire and use to an adequate extent the necessary articles and materials related to the rites or customs of a religion or belief;

(d) To write, issue and disseminate relevant publications in these areas;

(e) To teach a religion or belief in places suitable for these purposes;

(f) To solicit and receive voluntary financial and other contributions from individuals and institutions;

(g) To train, appoint, elect or designate by succession appropriate leaders called for by the requirements and standards of any religion or belief;

(h) To observe days of rest and to celebrate holidays and ceremonies in accordance with the precepts of one's religion or belief;

(i) To establish and maintain communications with individuals and communities in matters of religion and belief at the national and international levels.

### Article 7

The rights and freedoms set forth in the present Declaration shall be accorded in national legislation in such a manner that everyone shall be able to avail himself of such rights and freedoms in practice.

*Article 8*

Nothing in the present Declaration shall be construed as restricting or derogating from any right defined in the Universal Declaration of Human Rights and the International Covenants on Human Rights.

## 10. VIENNA CONCLUDING DOCUMENT (1989)[10]

*Principle 16.* In order to ensure the freedom of the individual to profess and practice religion or belief, the participating States will, *inter alia*,

16a. take effective measures to prevent and eliminate discrimination against individuals or communities, on the grounds of religion or belief in the recognition, exercise and enjoyment of human rights and fundamental freedoms in all fields of civil, political, economic, social and cultural life, and ensure the effective equality between believers and non-believers;

16b. foster a climate of mutual tolerance and respect between believers of different communities as well as between believers and non-believers;

16c. grant upon their request to communities of believers, practicing or prepared to practice their faith within the constitutional framework of their states, recognition of the status provided for them in their respective countries;

16d. respect the right of religious communities to establish and maintain freely accessible places of worship or assembly, organize themselves according to their own hierarchical and institutional structure, select, appoint and replace their personnel in accordance with their respective requirements and standards as well as with any freely accepted arrangements between them and their State, solicit and receive voluntary financial and other contributions;

16e. engage in consultations with religious faiths, institutions and organizations in order to achieve a better understanding of the requirements of religious freedom;

16f. respect the right of everyone to give and receive religious education in the language of his choice, individually or in association with others;

16g. in this context respect, *inter alia*, the liberty of parents to ensure the religious and moral education of their children in conformity with their own convictions;

16h. allow the training of religious personnel in appropriate institutions;

16i. respect the right of individual believers and communities of believers to acquire, possess, and use sacred books, religious publications in the language of their choice and other articles and materials related to the practice of religion or belief;

16j. allow religious faiths, institutions and organizations to produce and import and disseminate religious publications and materials;

16k. favorably consider the interest of religious communities in participating in public dialogue, *inter alia*, through mass media.

*Principle 17.* The participating States recognize that the exercise of the above-mentioned rights relating to the freedom of religion or belief may be subject only to such limitations as are provided by law and consistent with their obligations under international law and with their international commitments. They will ensure in their laws and regulations and in their application the full and effective implementation of the freedom of thought, conscience, religion or belief.

## 11. DOCUMENT OF THE COPENHAGEN MEETING OF THE CONFERENCE ON THE HUMAN DIMENSION OF THE CSCE (1990)[11]

*Article 9.* The participating States reaffirm that . . .
(9.4) everyone will have the right to freedom of thought, conscience and religion. This right includes freedom to change one's religion or belief and freedom to manifest one's religion or belief, either alone or in community with others, in public or in private, through worship, teaching, practice and observance. The exercise of these rights may be subject only to such restrictions as are prescribed by law and are consistent with international standards.

## 12. THE CAIRO DECLARATION ON HUMAN RIGHTS IN ISLAM (1990)[12]

*Article 10.* Islam is the religion of unspoiled nature. It is prohibited to exercise any form of compulsion on man or to exploit his poverty or ignorance in order to convert him to another religion or to atheism.

## 13. DECLARATION ON THE RIGHTS OF PERSONS BELONGING TO NATIONAL OR ETHNIC, RELIGIOUS, AND LINGUISTIC MINORITIES (1992)[13]

*Article 2.*
1. Persons belonging to national or ethnic, religious, and linguistic minorities (hereinafter referred to as persons belonging to minorities) have the right to enjoy their own culture, to profess and practise their own religion, and to use their own language, in private and in public, freely and without interference or any form of discrimination.
5. Persons belonging to minorities have the right to establish and maintain, without any discrimination, free and peaceful contacts with other members of their group and with persons belonging to other minorities, as well as contacts across frontiers with citizens of other States to whom they are related by national or ethnic, religious or linguistic ties.

## 14. FUNDAMENTAL AGREEMENT BETWEEN THE HOLY SEE AND THE STATE OF ISRAEL (1993)[14]

*Preamble*

*The Holy See and the State of Israel,*

*Mindful* of the singular character and universal significance of the Holy Land;

*Aware* of the unique nature of the relationship between the Catholic Church and the Jewish people, and of the historic process of reconciliation and growth in mutual understanding and friendship between Catholics and Jews;

*Having decided* on 29 July 1992 to establish a "Bilateral Permanent Working Commission," in order to study and define together issues of common interest, and in view of normalizing their relations;

*Recognizing* that the work of the aforementioned Commission has produced sufficient material for a first and Fundamental Agreement;

*Realizing* that such Agreement will provide a sound and lasting basis for the continued development of their present and future relations and for the furtherance of the Commissions task;

*Agree* upon the following Articles:

*Article 1*

1. The State of Israel, recalling its Declaration of Independence, affirms its continuing commitment to uphold and observe the human right to freedom of religion and conscience, as set forth in the Universal Declaration of Human Rights and in other international instruments to which it is a party.

2. The Holy See, recalling the Declaration on Religious Freedom of the Second Vatican Ecumenical Council, "Dignitatis humanae," affirms the Catholic Church's commitment to uphold the human right to freedom of religion and conscience, as set forth in the Universal Declaration of Human Rights and in other international instruments to which it is a party. The Holy See wishes to affirm as well the Catholic Church's respect for other religions and their followers as solemnly stated by the Second Vatican Ecumenical Council in its Declaration on the Relation of the Church to Non-Christian Religions, "Nostra aetate."

*Article 2*

1. The Holy See and the State of Israel are committed to appropriate co-operation in combating all forms of antisemitism and all kinds of racism and of religious intolerance, and in promoting mutual understanding among nations, tolerance among communities and respect for human life and dignity.

2. The Holy See takes this occasion to reiterate its condemnation of hatred, persecution and all other manifestations of antisemitism directed against the Jewish people and individual Jews anywhere, at any time and by anyone.

In particular, the Holy See deplores attacks on Jews and desecration of Jewish synagogues and cemeteries, acts which offend the memory of the victims of the Holocaust, especially when they occur in the same places which witnessed it.

### Article 3

1. The Holy See and the State of Israel recognize that both are free in the exercise of their respective rights and powers, and commit themselves to respect this principle in their mutual relations and in their co-operation for the good of the people.

2. The State of Israel recognizes the right of the Catholic Church to carry out its religious, moral, educational and charitable functions, and to have its own institutions, and to train, appoint and deploy its own personnel in the said institutions or for the said functions to these ends. The Church recognizes the right of the State to carry out its functions, such as promoting and protecting the welfare and the safety of the people. Both the State and the Church recognize the need for dialogue and co-operation in such matters as by their nature call for it.

3. Concerning Catholic legal personality at canon law the Holy See and the State of Israel will negotiate on giving it full effect in Israeli law, following a report from a joint sub-commission of experts.

### Article 4

1. The State of Israel affirms its continuing commitment to maintain and respect the "Status quo" in the Christian Holy Places to which it applies and the respective rights of the Christian communities thereunder. The Holy See affirms the Catholic Church's continuing commitment to respect the aforementioned "Status quo" and the said rights.

2. The above shall apply notwithstanding an interpretation to the contrary of any Article in this Fundamental Agreement.

3. The State of Israel agrees with the Holy See on the obligation of continuing respect for and protection of the character proper to Catholic sacred places, such as churches, monasteries, convents, cemeteries and their like.

4. The State of Israel agrees with the Holy See on the continuing guarantee of the freedom of Catholic worship.

### Article 5

1. The Holy See and the State of Israel recognize that both have an interest in favoring Christian pilgrimages to the Holy Land. Whenever the need for coordination arises, the proper agencies of the Church and of the State will consult and cooperate as required.

2. The State of Israel and the Holy See express the hope that such pilgrimages will provide an occasion for better understanding between the pilgrims and the people and religions in Israel.

### Article 6
The Holy See and the State of Israel jointly reaffirm the right of the Catholic Church to establish, maintain and direct schools and institutes of study at all levels; this right being exercised in harmony with the rights of the State in the field of education.

### Article 7
The Holy See and the State of Israel recognize a common interest in promoting and encouraging cultural exchanges between Catholic institutions worldwide, and educational, cultural and research institutions in Israel, and in facilitating access to manuscripts, historical documents and similar source materials, in conformity with applicable laws and regulations.

### Article 8
The State of Israel recognizes that the right of the Catholic Church to freedom of expression in the carrying out of its functions is exercised also through the Church's own communications media; this right being exercised in harmony with the rights of the State in the field of communications media.

### Article 9
The Holy See and the State of Israel jointly reaffirm the right of the Catholic Church to carry out its charitable functions through its health care and social welfare institutions, this right being exercised in harmony with the rights of the State in this field.

### Article 10
1. The Holy See and the State of Israel jointly reaffirm the right of the Catholic Church to property.

2. Without prejudice to rights relied upon by the Parties:

(a) The Holy See and the State of Israel will negotiate in good faith a comprehensive agreement, containing solutions acceptable to both Parties, on unclear, unsettled and disputed issues, concerning property, economic and fiscal matters relating to the Catholic Church generally, or to specific Catholic Communities or institutions.

(b) For the purpose of the said negotiations, the Permanent Bilateral Working Commission will appoint one or more bilateral submissions of experts to study the issues and make proposals.

(c) The Parties intend to commence the aforementioned negotiations within three months of entry into force of the present Agreement, and aim to reach agreement within two years from the beginning of the negotiations.

(d) During the period of these negotiations, actions incompatible with these commitments shall be avoided.

### Article 11

1. The Holy See and the State of Israel declare their respective commitment to the promotion of the peaceful resolution of conflicts among States and nations, excluding violence and terror from international life.

2. The Holy See, while maintaining in every case the right to exercise its moral and spiritual teaching-office, deems it opportune to recall that, owing to its own character, it is solemnly committed to remaining a stranger to all merely temporal conflicts, which principle applies specifically to disputed territories and unsettled borders.

### Article 12

The Holy See and the State of Israel will continue to negotiate in good faith in pursuance of the Agenda agreed upon in Jerusalem, on 15 July 1992, and confirmed at the Vatican, on 29 July 1992; likewise on issues arising from Articles of the present Agreement, as well as on other issues bilaterally agreed upon as objects of negotiation.

### Article 13

1. In this Agreement the Parties use these terms in the following sense:

(a) The Catholic Church and the Church including, inter alia, its Communities and institutions.

(b) Communities of the Catholic Church meaning the Catholic religious entities considered by the Holy See as Churches sui juris and by the State of Israel as Recognized Religious Communities;

(c) The State of Israel and the State—including, inter alia, its authorities established by law.

2. Notwithstanding the validity of this Agreement as between the Parties, and without detracting from the generality of any applicable rule of law with reference to treaties, the Parties agree that this Agreement does not prejudice rights and obligations arising from existing treaties between either Party and a State or States, which are known and in fact available to both Parties at the time of the signature of this Agreement.

### Article 14

1. Upon signature of the present Fundamental Agreement and in preparation for the establishment of full diplomatic relations, the Holy See and the State of Israel exchange Special Representatives, whose rank and privileges are specified in an Additional Protocol.

2. Following the entry into force and immediately upon the beginning of the implementation of the present Fundamental Agreement, the Holy See and the State of Israel will establish full diplomatic relations at the level of Apostolic Nunciature, on the part of the Holy See, and Embassy, on the part of the State of Israel.

*Article 15*

This Agreement shall enter into force on the date of the latter notification of ratification by a Party.

Done in two original copies in the English and Hebrew languages, both texts being equally authentic. In case of divergency, the English text shall prevail.

Signed in Jerusalem, this thirtieth day of the month of December, in the year 1993, which corresponds to the sixteenth day of the month of Tevet, in the year 5754.

## 15. COUNCIL OF EUROPE: FRAMEWORK CONVENTION FOR THE PROTECTION OF NATIONAL MINORITIES (1995)[15]

*Article 5.*

1. The Parties undertake to promote the conditions necessary for persons belonging to national minorities to maintain and develop their culture, and to preserve the essential elements of their identity, namely their religion, language, traditions and cultural heritage.

*Article 8.*

The Parties undertake to recognise that every person belonging to a national minority has the right to manifest his or her religion or belief and to establish religious institutions, organisations and associations.

*Article 17.*

1. The Parties undertake not to interfere with the right of persons belonging to national minorities to establish and maintain free and peaceful contacts across frontiers with persons lawfully staying in other States, in particular those with whom they share an ethnic, cultural, linguistic or religious identity, or a common cultural heritage.

2. The Parties undertake not to interfere with the right of persons belonging to national minorities to participate in the activities of non-governmental organizations, both at the national and international levels.

## 16. OSLO DECLARATION ON FREEDOM OF RELIGION AND BELIEF (1998)[16]

Whereas the Oslo Conference on Freedom of Religion or Belief meeting in celebration of the fiftieth anniversary of the Universal Declaration of Human Rights, reaffirms that every person has the right to freedom of religion or belief;

And whereas participants in the Oslo Conference have accepted the challenge to build an international coalition and to develop a strategic plan of action to achieve substantial progress in and give practical support to the implementation of Article 18 of the Universal Declaration of Human Rights, Article 18 of the International Covenants on Civil and Political Rights, and the 1981 United Nations Declaration on the Elimination of All Forms of Intolerance and of Discrimination Based on Religion or Belief;

Therefore, we the participants in the Oslo Conference:

Recognize that religions and beliefs teach peace and good will;

Recognize that religions and beliefs may be misused to cause intolerance, discrimination and prejudice, and have all too often been used to deny the rights and freedoms of others;

Affirm that every human being has a responsibility to condemn discrimination and intolerance based on religion or belief, and to apply religion or belief in support of human dignity and peace;

Consider the founding of the United Nations and the adoption of the Universal Declaration of Human Rights to be watershed events, in which the world community recognized for the first time that the existence of human rights transcends the laws of sovereign states;

Confirm that Article 18 of both the Universal Declaration of Human Rights and of the International Covenant on Civil and Political Rights together with other instruments create both a mandate for freedom of religion or belief and a universal standard around which we wish to rally;

Recognize that the U.N. has made significant accomplishments in strengthening this universal standard by passage of the 1981 U.N. Declaration on the Elimination of All Forms of Intolerance and of Discrimination Based on Religion or Belief, by the appointment of a Special Rapporteur to monitor its implementation, and by further defining freedom of religion or belief in the General Comment on Article 18 of the International Covenant on Civil and Political Rights;

Recommend that the U.N. Commission on Human Rights change the title of the Rapporteur to Special Rapporteur on Freedom of Religion or Belief;

Urge increased financial and personnel support to the U.N. to implement the work of the Special Rapporteur and his recommendations;

Request the U.N. High Commissioner for Human Rights to develop a coordinated plan to focus resources of the United Nations, including all specialized agencies and bodies such as UNESCO, ILO, UNDP, and UNHCR on problems involving freedom of religion or belief;

Call for UNESCO to expand its work for peace through religious and cultural dialogue and encourage intensified co-operation with UNESCO in this field;

Urge scholars and teachers to study and apply the Universal Declaration of Human Rights, the International Covenant on Civil and Political Rights and the 1981 Declaration as universal standards on freedom of religion or belief and as a way to solve problems of intolerance and discrimination caused by competing beliefs;

Challenge governments, religious bodies, interfaith associations, humanist communities, non-governmental organizations and academic institutions to create educational programs using the 1981 Declaration as a universal standard to build a culture of tolerance and understanding and respect between people of diverse beliefs;

Further urge U.N. member states to use the 1981 Declaration and other relevant instruments to mediate, negotiate, and resolve intolerance, discrimination, injustices and violence in conflicts where religion or belief plays a role;

Support research and development of other informational resources and methodologies for collecting information, monitoring compliance and initiating comparative country studies to strengthen the work of the United Nations and protect freedom of religion or belief;

Urge the organizers and sponsors of the Oslo Conference in consultation with Conference participants:

To review the discussions and recommendations of the Conference, with the purpose of creating an Oslo Coalition on Freedom of Religion or Belief, inviting support and participation by governments, religious or belief communities, academic institutions and non-governmental organizations; and

To develop a strategic plan of action and seek funding to carry out programs and projects based on its recommendations, in cooperation with the United Nations system.

# NOTES

## INTRODUCTION

1. See Samuel P. Huntington, "The Clash of Civilizations?" *Foreign Affairs* 72 (1993): 22, developed in 1996 into a book with several responses and the same title (Samuel P. Huntington, *The Clash of Civilizations and the Remaking of World Order* [1996]). His views caused considerable controversy. See, e.g., Jean Daniel, "The Clash That Matters Is Occurring within Society," *International Herald Tribune* (September 8, 1998): 10 (arguing that "the vertical divide that Huntington sees between civilizations is in fact a horizontal divide inside all the world societies"). For the shift from violence between sovereign states to conflict between ethnic and religious formations, see Susanne Hoeber Rudolph, "Introduction," in *Transnational Religion and Fading States*, ed. Susanne Hoeber Rudolph and James Piscatori (1997), 3-4.

2. Writing about the August 1998 terrorist attacks in Nairobi and Dar es Salaam, Johanna McGeary reported that eighteen out of twenty-four previous attacks were believed to have been done by Muslims and provided a list of Islamic groups accused of terrorist activities. Johanna McGeary, "Terror in Africa," *Time* (August 17, 1998): 32. President Clinton stressed the need to distinguish between such activities and Islam as a whole. See Thomas W. Lippman, "Pact Is Near on Plan for Pan Am Bomb Suspects Trial," *The Washington Post* (August 24, 1998): A1.

3. See, e.g., Louis Henkin and John Lawrence Hargrove, eds., *Human Rights: An Agenda for the Next Century* (1994). None of the seventeen chapters of this comprehensive and valuable book deals with the issue of religion and human rights. See also Mark W. Janis, "Panel on Religion and International Law," *American Society of International Law Proceedings* 82 (1988): 195-219. Some of the presentations of the panel were included in Mark W. Janis, ed., *The Influence of Religion on the Development of International Law* (1991). See, among others, James A. R. Nafziger, "The Functions of Religion in the International Legal System," in Janis, *The Influence of Religion on the Development of International Law*, 147-169. Already in 1978 Roger S. Clark complained that "the human rights literature is surprisingly sparse on the issue of religious intolerance" ("The United Nations and Religious Freedom," *New York University Journal of International Law and Politics* 11 [1978-79]: 197 n.1).

4. Symposium, "Soul Wars: The Problem of Proselytism in Russia," *Emory International Law Review* 12 (1998): 1-737.

5. Malcolm D. Evans, *Religious Liberty and International Law in Europe* (1997). The book contains, in addition to the European aspect, a substantial discussion of early and modern antecedents on the global arena (261 pages out of a total of almost 400).

6. Tad Stahnke and J. Paul Martin, eds., *Religion and Human Rights: Basic Documents* (1998).

7. Kevin Boyle and Juliet Sheen, eds., *Freedom of Religion and Belief: A World Report* (1997).

8. Bahiyyih G. Tahzib, *Freedom of Religion or Belief: Ensuring Effective International Legal Protection*, Ph.D. diss. (1996).

9. David Little, "Tolerance, Equal Freedom, and Peace: A Human Rights Approach," in *The Essence of Living in a Free Society*, ed. W. Lawson Taitte (1997), 151-90, refers to all fundamental beliefs as being covered by the 1981 Declaration.

10. *Stroud's Judicial Dictionary*, 5th ed. (1986), 2218.

11. *Black's Law Dictionary*, 6th ed. (1990), 1292.

12. *Davis v. Beeason,* 133 U.S. 333, 342 (1890).

13. 367 U.S. 488 (1961).

14. *Wisconsin v. Yoder,* 406 U.S. 205, 215-216 (1972).

15. Respectively 380 U.S. 163 (1965); 398 U.S. 333 (1970).

16. *Torcaso v. Watkins,* 367 U.S. 488, 495 (1961).

17. Note, "Towards a Constitutional Definition of Religion," *Harvard Law Review* 91 (1978): 1056-89, at 1089. For general discussions of religious rights in the United States, see John Witte Jr., *Religion and the American Constitutional Experiment* (1999); Wojciech Sadurski, "On Legal Definitions of Religion," *Australian Law Journal* 63 (1989): 834-843 (commenting on the *Church of New Faith* case decided by the Australian High Court and favoring a bifurcated definition that would permit reading the same word differently in the non-establishment and free exercise clauses). See also Michael S. Ariens and Robert A. Destro, *Religious Liberty in a Pluralistic Society* (1996), 947-995.

18. *Malnak v. Yogi,* 592 F.2d 197, 207-210 (3d Cir. 1979).

19. *Black's Law Dictionary,* 6th ed. (1990), 155.

20. Arcot Krishnaswami, *Study of Discrimination in the Matter of Religious Rights and Practices* (1960), 1 n.1. See also Little, "Tolerance, Equal Freedom, and Peace," 10.

21. On the imposition of beliefs such as folkish state and the *Führerprinzip,* see William L. Shirer, *The Rise and Fall of the Third Reich* (1960).

22. John Witte Jr., "Introduction," in *Religious Human Rights in a Global Perspective: Religious Perspectives*, ed. John Witte Jr. and Johan D. van der Vyver (1996), xxiv.

23. See detailed sources and discussion in chapter 1.

24. Freedom of conscience is frequently related to what is called conscientious objection, a subject that exceeds the area of religion alone and has engendered abundant case law in many countries. See Kent Greenawalt, *Conflicts of Law and Morality* (1987); Rafael Palomino, *Las Objeciones de Conciencia* (1994) (containing an updated and detailed bibliography on the subject); Chaim Gans, *Philosophical Anarchism and Political Disobedience* (1992); Rafael Navarro-Valls and Javier Martinez Torron, *Las Objeciones de Conciencia* (1995). The Human Rights Committee related the issue of freedom of conscience to the right to manifest one's religion or belief. General Comment No. 22(48) (Article 18), U.N. GAOR Hum. Rts. Comm., 48th Sess., Supp. No. 40, para. 11, U.N. Doc. A/48/40 (1993).

25. On individual, collective, and group rights, see chapters 1 and 3 below, and Natan Lerner, *Group Rights and Discrimination in International Law* (1991).

26. See the report submitted by Abdelfattah Amor, special rapporteur on Freedom of Religion and Belief to the Commission on Human Rights, U.N. ESCOR, 54th Sess., Agenda Item 18, at 28, U.N. Doc. E/CN.4/1998/6 (1998).

27. Ibid.

28. See Report by Amor, U.N. Doc. E/CN.4/1998/6/Add.2.

29. Ibid., 14.

30. Ibid., 16ff. The authorities, on their part, alleged that Scientology was a commercial enterprise, as established by a German Federal Labour Court, and all measures taken were according to law.

31. Ibid., 21ff.

32. Decree No. 980-890. A French parliamentary commission investigated the issue earlier.

33. See *Time* (January 27, 1997), which contains several articles on the issue.

34. Report by Amor, E/CN.4/1998/6/Add.2, at 23.

35. The Oslo Declaration on Freedom of Religion or Belief, adopted on August 11-15, 1998, at a conference convened under the auspices of the Norwegian government, for instance, does not refer to the problem of sects. For the text, see *Helsinki Monitor* 9 (1998): 101, and appendix 16 herein.

36. Recommendation 1412 (1999), adopted on June 22, 1999.

## 1. RELIGIOUS HUMAN RIGHTS UNDER THE UNITED NATIONS

1. Nehemiah Robinson, *Universal Declaration of Human Rights: Its Origin, Significance, Application, and Interpretation* (1958), 128ff. See also Martin Scheinin, "Article 18," in *The Universal Declaration of Human Rights: A Commentary*, ed. Asbjorn Eide et al. (1992), 263-274; Karl J. Partsch, "Freedom of Conscience and Expression, and Political Freedoms," in *The International Bill of Rights*, ed. Louis Henkin (1981), 209-245; John P. Humphrey, "The Universal Declaration of Human Rights: Its History, Impact and Judicial Character," in *Human Rights: Thirty Years after the Universal Declaration*, ed. B. G. Ramcharan (1979), 21.

2. Scheinin, "Article 18," 266.

3. Warwick McKean, *Equality and Discrimination under International Law* (1983), 121.

4. *Study of Discrimination in the Matter of Religious Rights and Practices*, U.N. Sales No. 60.XIV.2 (1960).

5. Ibid., 18.

6. Ibid., 35ff.

7. John Witte Jr. distinguishes seven principal patterns regarding state and religion: (1) state religions; (2) established churches; (3) state neutrality; (4) state concordats with the Catholic Church (there are also a few similar agreements with other religions, as we shall see later); (5) no official religion; (6) separation of church and state; and (7) protection of legally recognized religious groups. See, John Witte Jr., *The State of Religious Human Rights in the World: A Comparative Religious and Legal Study* (1993).

8. *Study of Discrimination*, 63-66.

9. Ibid., 71-74.

10. For the text of both covenants, see United Nations, *Human Rights: A Compilation of International Instruments*, at 8, 20, U.N. Sales No. E.93.XIV.1 (1983) [hereafter *Human Rights*]. Among the many works on the covenants, see generally Henkin, *The International Bill of Rights*; Theodor Meron, ed., *Human Rights Law-Making in the United Nations* (1986); Philip Alston, ed., *The United Nations and Human Rights* (1992); Dominic McGoldrick, *The Human Rights Committee* (1991). See also the reports of the Human Rights Committee, published as Official Records of the General Assembly (GAOR), Supplement No. 40.

11. See further discussion in chapter 4.

12. On limitations in the covenant, see Thomas Buergenthal, "To Respect and to Ensure: State Obligations and Permissible Derogations," in Henkin, *The International Bill of Rights,* 72-89, and Alexandre C. Kiss, "Permissible Limitations on Rights," in ibid., 290-310.

13. For a United States Supreme Court decision on animal sacrifices according to the Santeria rite, see *Church of the Lukumi Babalu Aye, Inc. v. City of Hialeah,* 508 U.S. 520 (1993).

14. See, inter alia, Donna J. Sullivan, "Gender Equality and Religious Freedom: Toward a Framework for Conflict Resolution," *New York University Journal of International Law and Politics* 24 (1992): 795-856, at 819-820; Leon Sheleff, "Tribal Rites and Legal Rights," *Israel Yearbook on Human Rights* 18 (1988): 153-172; Aviam Soifer, "Freedom of Association: Indian Tribes, Workers, and Communal Ghosts," *Maryland Law Review* 48 (1989): 350-383.

15. For the three mentioned instruments, see Convention against Discrimination in Education, in *Human Rights,* 1:101-107; Declaration on the Elimination of All Forms of Intolerance and of Discrimination Based on Religion or Belief, in ibid. 1:122-125; Convention on the Rights of the Child, in ibid., 1:171-173.

16. *Hartikainen v. Finland, Communication* No. 40/1978, in *Selected Decisions of the Human Rights Committee under the Optional Protocol,* 1:74-76, U.N. Doc. No. CCPR/C/OP/1, U.N. Sales No. E.84.XIV.2 (1985) [hereafter *Selected Decisions*].

17. Partsch, "Freedom of Conscience and Expression," 453-454 n.75.

18. Report of the Human Rights Committee, U.N. GAOR 38th Sess., Supp. No. 40, Annex VI, at 110, U.N. Doc. No. A/38/40 (1983).

19. For the text of the Convention, see International Convention on the Elimination of All Forms of Racial Discrimination, *Human Rights,* 1:66-79.

20. See Committee on the Elimination of Racial Discrimination, Positive Measures Designed to Eradicate All Incitement to, or Acts of, Racial Discrimination, U.N. Doc. No. CERD/2, U.N. Sales No. E.85.XIV.2 (1983). See also Natan Lerner, *The U.N. Convention on the Elimination of All Forms of Racial Discrimination* (1980). For a model national legislation against racial discrimination and incitement, see Elimination of Racism and Racial Discrimination, U.N. GAOR, 48th Sess., Agenda Item 107, U.N. Doc. A/48/558 (1993). Incitement on religious grounds is not specifically mentioned in this document.

21. See Colloquium, "International Colloquium on Racial and Religious Hatred and Group Libel," *Israel Yearbook on Human Rights* 22 (1992), especially articles by Natan Lerner, "Incitement in the Racial Convention: Reach and Shortcomings of Article 4," in ibid., 1-15, and Rudolf Bernhardt, "Human Rights Aspects of Racial and Religious Hatred under Regional Human Rights Conventions," in ibid., 17-29. See also Kevin Boyle, "Religious Intolerance and the Incitement of Hatred," in *Striking a Balance: Hate Speech, Freedom of Expression and Non-discrimination,* ed. Sandra Coliver (1992), 61-71. In 1993 the Committee on the Elimination of Racial Discrimination stated that the prohibition of the dissemination of racist ideas is compatible with the right to freedom of opinion and expression. Report of the Committee on the Elimination of Racial Discrimination, U.N. GAOR 42nd Sess., Supp. No. 18, at 115-116, U.N. Doc. No. A/42/18 (1987).

22. *Wisconsin v. Mitchell,* 508 U.S. 478 (1993).

23. Report of the Human Rights Committee, U.N. GAOR 48th Sess., Supp. No. 40, Annex VI, U.N. Doc. A/48/40 (1993).

24. Ibid., para. 2.

25. These issues have engendered interesting judicial decisions in some countries. See Leon Shaskolsky Sheleff, "Rabbi Captain Goldman's Yarmulke, Freedom of Religion and Conscience, and Civil (Military) Disobedience," *Israel Yearbook on Human Rights* 17 (1987): 197-221. In *Goldman v. Weinberger*, 475 U.S. 503 (1986), the United States Supreme Court decided that an Air Force regulation on the dress code took precedence over religious traditions. The issue was solved by legislative means. See 10 U.S.C.A. sec. 774 (1988). See also the well-known Sikh cases *Mandla v. Dowell Lee*, 1108 All E.R. (Eng. C.A. 1982) and *Panesar v. Nestle Co. Ltd.*, 1980 I.C.R. 144 (Eng. C.A.). In France, after contradictory decisions of the Conseil d'Etat, the Ministry of Education, with the support of the teachers' unions, prohibited in 1994 in public schools the traditional head coverage used by Muslim girls. The ban includes all ostentatious religious identifications, as distinguished from discrete signs such as small crosses, stars of David, or the name of Allah. The issue was described in newspaper articles as a national psychodrama. See Robert Sole, "Derrier le foulard islamique," *Le Monde* (September 13, 1994): 1. In Israel, the Supreme Court affirmed a decision of a Christian private school in Nazareth to reject a Muslim girl student who insisted on using the traditional veil. Some cases came before the European human rights bodies. In *X. v. United Kingdom*, App. No. 7992/77, 14 European Commission of Human Rights Decisions and Reports 234 (1978), the duty of a Sikh motorcyclist to remove his turban and wear a crash helmet was seen as interfering with his religious freedom justified for the protection of public health.

26. Report of the Human Rights Committee, para. 8.

27. Ibid., para. 9-10. The issue of blasphemy, an offense in some legislations (Britain, Egypt, and Iran, for instance), caused public controversy as a result of the publication in 1988 of Salman Rushdie's *The Satanic Verses* in Great Britain. The author was condemned to death by the Khomeini regime in 1989. Restrictions on publications considered blasphemous against the Church of England were declared compatible with Article 10(2) of the European Convention on Human Rights by the European Commission on Human Rights. See *Gay News v. U.K.*, 5 E.H.R.R. 123 (1983). The Bangladesh government has brought criminal charges against the writer Taslim Nasreem for blasphemy. On blasphemy generally, see Leonard W. Levy, *Blasphemy: Verbal Offense against the Sacred, from Moses to Salman Rushdie* (1993).

28. See generally, Rafael Palomino, *Las Objeciones de Conciencia* (1994); Chaim Gans, *Philosophical Anarchism and Political Disobedience* (1992); Kent Greenawalt, *Conflicts of Law and Morality* (1987); Joseph Raz, *The Authority of Law* (1979); Rafael Navarro-Valls and Javier Martinez Torrón, *Las Objeciones de Conciencia* (Torino, 1997). The European Commission on Human Rights dealt with the meaning of *conscientious objection* in, inter alia, *Grandrath v. Germany*, 1967 Yearbook of the European Convention on Human Rights 626. The European Convention on Human Rights refers to conscientious objection in Article 4 and not in connection with religion. The U.S. Supreme Court granted exemptions not only on religious premises. In *Welsh v. United States*, 398 U.S 333 (1970), for instance, the Supreme Court granted such exemption on secular grounds.

29. While the General Comments are neither scholarly studies nor secondary legislative acts, and are couched in general terms, they represent an important body of experience in considering matters from the angle of the covenant. Torkel Opsahl, "The Human Rights Committee," in Alston, *The United Nations and Human Rights*, 369-443, at 415.

30. Report of the Human Rights Committee, U.N. GAOR 47th Sess., Supp. No. 40, at 15-16, U.N. Doc. No. A/47/40 (1994).

31. Ibid., 24-25.

32. Ibid., 89.

33. Report of the Human Rights Committee, U.N. GAOR 46th Sess., Supp. No. 40, at 100, U.N. Doc. No. A/46/40 (1991).

34. Ibid., 127; also, Report of the Human Rights Committee, U.N. GAOR 53rd Sess., Supp. No. 40., at 25, U.N. Doc. No. A/53/40 (1998).

35. For Argentina, see Report of the Human Rights Committee, U.N. GAOR 45th Sess., Supp. No. 40, at 49, U.N. Doc. No. A/45/40 (1990); for Lithuania, see U.N. GAOR 53rd Sess., Supp. No. 40, at 32, U.N. Doc. No. A/53/40(40); for Israel, Ibid., 49. In this respect the committee expressed concern regarding the application of religious law to matters of personal status.

36. Ibid., 26. In its last report before this writing the committee dealt with discrimination on religious grounds in Iraq. Ibid., 21.

37. CCPR/C/74/Add.3.

38. A/53/40, pp. 38-39.

39. *Selected Decisions,* vols. 1 and 2, in Selected Decisions of the Human Rights Committee under the Optional Protocol, U.N. Doc. CCPR/C/OP/2, U.N. Sales No. E.89.XIV.1 (1990).

40. For the text, see *Human Rights,* 1:8-19.

41. See generally, Philip Alston, "The Committee on Economic, Social and Cultural Rights," in Alston, *The United Nations and Human Rights,* 473-508.

42. For the text, see *Human Rights,* 1:122-125. For an analysis of the declaration, see Natan Lerner, *Group Rights and Discrimination in International Law* (1991), 75-96; Donna J. Sullivan, "Advancing the Freedom of Religion or Belief through the U.N. Declaration on the Elimination of Religious Intolerance and Discrimination," *American Journal of International Law* 82 (1988): 487-520.

43. Lerner, *Group Rights and Discrimination,* 46. For the reasons for the difference of treatment by the U.N. of the religious issue as compared to other human rights, see also Antonio Cassese, "The General Assembly: Historical Perspective 1945-1989," in Alston, *The United Nations and Human Rights,* 25-54, at 37.

44. *Webster's Third New International Dictionary* (1986) defines *intolerant* as "refusing to allow others the enjoyment of their opinion or worship," and as equivalent to bigoted. Elizabeth Odio Benito, *Study of the Current Dimensions of the Problem of Intolerance and Discrimination Based on Religion or Belief,* U.N. ESCOR 39th Sess., Agenda Item 13, at 3, U.N. Doc. E/CN.4/Sub.2/1987/26 (1986), states that manifestations of intolerance go in many cases much further than discrimination and involve the stirring up of hatred against, or even the persecution of, individuals or groups of a different religion or belief. In its resolution 48/126, of December 20, 1993, on the 1995 Year for Tolerance, the General Assembly described tolerance as the recognition and appreciation of others, the ability to live together with and to listen to others, and as a sound foundation of any civil society and of peace. U.N. Press Release GA/8637, January 20, 1994, at 382-384.

45. See, inter alia, Partsch, "Freedom of Conscience" and Reports of the Human Rights Committee and its authoritative General Comment on Article 18 of the Covenant, summarized above.

46. See Odio Benito, E/CN.4/Sub.2/1987/26, at 37.

47. On several occasions the Human Rights Committee and the European Court on Human Rights dealt with the scope of permissible limitations. The European Court clarified the notion of morals in the *Handyside Case*, 24 European Court of Human Rights (ser. A) (1976).

48. Difficulties arose in the case of elections taking place on days that are holy for some religious minorities in the country who prohibit work and traveling on such days. Flexibility and good will are necessary in such situations, which may be difficult to foresee.

49. Krishnaswami points out that an identical formal relationship between the state and religion may result in discrimination in some cases, but not in others. See the Krishnaswami study, 46. Odio Benito, on the other hand, maintains that the establishment of a religion or belief by the state amounts to preferences and privileges that may be discriminatory. E/CN.4/Sub.2/1987/26, at 21.

50. Odio Benito, E/CN.4/Sub.2/1987/26, at 25.

51. For the texts of the declaration and the convention, see *Human Rights* 1:171 and 174, respectively. On the subject generally, see Geraldine Van Bueren, *The International Law on the Rights of the Child* (1995); Lawrence J. LeBlanc, *The Convention on the Rights of the Child: United Nations Lawmaking on Human Rights* (1995).

52. See Stephen Schwebel, "The Effect of Resolutions of the U.N. General Assembly on Customary International Law," *American Society of International Law, Proceedings of the 73rd Annual Meeting* (1979): 301. Odio Benito, E/CN.4/Sub.2/1987/26, at 49, refers to concrete obligations of conduct for states and individuals.

53. On the seminar, see the report by Kevin Boyle, United Nations Seminar on the Encouragement of Understanding, Tolerance, and Respect in Matters Relating to Freedom of Religion or Belief, U.N. Doc. ST/HR/Ser.A/16 (1984), particularly para.102(q), on the possibility of a convention.

54. See, for instance, U.N. Doc. A/54/100 (June 15, 1999). Formerly, in its resolution 41/20 of December 4, 1986, the General Assembly stated that standard setting should proceed with adequate preparation.

55. For the Vienna Declaration and Programme of Action, see 32 I.L.M. 1661 (1993).

56. Theo van Boven, Elimination of All Forms of Intolerance and Discrimination Based on Religion of Belief: Working Paper, U.N. SCOR 41st Sess., Agenda Item 11, U.N. Doc. E/CN.4/Sub.2/1989/32 (1989). Van Boven mentions suggestions to frame a new binding instrument in the form of a protocol to the ICCPR, in which case the Human Rights Committee would become the implementation machinery. He also points out the practical difficulties for the establishment of a new treaty body (ibid., 27). See also Theo Van Boven, "Advances and Obstacles in Building Understanding and Respect between People of Diverse Religions and Beliefs," *Human Rights Quarterly* 13 (1991): 437-449, an adapted version of the Arcot Krishnaswami Lecture at a conference of experts on ways to promote the 1981 Declaration, Project Tandem, New Delhi, 1991.

57. Yoram Dinstein and Mala Tabory, eds., *The Protection of Minorities and Human Rights* (1992), 179.

58. Elimination of All Forms of Religious Intolerance: Note by the Secretary-General, U.N. GAOR 25th Sess., Agenda Item 56, U.N. Doc. A/7930 (1970). See Appendix, p. 131 above.

59. For the seven reports, see U.N. Doc. E/CN.4/1987/35; E/CN.4/1988/45 and E/CN.4/1988/45/Add.1; E/CN.4/1989/44; E/CN.4/1990/46; E/CN.4/1991/56; E/

CN.4/1992/52; E/CN.4/1993/62 revised by E/CN.4/1993/62/Corr.1 and E/CN.4/1993/62/Add.1.

60. Odio Benito, E/CN.4/Sub.2/1987/26.

61. Until this writing, U.N. Doc. E/CN.4/1994/79; E/CN.4/1995/91; E/CN.4/1996/95 revised by E/CN.4/1996/95/Corr.1 and E/CN.4/1996/95/Add. 1 and E/CN.4/1996/95/Add.2; E/CN.4/1997/91 and E/CN.4/1997/91Add.1; E/CN.4/1998/6 and E/CN.4/1998/6/Add.1 and E/CN.4/1998/6/Add.2.

62. See U.N. Doc. E/CN.4/1995/91.

63. On the visits, see U.N. Doc. E/CN.4/1995/91, E/CN.4/1996/95/Add.1 and E/CN.4/1996/95/Add.2, E/CN.4/1997/91/Add.1, as well as Human Rights Questions, Including Alternative Approaches for Improving the Effective Enjoyment of Human Rights and Fundamental Freedoms: Note by the Secretary-General, U.N. GAOR 51st Sess., Agenda Item 110(b), Add.1, U.N. Doc. A/51/542/Add.1 and ibid., Add.2, and U.N. Doc. E/CN.4/1998/6/Add.1 and E/CN.4/1998/6/Add.2.

64. U.N. Doc. E/CN.4/1996/95.

65. Ibid., 14.

66. U.N. Doc. E/CN.4/1998/6.

67. UNP Sales No. E.91. XIV.2.

68. The bibliography on minorities is enormous. For an early list, see Definition and Classification of Minorities, at 26-51, U.N. Doc. E/CN.4/Sub.2/85, U.N. Sales No. E.50.XIV.3. For recent literature in addition to Capotorti's Study, see, inter alia, Felix Ermacora, "The Protection of Minorities Before the United Nations" 182, vol. 4, *Recueil des Cours* (1983): 247-370; Louis B. Sohn, "The Rights of Minorities," in Henkin, *The International Bill of Rights,* 270-289; Lerner, *Group Rights*; Patrick Thornberry, *International Law and the Rights of Minorities* (1991); Dinstein and Tabory, eds., *The Protection of Minorities and Human Rights*; Catherine Brolman et al., eds., *Peoples and Minorities in International Law* (1993).

69. On this early period, see Thornberry, *International Law and the Rights of Minorities,* 25ff.; Malcolm D. Evans, *Religious Liberty and International Law in Europe* (1997), 42-74.

70. For an authoritative interpretation of the system and the context in which it worked, see Jacob Robinson et al., *Were the Minorities Treaties a Failure?* (1943).

71. In relation to this interesting and rare case, see Stephen J. Roth, "The Impact of the Holocaust on the Legal Status of Jews and Jewish Communities," *Israel Yearbook on Human Rights* 9 (1979): 121-139, at 128.

72. *Minority Schools in Albania,* 1935 P.C.I.J. (ser. A/B) No. 64, at 17.

73. The interpretation of Article 27 provoked a debate among scholars. See Thornberry, *International Law and the Rights of Minorities,* 149ff.; Francesco Capotorti, "Are Minorities Entitled to Collective International Rights?" *Israel Yearbook on Human Rights* 20 (1990): 351-357; Lerner, *Group Rights,* 14ff.; Lerner, "The Evolution of Minority Rights in International Law," in Brolman et al., *Peoples and Minorities in International Law,* 88ff.; Yoram Dinstein, "Freedom of Religion and the Protection of Religious Minorities," in Dinstein and Tabory, *The Protection of Minorities and Human Rights,* 154ff.

74. On the declaration, see Natan Lerner, "The 1992 U.N. Declaration on Minorities," *Israel Yearbook on Human Rights* 23 (1993): 111-128.

75. See Dusan Janjic et al., eds., *Democracy and Minority Communities, Theses for the Law on Freedoms and Rights of Minority Communities and Their Members* (1993), 34.

76. For the 1949 humanitarian law conventions, see International Committee of the Red Cross, *The Geneva Conventions of August 12, 1949* (1949), as well as Jean S. Pictet, *International Committee of the Red Cross, Commentary: Geneva Convention* (1952).

77. For the texts of the declaration and the Convention on the Elimination of All Forms of Discrimination against Women, see *Human Rights*, 1:145-149 and 1:150-163. On the convention generally, see Theodor Meron, *Human Rights Law-Making in the United Nations* (1986), 53-82; Donna J. Sullivan, "Gender Equality and Religious Freedom: Toward a Framework for Conflict Resolution," *New York University Journal of International Law and Politics* 24 (1991-92): 795-856; Kathleen E. Mahoney and Paul Mahoney, eds., *Human Rights in the Twenty-First Century* (1993).

78. For the text, see Convention against Discrimination in Education, *Human Rights*, 1:101.

79. See chap. 1, note 51.

80. For the American case law, see M. Glenn Albernathy, *Civil Liberties under the Constitution* (1993), 172-220, 345-376; for some of the European cases, see *Case of Kjeldsen, Busk Madsen and Pedersen*, 23 European Court of Human Rights (ser. A) at 25 (1976), and *Angelini v. Sweden,* European Commission on Human Rights, App. No. 1049, 10 E.H.R.R. 123 (1988); on the global level, *Hartikainen v. Finland*, Communication No. 40/1978, in *Selected Decisions*, 1:74. This case was also considered by the European Human Rights Committee.

81. For the text, see Discrimination (Employment and Occupation) Convention, *Human Rights*, 1:96.

82. See, inter alia, the decision of the Court of Justice of the European Communities in Case 130/75, *Preis v. Council of the European Communities* [1976] 2 Common Market Law Reports 708 (1976). The court stated that if a candidate for a job or a religious organization applies in time for a change in dates for a job examination, for religious reasons, that should be taken into account, if possible. For a different stand by the European Commission, see *M. v. Austria*, 1993 CD 25. The commission rejected a complaint against the denial of an adjournment of a hearing for religious motives because of the complexity of the case.

83. For the 1989 convention, see Convention (No. 169) concerning Indigenous and Tribal Peoples in Independent Countries, *Human Rights*, 1:471. For its analysis, see Lerner, *Group Rights*, 99-114. For the U.N. draft declaration, see Commission on Human Rights, Discrimination against Indigenous Peoples: Technical Review of the United Nations Draft Declaration on the Rights of Indigenous Peoples: Note by the Secretariat, U.N. ESCOR 46th Sess., Agenda Item 15, U.N. Doc. E/CN.4/Sub.2/1994/2 (1994) and U.N. Doc. E/CN.4/Sub.2/1994/2/Add.1; Work Group on Indigenous Populations, Commission on Human Rights, Discrimination against Indigenous Peoples, U.N. ESCOR 46th Sess., Agenda Item 5, U.N. Doc. E/CN.4/Sub.2/1994/30 revised by U.N. Doc. E/CN.4/Sub.2/1994/30/Corr.1 (1994).

84. For the text, see International Convention on the Protection of the Rights of All Migrant Workers and Members of Their Families, *Human Rights*, 1:550. For its analysis, see Ved P. Nanda, "The Protection of the Rights of Migrant Workers," *Asian and Pacific Migration Journal* 2 (1993): 161 177.

## 2. REGIONAL PROTECTION OF RELIGIOUS HUMAN RIGHTS

1. For the European human rights system in general, see Mark W. Janis et al., *European Human Rights Law* (1995); Mirielle Delmas-Marty, ed., *The European*

*Convention for the Protection of Human Rights* (1992); Peter Van Dijk and G. J. H. Van Hoof, *Theory and Practice of the European Convention on Human Rights* (1998); Donna Gomien et al., *Law and Practice of the European Convention on Human Rights and the European Social Charter* (1996).

2. See, inter alia, J. G. Merrills, *The Development of International Law by the European Court of Human Rights* (1993); Arie Bloed et al., eds., *Monitoring Human Rights in Europe* (1993).

3. For a comprehensive and updated survey, including the historical development, see Malcolm D. Evans, *Religious Liberty and International Law in Europe* (1997). See also Malcolm N. Shaw, "Freedom of Thought, Conscience and Religion," in *The European System for the Protection of Human Rights*, ed. Ronald St. J. Macdonald et al. (1993), 445-463. See also 9 (3) *Helsinki Monitor* (1998), a special issue on freedom of religion or belief.

4. 213 U.N.T.S. 211. The convention has its origin in a draft prepared in 1949 by the European Movement. It included a reference to freedom of religious belief, practice, and teaching.

5. For the CSCE documents, see Directorate of Human Rights, Council of Europe, *Human Rights in International Law: Basic Texts* (1992). For the work of the CSCE in general, see Arie Bloed, ed., *The Conference on Security and Cooperation in Europe: Analysis and Basic Documents* (1993).

6. Such were the cases of Sweden and Turkey. The issue was solved allowing reservations in respect of possible contradictions between the convention and national laws not in conformity with it. For the drafting process, see Evans, *Religious Liberty and International Law in Europe*, 264-272.

7. Ibid., 272ff. Gomien et al., *Law and Practice of the European Convention*, 264, points out that Article 9 is the only one among the articles with a similar structure that does not allow invocation of national security to restrict the protected rights.

8. On Principles 16 and 17, see W. Cole Durham Jr., "Perspectives on Religious Liberty: A Comparative Framework," in *Religious Rights in Global Perspective: Legal Perspectives*, ed. Johan D. van der Vyver and John Witte Jr. (1996): 1-44, at 33ff.

9. For a detailed and updated survey on European case law with emphasis on religious liberty, see Evans, *Religious Liberty and International Law in Europe*. For a critical commentary on the negative side of the Strasbourg case law, because of its inclination toward enshrining the absolute supremacy of neutral laws over the individual conscience and what the authors call "secular intolerance" and "aggressive and compulsory secularism (*laicité*)," see Javier Martinez-Torrón and Rafael Navarro-Valls, "The Protection of Religious Freedom in the System of the European Convention on Human Rights," in 9 (3) *Helsinki Monitor* (1998). On the role of the European Court of Justice, see Iris Canor, *The Limits of Judicial Discretion in the European Court of Justice* (1998), emphasizing security and foreign affairs issues.

10. *Arrowsmith v. United Kingdom*, App. No. 7050/75, 8 Eur. Commn H.R. Dec. & Rep. 123 (1978).

11. Case of Campbell and Cosans, 48 Eur. Ct. H.R. (ser. A) (1982).

12. See Evans, *Religious Liberty and International Law in Europe*, 290, citing the relevant case law. Evans points out that when there are doubts concerning the status of an alleged religion, the applicant must demonstrate its existence. In *Hazar v. Turkey*, App. No. 16311/90, 16312/90 and 16313/90, 72 Eur. Commn H.R. Dec. & Rep. 200 (1991), the commission accepted, for the purposes of admissibility, that Communism fell within the terms of Article 9.

13. *Chappel v. United Kingdom*, App. No. 12587/86, 53 Eur. Commn H.R. Dec. & Rep. 241 (1987).

14. For the commission, see *Otto-Preminger-Institut v. Austria*, App. No. 13470/87, 69 Eur. Commn H.R. Dec. & Rep. 173 (1993); for the court, see *Otto-Preminger-Institut v. Austria*, 295 Eur. Ct. H.R. (ser. A) (1994).

15. The court's decision was criticized on the grounds that it granted too much margin of discretion to the state and that the convention did not contain any reference to the need to respect the religion of others. See Evans, *Religious Liberty and International Law in Europe*, 337-339. See also the *Gay News* case, *X Ltd. v. United Kingdom*, App. No. 8710/79, 28 Eur. Commn H.R. Dec. & Rep. 77 (1982) and *Wingrove v. United Kingdom* (1996).

16. See Evans, *Religious Liberty and International Law in Europe*, 286-289, also citing the relevant decisions.

17. 48 Eur. Ct. H.R. (ser. A) (1982), para. 53. See also *Angelini v. Sweden*, app. No. 1049/83, 10 E.H.R.R. (1988) 123; *Hartikainen et al. v. Finland* (R.9/40) HRC 36, 147, also considered by the Human Rights Committee, *Hartikainen v. Finland*, Communication No. 40/1978, in *Selected Decisions*.

18. See *Bernard v. Luxembourg*, App. No. 17187/90, 75 Eur. Commn H.R. Dec. & Rep. 57 (1993).

19. Evans, *Religious Liberty and International Law in Europe*, 295. The commission also stated that it is permissible to require an Orthodox Jew to send a letter of repudiation to his ex-wife, or to pay damages if he refuses to do so. No violation of religious rights is involved because Jewish religious norms are not affected. *D. v. France*, App. No. 10180/82, 35 Eur. Commn H.R. Dec. & Rep. 199 (1983).

20. App. No. 11581/85, Rep.1989, paras 50-51.

21. For the text and Explanatory Report, see Council of Europe, Framework Convention for the Protection of National Minorities (Strasbourg, 1995). See also Patrick Thornberry and M. A. Martin Estebanez, *The Council of Europe and Minorities* (1994); Geoff Gilbert, "The Council of Europe and Minority Rights," *Human Rights Quarterly* 18 (1996): 160-189; Jane Wright, "The OSCE and the Protection of Minority Rights," *Human Rights Quarterly* 18 (1996): 190-205.

22. For the text, see O.A.S. Treaty Series No. 36. On the subject generally, see Thomas Buergenthal, "The Inter-American System for the Protection of Human Rights," in *Human Rights in International Law*, ed. Theodor Meron (1983); Thomas Buergenthal et al., *Protecting Human Rights in the Americas* (1995); Scott Davidson, *The Inter-American Human Rights System* (1997); Scott Davidson, *The Inter-American Court of Human Rights* (1992).

23. See Case 9178, Inter-American Commission on Human Rights, reported in *Human Rights Law Journal* 6 (1985): 211. Costa Rica asked the court to interpret Article 13 and give an advisory opinion on it.

24. See Davidson, *Inter-American Human Rights System*, 260.

25. See OEA/Ser. L/V./II.49,doc. 19, corr. 1, 251-254 (1980). See also Buergenthal et al., *Protecting Human Rights in the Americas*, 391-392 n.70.

26. See OEA/Ser. P.AG/Com.I/Acta 5/80 (1980).

27. See, OEA/Ser. L/V/II.54, doc.9, rev.1, 25 (1981).

28. See, OEA/Ser. L/V/II.53, doc. 21, rev.2, 72-83 (1981).

29. For the text, see African Charter on Human and Peoples' Rights, January 7-19, 1981, 21 I.L.M. 58 (1982). On the system generally, see Fatsah Ouguergouz, *La Charte Africaine des Droits de l'Homme et des Peuples* (1993); U. Oji Umozurike,

*The African Charter on Human and Peoples' Rights* (1997); Evelyn A. Ankumah, *The African Commission on Human and Peoples' Rights* (1996).

30. For a detailed analysis of the procedural rules of the Commission, see Ankumah, *The African Commission on Human and Peoples' Rights*, chaps. 2 and 3.

31. Umozurike, *The African Charter on Human and Peoples' Rights*, 67ff. Umozurike is a former chairman of the African Commission on Human Rights.

32. Ankumah, *The African Commission on Human and Peoples' Rights*, 134.

33. For the charter, see 914 U.N.T.S. 103.

34. For the text of the Cairo Declaration on Human Rights, see Tad Stahnke and J. Paul Martin, eds., *Religion and Human Rights: Basic Documents* (1998), 185.

35. Juliane Kokott, "The Protection of Fundamental Rights Under German and International Law," *African Journal of International and Comparative Law* 8 (1996): 347.

36. Ibid., 387.

37. See Felix Ermacora et al., eds., *International Human Rights: Documents and Introductory Notes* (1993), 324.

38. Abdullah Ahmed An-Na'im, "Islamic Foundations of Religious Human Rights," in van der Vyver and Witte, *Religious Human Rights in Global Perspective: Religious Perspectives*, 337-359.

39. Donna E. Arzt, "The Treatment of Religious Dissidents Under Classic and Contemporary Islamic Law," in van der Vyver and Witte, *Religious Human Rights in Global Perspective: Religious Perspectives*, 387-453, at 423.

40. See Natan Lerner, "Religious Human Rights under the United Nations," in van der Vyver and Witte, *Religious Human Rights in Global Perspective: Legal Perspectives*, 79-134. Also see Stahnke and Martin, *Religion and Human Rights*, 183ff., which contains a selection of texts from agreements and pertinent legislation.

41. For the text, see Holy See—Israel: Fundamental Agreement, December 30, 1993, 33 I.L.M. 153 (1994). On this agreement, see Rafael Palomino Lozano, "El Acuerdo Fundamental entre la Santa Sede y el Estado de Israel," XXII *El Olivo* (1998): 69-93; Silvio Ferrari, "Concordats Were Born in the West," 12/13 *La Porta D'Oriente* (1998): 37-44; Natan Lerner, "Protecting Religious Human Rights by Bilateral Arrangements," 12/13 *La Porta D'Oriente* (1998): 45-55.

42. Ferrari, "Concordats Were Born in the West," 37-38, 44.

43. See Stahnke and Martin, *Religion and Human Rights*, 183ff.; Ministry of Justice of Spain, Libertad Religiosa (Normas reguladoras) (1998); Laws 24, 25 and 26/1992, approving the special agreements, BOE 272 (1992), 38209ff. For the agreements with the Holy See, see Spanish Ministry for Foreign Affairs, Acuerdos entre España y la Santa Sede (1976-1979).

44. Report of the Human Rights Committee, U.N. GAOR 47th Sess., Supp. No. 40, 97, U.N. Doc. A/47/40 (1992).

45. Italy—The Holy See: Agreement to Amend the 1929 Lateran Concordat, February 18, 1984, 24 I.L.M. 1589 (1985). See also Giorgio Sacerdoti, "Jewish Rights under a New Italian Concordat," *Patterns of Prejudice* 12 (1978): 26 n.1.

46. For the text, see International Catholic-Jewish Liaison Committee, *Fifteen Years of Catholic-Jewish Dialogue, 1970-1985* (1988), 291.

47. For the text, see ibid., 293.

48. For the text, see Stahnke and Martin, *Religion and Human Rights*, 207.

### 3. PROTECTING RELIGIOUS GROUPS FROM PERSECUTION AND INCITEMENT

1. For the text, see *Human Rights: A Compilation of International Instruments* (1993), at 669, U.N. Sales No. E.88.XIV.1 (1988) [hereafter *Human Rights*].

2. *Beauharnis v. Illinois*, 343 U.S. 250, 263 (1952).

3. See, for instance, the controversial International Religious Freedom Act 1998 (H.R. 2431), signed by the United States president on October 27, 1998, calling upon the president to "take diplomatic and other appropriate action with respect to any country that engages in or tolerates violations of religious freedom." See the Annual Report on International Religious Freedom for 1991, Bureau for Democracy, Human Rights and Labor, Washington (1999). See also the detailed list of violations of religious rights in several countries included in the reports of Special Rapporteur Abdelfattah Amor (see chap. 1); Kevin Boyle and Juliet Sheen, eds., *Freedom of Religion and Belief: A World Report* (1997) (covering persecution against different religious groups in many countries); and Paul Marshall with Lela Gilbert, *Their Blood Cries Out* (1997) (dealing with the persecutions and discrimination of hundreds of millions of Christians in over sixty countries).

4. See the definition in Article 1 of the Convention on Racial Discrimination. For the text, see *Human Rights*, 66.

5. See Jose D. Ingles, *Study on the Implementation of Article 4 of the Convention on the Elimination of All Forms of Racial Discrimination, CERD, Positive Measures Designed to Eradicate All Incitement to, or Acts of Racial Discrimination*, U.N. Doc. A/CONF.119/10.CERD/2, U.N. Sales No. E.85.XIV.2 at 38 (1986).

6. See Ian Brownlie, *Principles of Public International Law*, 4th ed. (1980), 513 n. 29.

7. *Human Rights*, 20.

8. For the text, see Council of Europe, *European Convention on Human Rights: Collected Texts* (1974).

9. For the text, see 9 I.L.M. 1970.

10. *Human Rights*, 122.

11. Ibid., 132.

12. See, S. J. Roth, "The CSCE 'Charter of Paris for a New Europe,'" *Human Rights Law Journal* 11 (1990): 373, 379.

13. See generally Natan Lerner, *The U.N. Convention on the Elimination of All Forms of Racial Discrimination* (1980); Theodore Meron, *Human Rights Law-Making in the United Nations* (1986); E. Schwelb, "The International Convention on the Elimination of All Forms of Racial Discrimination," *International and Comparative Law Quarterly* 15 (1966); G. Tenekides, "L'Action des Nations Unies contre la Discrimination Raciale," *Recueil des Cours* III (1980): 269. On the implementation of the convention, see Thomas Buergenthal, "Implementing the U.N. Racial Convention," *Texas International Law Journal* 12 (1977): 187. See also the Reports of the Committee on the Elimination of Racial Discrimination (GAOR, Supplements No. 18, the last of which until this writing is A/54/18, 1999).

14. See Ingles, *Study*; Lerner, *The U.N. Convention*.

15. Lerner, *The U.N. Convention*, 46.

16. Ingles, *Study*, 1. See also, Natan Lerner, "Incitement in the Racial Convention: Reach and Shortcomings of Article 4," *Israel Yearbook on Human Rights* 222 (1992): 1.

17. U.N. Doc A/PV. 1406, at 42-43 (1965).

18. President's Message, 95th Cong., 2d Sess. (February 23, 1978).

19. Lerner, *The U.N. Convention*, 183-84.

20. United Nations, *Multilateral Treaties in Respect of which the Secretary-General Performs Depository Functions* (1978), 97-98. The text of the United Kingdom reservation interpreting Article 4 is also quoted in Lerner, *The U.N. Convention*, 160. See also Sandra Coliver, ed., *Striking a Balance* (1992), with an annex on reservations and declarations regarding Article 4 (pp. 394ff.)

21. U.N. Doc. A/46/18, at 58 (1991).

22. U.N. GAOR supp. (No. 18) at 37, U.N. Doc. A/8718 (1972).

23. Ingles, *Study*, 37.

24. Ibid.

25. Ibid. See also *Statement of CERD at the World Conference to Combat Racism and Racial Discrimination*, U.N. GAOR Supp. (No.18) at 110, U.N. Doc. A/33/18 (1978).

26. Meron, *Human Rights Law-Making*, 28.

27. Ingles, *Study*, 39.

28. For a discussion of the drafting process, see Lerner, *The U.N. Convention*, 1-6, 43-53.

29. On the penalization of the denial of the facts of the Holocaust, see S. J. Roth, "Anti-Semitism and International Law," *Israel Yearbook on Human Rights* 13 (1983): 208, 223.

30. Ingles, *Study*, 18; Meron, *Human Rights Law-Making*, 33.

31. Statement of the U.S. Representative to the General Assembly, U.N. Doc. A/PV. 1406, at 53-55 (1965).

32. See Lerner, *The U.N. Convention*, 95.

33. Ingles, *Study*, 37.

34. *Statement of CERD at the World Conference to Combat Racism and Racial Discrimination*.

35. U.N. GAOR, U.N. Doc. A/38/40 (1983).

36. For a discussion on the broad scope of the convention, see Lerner, *The U.N. Convention*, 9.

37. For several judicial decisions in Great Britain, the United States, the Netherlands, and New Zealand dealing with group identity and stressing the relevance of self-perception and external perception in order to determine the existence of a distinct discriminated group, see Natan Lerner, *Group Rights and Discrimination in International Law* (1991), 33ff.

38. Meron, *Human Rights Law-Making*, 35. Professor Michael Banton, a member of CERD, wrote that "the Convention's potentiality for action against discrimination based upon colour or descent, and for linking these with the more general principle of non-discrimination . . . or for reducing the racial discrimination that has other causes, has scarcely been recognized." Michael Banton, "The International Defence of Racial Equality," *Ethnic and Racial Studies* 13 (1990): 568, 582.

39. *Human Rights*, 141.

40. Cf. U.N. Doc. A/C.3/SR.1315,at 2 (1965).

41. H.C. (High Court) 399/85, 41(3) Piskei Din (Judgments of the Supreme Court of Israel), 255-80, at 259. For a summary of the case in English, see *The Jerusalem Post* (August 3, 1987). In 1998 the Israeli Supreme Court decided an interesting case related to offenses against religious feelings committed by a Jewish girl who dissemi-

nated leaflets with the figure of a pig and the legend "Mohammed." The court upheld the conviction of the accused. See penal appeal 697/98. The well-known *Skokie*
case in the United States, discussed below, may also be relevant in this connection.

42. Article 9 (3) of the declaration, in *Human Rights*, 61.

43. Cf. U.N. Doc. E/CN.4/Sub.2/SR.418 (1964).

44. See U.N. Doc. A/46/18, at 107 (1991).

45. Ibid.

46. For this discussion, see, inter alia, Natan Lerner, "Group Libel Revisited,"
*Israel Yearbook on Human Rights* 17 (1987): 184; Kenneth Lasson, "Racial Defa-
mation as Free Speech: Abusing the First Amendment," *Columbia Human Rights
Law Review* 17 (1985): 11; Kathleen Mahoney, *Hate Vilification Legislation: Where
Is the Balance?* (1994); Raphael Cohen Almagor, "Harm Principle, Offence Prin-
ciple, and the Skokie Affair," *Political Studies* 41 (1993): 453-470. *New York Law
Forum* 14 (1968) also has several articles on the issue.

47. See citations in note 41 above.

48. This is the case in the United Kingdom. Cf. Anthony Dickey, "English Law
and Race Defamation," *New York Law Forum* 14 (1968). In Israel the law on racist
incitement enacted on August 5, 1986, requires the written consent of the attorney
general before criminal proceedings may be initiated.

49. Lasson, "Racial Defamation as Free Speech," 48.

50. *Beauharnais v. Illinois*, 343 U.S. at 256-257.

51. Eur. Consult. Ass. Deb. 17th Sess. 737-38 (January 27, 1966)

52. See Lerner, *The U.N. Convention*, 165-203.

53. *Beauharnais v. Illinois*, 343 U.S. at 256.

54. *Collin v. Smith*, 578 F.2d 1197 (7th Cir. 1978).

55. Lasson, "Racial Defamation as Free Speech," 18, 23, 30. For Lasson, racial
defamation is subversive speech and cannot be protected by the First Amendment.
He is inclined not to include defamation of religious groups within the prohibition,
because of the risk of "excessive entanglement" with the free exercise of religion.
Ibid., 35 n.174. This argument does not seem to be justified. There is no basic reason
to deny a religious group the same protection to which an ethnic group is entitled.

56. *Laws of the State of Israel*, 19:254.

57. See Izhak Zamir, "Herut Habitui K'neged Lashon Hara V'alimut Milulit"
(Freedom of Expression *vs.* Defamation and Verbal Violence), in *Sefer Sussman* 149
(1984).

58. See Lerner, *The U.N. Convention,* 204-209.

59. See, particularly, Articles 11.1 and 13.5.

60. See, particularly, Articles 10.2 and 11.2.

61. For the text, see *Human Rights*, 669.

62. In some cases ratification was discussed during several decades. That was the
situation in the United States, where ratification was only made possible in October
1988, almost forty years after the convention was transmitted by President Truman
to the Senate, and following a series of hearings at which strong opposition to ratification was voiced.

63. Reservations to the Convention on Genocide case, ICJ Reports (1 95 1), 15-
69, at 23.

64. Cf. Barcelona Traction, Light and Power Co. case, ICJ Reports (1970), paras.
33-34. See also Warwick McKean, *Equality and Discrimination under International
Law* (1983), 277ff.

65. Raphael Lemkin, *Axis Rule in Occupied Europe* (1944); idem, "Genocide: A New International Crime," *Revue Internationale de Droit Penal* (1946): 360; idem, "Genocide as a Crime in International Law," *American Journal of International Law* 41 (1947): 145. The term *genocide* appears in the indictment of the German War criminals at Nuremberg in 1945. For the Nuremberg Judgment, see *American Journal of International Law* 41 (1947): 172.

66. For an authoritative commentary, see Nehemiah Robinson, *The Genocide Convention* (1960), incorporating texts of drafts and relevant resolutions as well as reservations to the convention. See also, e.g., Leo Kuper, *Genocide: Its Political Use in the Twentieth Century* (1981); idem, *The Prevention of Genocide* (1985); Irving Horowitz, *Taking Lives: Genocide and State Power* (1980).

67. E/CN.4/Sub.2/416 (4 July 1978), and E/CN.4/Sub.2/1985/6 and Corr. 1 (2 July and 29 August 1985), respectively.

68. See, inter alia, the statement by the representative of the World Jewish Congress, Daniel Lack, E/CN.4/Sub.2/1984/SR.4.

69. Cf. Robinson, *The Genocide Convention*, 54. The resolution also protected "political groups" and dealt with cultural genocide.

70. Robinson, on the basis of the preparatory work, points out that the convention did not adopt the principle of universal repression (ibid., 32). This has to be seen in the light of the evolving approach of international law to the question of universal jurisdiction.

71. Kuper, *Genocide*, 23ff., takes the view that the convention was the proper instrument for the protection of political groups as well. This view is shared by Whitaker, who also recommends that the definition should be extended to "include a sexual group such as women, men, or homosexuals." See the Whitaker study cited in note 67, 16-18. Ruhashyankiko takes the opposite stand in his study (ibid., 23). The more restrictive approach seems to be the correct one.

72. Cf. Kuper, *Genocide*, 33-35; also Robinson, *The Genocide Convention*, 60-61.

73. Robinson, *The Genocide Convention*, 63. According to Kuper, genocide is a crime against a collectivity, by massive slaughter, and carried out with explicit intent (Kuper, *Genocide*, 86).

74. The document cited in note 68, above, states: "Contemporary examples abound on the denial of cultural facilities, the violation of cultural rights, as well as damage to and destruction of cultural property, which could lead to the annihilation of national, ethnic or religious groups." By contrast, McKean maintains that the decision to delete the reference to cultural genocide was a correct one (McKean, *Equality and Discrimination*, 110). There were also proposals to include ecocide—the destruction of the environment—in the notion of genocide.

75. Such legislation was adopted by some countries, such as Denmark, the Federal Republic of Germany, and Israel. Israel enacted a special law, No. 5710/50, on the prevention and punishment of the crime of genocide. For the text in English, see *Laws of the State of Israel (LSI)* (5710-1949/50), 4:101. Section Ib of the law reproduces the language of Article II of the convention. See Eichmann case, H.C. 336/61, 16 P.D. 2033.

76. Articles 7 and 8 of the Convention on Torture. For the text, see *Human Rights*, 293.

77. ICJ Reports (1951), 20.

78. See the 1996 Draft Code against the Peace and Security of Mankind, Article 18 e) and f). For the text, see doc. A/CN.4/L.532 (1996).

79. For the text, see *Human Rights*, 147. See Natan Lerner, "The Convention on the Non-Applicability of Statutory Limitations to War Crimes," *Israel Law Review* 4 (1969): 512. In 1979 the Federal Republic of Germany abolished the statutory limitation that would have prevented the punishment of genocide as of December 31, 1979.

80. See the Whitaker study, cited in note 67, 41, on steps suggested to fight genocide. See recommendations concerning the prevention of genocide in the Ruhashyankiko study, cited in note 67, 172ff. and 184ff. See also U.N. General Assembly Resolution 3074 (XXVIII), of December 3, 1973, on international cooperation in the detection, arrest, extradition, and punishment of persons guilty of war crimes and crimes against humanity.

81. The U.N. Security Council and the General Assembly, as well as other U.N. organs and treaty bodies, adopted numerous resolutions on "ethnic cleansing." The International Court of Justice has dealt with the subject. For scholarly comments, see, inter alia, Theodore Meron, "The Case for War Crimes Trials in Yugoslavia," *Foreign Affairs* 72 (1993): 122; idem, "Rape as a Crime under International Law," *American Journal of International Law* 87 (1993): 424; H. McCoubrey, "The Armed Conflict in Bosnia and Proposed War Crimes Trials," *International Relations* 11 (1993): 411-32; P. Akhavan, "Punishing War Crimes in the Former Yugoslavia: A Critical Juncture for the New World Order," *Human Rights* 15 (1993): 262; James C. O'Brien, "The International Tribunal for Violation of International Humanitarian Law in the Former Yugoslavia." *American Journal of International Law* 87 (1993): 639.

82. *Time* (October 25, 1993): 42.

83. See P. Mass, "In Czech Republic, a Surge of Racism against Gypsies," *International Herald Tribune* (August 14-15, 1993): 2.

84. See with respect to those two situations, respectively, M. S. Serrill, "Rain-Forest Genocide," *Time* (September 6, 1993): 42; A. Purvis, "A Demon Is Unleashed," *Time* (November 15, 1993): 50-51. Professor Shabtai Rosenne called my attention to the fact that, according to information from Yugoslavia, the term *ethnic cleansing* was first used in the U.S. media by *New York Newsday* journalist Roy Gutman, solely in connection with acts of the Bosnian Serbs, although such acts were committed by all sides in the civil war in Bosnia (letter to the author dated January 30, 1994).

85. U.N. Doc. E/CN.4/1993/62, at 119. Kris Janowski, Sarajevo spokesman for the U.N. high commissioner for refugees, accused Serbian gunmen of "erasing all traces of a Muslim religious and cultural presence." See *New York Times* (January 30, 1994).

86. See International Court of Justice, Case concerning Application of the Convention on the Prevention and Punishment of the Crime of Genocide (Bosnia and Herzegovina v. Yugoslavia (Serbia and Montenegro)), request for the Indication of Provisional Measures (March 20, 1993), 14.

87. See U.N. Doc. E/1992/22, E/CN.4/1992/84/Add.1(1992), and 1992/S-1/1 Annex (1992), respectively. For a similar resolution of the second special session of the Commission on Human Rights, see E/CN.4/1992/S-2/6 (1992). See also the "Statement of Principles" approved by the conference on Yugoslavia that met in London in August 1992.

88. For the text, see 31 I.L.M. 1470 (1992).
89. See Press Release G.A./8470 (February 1, 1993), at 276.
90. For the text, see 31 I.L.M. 1476 (1992).
91. Annex 1 to the U.N. Secretary-General Doc. S/25274 (1993).
92. Meron, "The Case for War Crimes Trials," 132.
93. McCoubrey, "The Armed Conflict," 424.
94. See Order on Application, April 8, 1993, 87 AJIL. 505-521 (1993); Order, September 13, 1993 (mimeographed text).
95. Ibid., 22-23.
96. Adopted on December 18, 1992.
97. S/25792 (1993) Annex and E/CN.4/1994/4, May 19, 1993.
98. For the U.N. Secretary-General's Report on the Tribunal (May 3, 1993), its Annex, with the Statute of the International Tribunal, and Security Council Resolution 827 (1993), adopted on May 25, 1993, approving the Report and deciding to establish the Tribunal, see 32 I.L.M. 1159-1205 (1993).
99. Ibid., 1173.
100. Ibid., 1203-1205
101. Adopted without a vote. See Press Release GA/8470, February 1, 1993, at 276.
102. For a listing of previous Security Council resolutions regarding the situation in former Yugoslavia, see 31 I.L.M. 1427 (1992).
103. U.N. Doc. A/CONF.157/DC/1, June 15, 1993.
104. See A/48 U.N. GAOR Supp. (No. 40), U.N. Doc. A/48/40 (Part I) (1993).
105. Ibid., 69.
106. See 48 U.N. GAOR Supp. (No. 12), U.N. Doc. A/48/18 (1993).
107. U.S.L.W. 4575-79 (1993).
108. In Israel, in July 1994, the Knesset passed a law amending Sec. 144 (d) of the Penal Law of 1977, doubling the penalty for offenses committed with a racist motive.

## 4. Proselytism and Change of Religion

1. Michael S. Serrill, "What the Pope Will Find When John Paul II Returns to a Region Where Catholic Marxism Is Out of Favor. The Big Threat: Evangelicals," *Time (Int'l)* (February 12, 1996): 28. In the poorer regions of Latin America the people view evangelical religions as a protest against Catholicism and the existing power structure that remains powerless to effectuate change (ibid.). See further, Paul E. Sigmund, ed., *Religious Freedom and Evangelization in Latin America: The Challenge of Religious Pluralism* (1999).
2. Human Rights Committee, General Comments Adopted under Article 40, Paragraph 4, of the International Covenant on Civil and Political Rights: General Comment No. 22(48) (Article 18), U.N. GAOR Hum. Rts. Comm., 48th Sess., Supp. No. 40, at 208, U.N. Doc. A /48/40 (1993) [General Comment No. 22(48)].
3. Report of the Human Rights Committee, U.N. GAOR, 50th Sess., Supp. No. 40, at 30, 34, U.N. Doc. A/50/40 (1995).
4. Report of the Committee on the Elimination of Racial Discrimination, U.N. GAOR, 50th Sess., Supp. No. 18, U.N. Doc. A/50/18 (1995).
5. See Consolidated Summary of the Seminar, OSCE, Warsaw, 1996.
6. G.A. Res. 217A, GAOR, 3d Sess. (December 10, 1948).
7. 999 U.N.T.S. 171 (March 23, 1976).

8. G.A. Res. 36155, U.N. GAOR, 36th Sess., Supp. No. 51, U.N. Doc. A/36/55 (1981).

9. See European Court of Human Rights, *Kokkinakis v. Greece, European Human Rights Report* 17, Part 5 (1994): 397. Mentioning this case and the prohibition of proselytism in Greece, Silvio Ferrari points out the preferential treatment given to the principal church over the followers of all other religious faiths, including new religions, cults, and nonrecognized religious communities, which are perceived as foreign to the nation. See Silvio Ferrari, "The New Wine and the Old Cask: Tolerance, Religion and the Law in Contemporary Europe," *Ratio Juris* 10 (1997): 75, 83.

10. Fernando Volio, "Legal Personality, Privacy and the Family," in *The International Bill of Rights: The Covenant on Civil and Political Rights*, ed. Louis Henkin (1981), 190, 193. Volio mentions a declaration of the 1967 Nordic Conference in Stockholm that connected the right to privacy with intimacy (defined as the right to live one's life in an independent manner, without outside interference), which can be violated by intrusive communication, either verbal or written.

11. *Gay News v. United Kingdom*, Eur. Ct. H.R. 5 (1983): 123.

12. *Choudhury v. The United Kingdom*, Application No. 17439/90, reprinted in *Human Rights Law Journal* 12 (1991): 172.

13. Kevin Boyle, "Religious Intolerance and the Incitement of Hatred," in *Striking a Balance: Hate Speech, Freedom of Expression and Non-Discrimination*, ed. Sandra Coliver (1992), 61, 68.

14. See Barry Lynn et al. eds., *The Right to Religious Liberty* (1995), 70-71.

15. Ibid., 21-22; see also *DeNooyer v. Livonia Public Schools*, 799 F. Supp. 744 (E.D. Mich. 1992).

16. See *Kjeldsen, Busk Madsen & Pedersen v. Denmark*, 1 Eur. H.R. Rep. 711 (1976) (court decision).

17. The military authorities in Israel had to restrict the free access of one Jewish religious group to military quarters when its representatives tried to induce soldiers, also Jewish, to return to strict expressions of Jewish religiosity.

18. See Arcot Krishnaswami, *Study of Discrimination in the Matter of Religious Rights and Practices* (1960).

19. Ibid. See also Asher Maoz, "Human Rights in the State of Israel," in *Religious Human Rights in Global Perspective: Legal Perspectives*, ed. Johan D. van der Vyver and John Witte Jr. (1996), 349, 360.

20. See Cecil M. Robeck Jr., "Mission and the Issue of Proselytism," *International Bulletin of Missionary Research* 20 (1996): 2.

21. Ibid., 2. See also Eugene P. Heideman, "Proselytism, Mission, and the Bible," *International Bulletin of Missionary Research* 20 (1996): 10.

22. For a recent study on the Jewish orthodox view of proselytism and conversion, see Menachem Finkelstein, *Proselytism, Halakha and Practice* (1994). For a human rights-oriented reference to conversion, apostasy, and blasphemy in Jewish law, see Haim H. Cohn, *Human Rights in Jewish Law* (1984).

23. See Robeck, "Mission and the Issue of Proselytism," 1.

24. *Webster's New Dictionary of Synonyms* (1973), 189, 646.

25. Heideman, "Proselytism, Mission, and the Bible," 10.

26. *Webster's Third New International Dictionary* (1993), 102.

27. Ibid., 1445.

28. A. Bradney, *Religions, Rights and Laws* (1993), 5. Leo Pfeffer also saw as "an article of organic law that the relations between man and his Maker were a private

concern, into which other men have no right to intrude" (Leo Pfeffer, *Church, State, and Freedom* [1953], ix).

29. See, K. J. Partsch, "Freedom of Conscience and Expression, and Political Freedoms," in Henkin, *International Bill of Rights.* Partsch does not refer at all to freedom of thought. Martin Scheinin, "Article 18," in *The Universal Declaration of Human Rights: A Commentary,* ed. Asbjorn Eide (1992), 263, writes that "states have not considered it difficult to allow their citizens the freedom to think. Difficulties start in relation to the right to express convictions, or act in accordance."

30. Theodore S. Orlin, "Religious Pluralism and Freedom of Religion: Its Protection in Light of Church/State Relationships," in *The Strength of Diversity—Human Rights and Pluralist Democracy,* ed. Allan Rosas and Jan Holgensen (1992), 94 (pointing out that the minority treaties system failed to universalize freedom of religion and did not reflect the growing need to protect religions and beliefs not seen as irritants to the peace or not linked to politically unstable situations).

31. See Natan Lerner, *Group Rights and Discrimination in International Law* (1991); Warwick McKean, *Equality and Discrimination Under International Law* (1983).

32. For human rights in the Charter, see generally Hersch Lauterpacht, *International Law and Human Rights* (1950). For the text, see 1 U.N.T.S. XVI.

33. Universal Declaration of Human Rights, G.A. Res. 217, U.N. GAOR, 3d Sess., Supp. (1948).

34. J. A. Walkate, "The Right of Everyone to Change His Religion or Belief," *Netherlands International Law Review* 2 (1983): 146, 152. The Lebanese representative, Charles Malik, a Christian, defended the text and participated in its preparation. The representative of Pakistan took a similar position.

35. Nehemiah Robinson, *The Universal Declaration of Human Rights,* 129.

36. See Walkate, "The Right of Everyone to Change His Religion or Belief."

37. See, in this respect, a letter sent by the 1981 chairman of the Third Committee, Dr. Declan O'Donovan, to Roger S. Clark, mentioned in Clark's article, "The United Nations Declaration on the Elimination of All Forms of Intolerance and of Discrimination Based on Religion or Belief," in *Chitty's Law Journal* 31 (1983): 23, n.36.

38. Krishnaswami, *Study of Discrimination in the Matter of Religious Rights and Practices,* 3.

39. Ibid., 21.

40. Ibid., 24.

41. Ibid., 30.

42. Ibid., 40 n.1.

43. Ibid., 40.

44. See Leonard W. Levy, *Blasphemy: Verbal Offense Against the Sacred, from Moses to Salman Rushdie* (1993).

45. Krishnaswami, *Study of Discrimination,* 41.

46. Ibid., 63.

47. Ibid., 71.

48. Ibid., 72-73.

49. For the situation in some societies, such as India, see Subash C. Kashyap, *Delinking Religion and Politics* (1993). Kashyap emphasizes that proselytism promotes religious conflict, particularly when conversion is alien to the nonmissionary

nature of the religion of the majority community and also is likely to be brought about by illegitimate or unfair means in the context of rampant illiteracy and poverty (ibid., 25).

50. See Partsch, "Freedom of Conscience and Expression, and Political Freedoms"; Scheinin, "Article 18." See also Walkate, "The Right of Everyone to Change His Religion or Belief" (summarizing the history of the amendments and votes that finally led to the adopted text).

51. See Walkate, "The Right of Everyone to Change His Religion or Belief."

52. See Partsch, "Freedom of Conscience and Expression, and Political Freedoms," 447 nn.5-8. Partsch takes the view that, despite the changes in wording in comparison to the Universal Declaration, the text confirms the freedom to change one's religion or beliefs (ibid., 211).

53. See Walkate, "The Right of Everyone to Change His Religion or Belief," 153.

54. See United Nations, *Human Rights: A Compilation of International Instruments* (1993) [hereafter *Human Rights*], 101, 122, 176.

55. See *Erki Hartikainen v. Finland*, Communication No. 40/1978, in *United Nations Selected Decisions of the Human Rights Commitee under the Optional Protocol*, 74 U.N. Doc. CCPR/C/OP 1, 10.4 (1985). Finland took into consideration the committee's views and introduced changes in its teaching program.

56. U.N. GAOR, 48th Sess., Supp. No. 40, U.N. Doc. No. A/48/40, Annex VI (1993), para. 2.

57. Issued as General Assembly Official Records (GAOR), Supp. No. 40.

58. See U.N. GAOR, Supp. No. 40 (summary of the discussion of the respective country reports).

59. For the text of the Covenant on Economic, Social and Cultural Rights, see *Human Rights*, 8. On the respective Committee, see generally Philip Alston, "The Committee on Economic, Social and Cultural Rights," in *The United Nations and Human Rights: A Critical Appraisal*, ed. Philip Alston (1992) See generally Asbjorn Eide et al., eds., *Economic, Social and Cultural Rights* (1995).

60. For the text, see *Human Rights*, 122. For an analysis of the declaration see Lerner, *Group Rights*, 75-96; Donna J. Sullivan, "Advancing the Freedom of Religion or Belief through the U.N. Declaration on the Elimination of Religious Intolerance and Discrimination," *American Journal of International Law* 82 (1988): 487.

61. Consider the judgment of the International Court of Justice in North Sea Continental Shelf Cases, 1969 ICJ, at 22 (discussing the formation of new rules of customary law on the basis of what was a purely conventional rule).

62. See Clark, "The United Nations Declaration on the Elimination of All Forms of Intolerance and of Discrimination Based on Religion or Belief," 38.

63. Walkate, "The Right of Everyone to Change His Religion or Belief."

64. Ibid., 150.

65. Ibid., 151. The meaning of reservations to General Assembly declarations, is, of course, involved, particularly in the case of states that ratified the covenant without reservations. It should be remembered that Article 18 of the covenant, which follows the text of the Universal Declaration, is among the nonderogable articles according to Article 4 of the covenant. The covenant as a whole was adopted unanimously. The question is, therefore, to what extent the interpretations and/or declarations formulated with regard to the 1981 Declaration can be seen as implying a legally significant weakening of Article 18 of both the Universal Declaration and the

covenant, or at least denying it the character of customary international law with regard to the Muslim states. This may also involve, in some countries, the legality of steps restricting proselytism because of its clash with the prohibition of conversion.

66. Sami A. Aldeeb Abu-Sahlieh, "The Islamic Conception of Migration," *International Migration Review* 30 (1996): 37. For a detailed description of the Islamic attitude toward proselytism and conversion, see Sami A. Aldeeb Abu-Sahlieh, *Les Musulmans Face aux Droits de L'Homme: Religion et Droit et Politique: Étude et Documents* (1994).

67. See Bat Yeor, *The Decline of Eastern Christianity under Islam—From Jihad to Dhimmitude* (1996).

68. See Bertie Ramcharan, "Towards a Universal Standard of Religious Liberty," in World Council of Churches, *Religious Liberty* (1987), 8-13. In the same publication Theo van Boven stresses that the freedom to change one's religion or belief is no longer explicitly included in the declaration ("Religious Witness and Practice in Political and Social Life as an Element of Religious Liberty," in WCC, *Religious Liberty*, 19). In a 1989 working paper van Boven refers to the consistency requirement as expressed in Article 8 of the 1981 Declaration, which excludes any interpretation restricting or derogating from rights recognized in the Universal Declaration or in the covenants. U.N. Doc. E/CN.4/Sub.2/ 1989/321, at 29.

69. Sullivan, "Advancing the Freedom of Religion," 495.

70. See U.N. Doc. E/CN.4/Sub.2/1987/26 (1986), particularly paras. 20 and 21. For the work of the special rapporteurs appointed by the Commission on Human Rights and the Subcommission on the Prevention of Discrimination and Protection of Minorities, see Bahiyyih G. Tahzib, *Freedom of Religion or Belief: Ensuring Effective International Legal Protection* (1996), 190; Brice Dickson, "The United Nations and Freedom of Religion," *International and Comparative Law Quarterly* 44 (1995): 347.

71. See U.N. Doc. E/CN.4/Sub.2/1987/26 (1986), para. 201.

72. See ibid., paras. 52-81.

73. See ibid., paras. 108-110.

74. See, e.g., *Kjeldsen, Busk Madsen & Pedersen, European Human Rights Report* 1 (1976: 711 (court decision). The case dealt with objections to sex education in public schools, but similar principles would apply to state-imposed religious education. The court declared that "the state is forbidden to pursue an aim of indoctrination that might be considered as not respecting parents' religious and philosophical convictions. . . . " See also *Angelini v. Sweden*, App. No. 10491/83, Eur. Comm. H. R. Dec. & Rep. 10, 123 (1988); Article 14 of the 1989 Convention on the Rights of the Child (for the text, see *Human Rights*, 174).

75. U.N. Docs. E/CN.4/1987/35, 1988/45 and Add.1 and Corr.1, 1989/44, 1990/ 46, 1991/56/ 1992/52, and 1993/62 and Add.1.

76. U.N. Doc. E/CN.4/1992/52, at 173.

77. See ibid., 177.

78. U.N. Docs. E/CN.4/1994/79; E/CN.4/1995/91/ and Add.1/Corr.1; E/CN. 4/ 1996/95, Add.1 and 2; E/CN.4/1997/91 and Add.1, E/CN.4/1998/6, and E/CN.4/ 1999/58.

79. U.N. Doc. E/CN.4/1996/95/Add.2, paras. 92 and 116.

80. See ibid., para. 116.

81. Ibid., paras. 21 and 22.

82. U.N. Doc. E/CN.4/1996/95/Add.1, paras. 31 and 32.

83. See U.N. Doc. E/CN.4/1996/95.

84. See ibid., Add.1.

85. U.N. Doc. E/CN.4/1995/91.

86. U.N. Doc. E/CN.4/1997/91 and Add.1.

87. Ibid., 19.

88. See E/CN.4/1998/6, p. 27.

89. See ibid., 28.

90. For the text, see *Human Rights*, 550.

91. U.N. Doc. E/CN.4/Sub.2/1985/22, Annex II.

92. For the text, see *Human Rights*, 471.

93. For the texts of the declaration and the convention, see *Human Rights*, 171, 174. On the subject, see generally Geraldine van Bueren, *The International Law on the Rights of the Child* (1995) and Lawrence J. LeBlanc, *The Convention on the Rights of the Child* (1995).

94. Tahzib, *Freedom of Religion or Belief*, 101.

95. See *Kjeldsen, Busk Madsen & Pedersen*. See also *Hoffman v. Austria*, 255C Eur. Ct. H. R. (ser. A) (1993). The issue was a complaint by a mother, a Jehovah's Witness, that she had been denied the custody of her children because of her religious convictions.

96. For the text, see *Human Rights*, 101.

97. For the draft as amended, see U.N. Doc. A/7930 (1970). See also, Appendix 6.

98. See Inter-American Commission on Human Rights, Case 9178 (Stephen Schmidt) (Costa Rica, 1984) (1985), *Human Rights Law Journal* 6 (1985): 211.

99. See OSCE, Office for Democratic Institutions and Human Rights, Human Dimensions Seminar, Constitutional, Legal, and Administrative Aspects of the Freedom of Religion, Consolidated Summary, Warsaw (April 16-19, 1996), 6.

100. Ibid., 23-24.

101. Ibid., 25.

102. The text does not define national minorities. The phrase is a complicated notion that, in the author's opinion, is frequently used incorrectly.

103. For the European Court's decisions, see chapter 3. See also Francois Rigaux, "L'incrimination du prosélytisme face à la liberté d'expression," *Revue Trimestrielle des Droits de l'Homme* 17 (1994): 144-150, calling attention to the hostility shown by governments and courts toward Jehovah's Witnesses, primarily because they present a more radical version of the Christian faith. See also *Manoussakis and Others v. Greece*, 59/1995/565/651 (September 26, 1996).

104. 295 Eur. Ct. H.R. (ser. A) (1994).

105. *Kokkinakis v. Greece*, 260 Eur. Ct. H.R. (ser. A) (1993) 17 Eur. H.R. Rep., Part 5 (1994), 397-440.

106. See T. Jeremy Gunn, "Adjudicating Rights of Conscience under the European Convention on Human Rights," in van der Vyver and Witte, *Religious Human Rights in Global Perspective: Legal Perspectives*, 305-330; Alain Garay, "Liberté religieuse et prosélytisme: l'expérience européenne," *Revue Trimestrielle des Droits de l'Homme* 17 (1994): 7; Rigaux, "L'incrimination du prosélytisme," 137.

107. *Kokkinakis*, 17 Eur. H.R. Rep., 422.

108. See, e.g., Rigaux, "L'incrimination du prosélytisme," 146-147.

109. *Kokkinakis*, 17 Eur. H.R. Rep., 425.

110. Ibid., 426.

111. Ibid., 427.

112. Ibid., 428.
113. Ibid., 429.
114. Ibid., 439.
115. Ibid., 432-439.
116. See, e.g., *Kjeldsen*, 1 Eur. H.R. Rep. 711.
117. *Darby v. Sweden*, 187 Eur. Ct. H.R. (ser. A) (1990).
118. Gunn, "Adjudicating Rights of Conscience," 323ff.
119. Ibid., 328.
120. Rigaux, "L'incrimination du prosélytisme."
121. Garay, "Liberté religieuse et prosélytisme," 20. Garay deals particularly with the situation regarding freedom of religion and conscience in France. Three and a half years after Garay's comments, a decision of a Lyon court to recognize the right of Scientology to define itself as a religion engendered criticism in France and elsewhere.
122. See, on this case, the press release issued by the Registrar of the Court, No. 126, February 24, 1998.
123. See, for the definition of proselytism in that section, the text on page 113.
124. Paragraphs 32-35 of the judgment and point 1 of the operative provisions.
125. Paragraphs 36-61 of the judgment and points 2-4 of the operative provisions.
126. Paragraph 64 and paragraphs 65-69 of the judgment and points 5 and 6-7 of the operative provisions, respectively.

## APPENDIX

1. Adopted and proclaimed by United Nations General Assembly Resolution 217A(III) on December 10, 1948.

2. Adopted and opened for signature by United Nations General Assembly Resolution 260A (III) on December 9, 1948. Entered into force January 12, 1951.

3. Opened for signature by the Council of Europe on November 4, 1950. Entered into force September 3, 1953.

4. Adopted and opened for signature by United Nations General Assembly Resolution 2106A(XX) on December 21, 1965. Entered into force January 4, 1969.

5. Adopted and opened for signature by United Nations General Assembly Resolution 2200A (XXI) on December 16, 1966. Entered into force March 23, 1976.

6. Adopted by the commission at its twenty-first, twenty-second, and twenty-third sessions (1965-67).

7. Signed by the Organization of American States on November 22, 1969. Entered into force July 18, 1978.

8. Adopted by the Organization of African Unity on June 17, 1981. Entered into force October 21, 1986.

9. Proclaimed by United Nations General Assembly Resolution 36/55 on November 25, 1981.

10. Concluding Document of the Vienna Meeting of Representatives of the Participating States of the Conference on Security and Cooperation in Europe, adopted in Vienna, January 17, 1989.

11. Adopted in Copenhagen on June 29, 1990.

12. Adopted and issued at the Nineteenth Islamic Conference of Foreign Ministers in Cairo on August 5, 1990.

13. Adopted and proclaimed by United Nations General Assembly Resolution 47/135 on December 18, 1992.

14. Signed by the State of Israel and the Holy See on December 30, 1993.

15. Opened for signature by the Council of Europe on February 1, 1995, European Treaty Series No. 157.

16. Adopted on August 15, 1998, at the Oslo Conference on Freedom of Religion or Belief.

# INDEX